Learning Democracy and Citizenship
international experiences

Learning Democracy and Citizenship
international experiences

Edited by
Michele Schweisfurth
Lynn Davies
Clive Harber

SYMPOSIUM
BOOKS

Symposium Books
PO Box 65 Wallingford, Oxford OX10 0YG, United Kingdom
www.symposium-books.co.uk

Published in the United Kingdom, 2002

ISBN 1 873927 29 0

© Symposium Books, 2002

Typeset in Melior by Symposium Books
Printed and bound in the United Kingdom by Biddles Ltd, *www.biddles.co.uk*

Contents

Preface

The theme and chapters of this volume are based on the millennium year British Association for International and Comparative Education (BAICE) conference, which was held at the University of Birmingham, 8-10 September 2000. The theme of the conference was 'Learning Democracy and Citizenship', and its aims were:

> to bring together researchers and practitioners working in the field of democracy and citizenship internationally;
> to give a voice to students and teachers in this field;
> to examine democratisation at all levels and sites connected with learning: schools, colleges, ministries, non-formal education, teacher training, governor and parent bodies, education authorities, regional governments and aid agencies; and
> to highlight new theorising about and new action on democracy and citizenship.

The conference was hosted by the Centre for International Education and Research (CIER) of the School of Education, University of Birmingham. CIER puts education for democracy and citizenship at the heart of its teaching and research agenda, but we are not alone. In recent years, there has been a shift in discourse of major international agencies towards a greater recognition of the importance of democratic governments and institutions, and an explicit support for the development of democracy and citizenship through education. As UN Secretary-General Kofi Annan has stated, 'Education is a human right with immense power to reform. On its foundation rest the cornerstones of freedom, democracy and sustainable human development'.

These global trends reflect a heightened awareness of, and demand for, democracy and human rights, and an unprecedented number of countries have achieved democratic governments in the last decade, including zeitgeist-moving cases in eastern Europe and South Africa. Some would attribute these movements to globalisation, linked to a ubiquitous and imperative push for free markets. We, however, would argue for the plural 'globalisations', as these movements take different forms – neo-liberalism being only one of them. Democracy and human rights are others.

These macro-issues of democracy have parallels at the micro-level at which young people learn (see Harber [1997] for further discussion). In a recent competition run by the *Guardian* newspaper in the United Kingdom, 15,000 children expressed their views on 'the school we'd like'. Among the most commonly recurring themes were demands for a listening school, with opportunities for representation on governing bodies, and the right to have input on such issues as the employment of teachers, the use of resources, and the content of the curriculum. There were also calls for a more respectful school, where learners are treated as individuals. Respect was the single most commonly used word by entrants; it is, of course, one of the foundations of a democratic culture.

In editing this volume, attempts have been made to reflect the democratic ethos which governed the conference. The voices of pupils and students are present, with minimal editorial control; in fact, the very first chapter after this introduction is comprised of statements by young learners. Within the volume, it was not possible to include every paper that was presented, but those which have been included represent a 'broad church' in terms of how they have interpreted the issues at hand. Inevitably, the editors do not necessarily agree with all that has been written, but this volume provides an inclusive forum for these varying perspectives, and for important debates in this field.

In the 'right spirit' of good comparative education, the volume holds up no national models in terms of how democracy should be learned or done. The issues are far too complex, and too embedded in national and local contexts and cultures, to lend themselves to prescriptions or simplistic cross-national transfer. Nor does the traditional 'developed' and 'developing' countries dichotomy emerge from the papers. The learning of democracy and citizenship in all countries is problematised, and there is as much to learn from 'South' to 'North' as there is the other way around. In fact, as the title of the conference and of this volume suggests, we are all learners: students, teachers, policy-makers and researchers alike. In the context of this volume, we have chosen not to rehearse the issues surrounding theories and definitions of democracy, although CIER members have written about these elsewhere (e.g. Davies, 1999). Instead, the breadth of the discussion has been permitted to emerge from the papers themselves.

This book is, therefore, relatively unusual in the range of voices it includes, and how it attempts to incorporate them. Not surprisingly, most participants at a BAICE conference are United Kingdom-based academics, graduate students and practitioners. However, we have tried to allow other perspectives to be included as well. Inevitably, as inclusive as one may try to be, there will be gaps, both at the level of participation and in the content of the book. We acknowledge that this is the case, inviting further contributions, wider discussion and a continuation of the established research agendas in this area.

The book is divided into five parts. Each part book is prefaced with a brief introduction that outlines the chapters and draws out the links between them. The first part explores 'Pupil and Student Voice', first, by giving pupils voice, and also by exploring practices internationally in pupil representation, and by examining the related issue of children's rights. In the next part, 'Identities and Contexts for Democracy and Citizenship', themes are explored within different national and institutional perspectives. The chapters within Part 3, 'Democratic Ways of Working and Researching', consider democratic behaviours in educational research and in relationships in and between groups working for a common cause. The fourth part, 'Curriculum and Learning for National Identity', offers four case studies of the relationship between curriculum and the development of citizenship skills and attitudes. Finally, to remind us that learning democracy and citizenship is a lifelong endeavour, we finish with a group of chapters that examine issues in adult education.

Michele Schweisfurth, Lynn Davies & Clive Harber
Editors

References

Annan, Kofi (1998) Foreword, in *The State of the World's Children 1999: education*. New York: UNICEF.

Davies, Lynn (1999) Comparing Definitions of Democracy in Education, *Compare*, 29, pp. 127-140.

Guardian (Education Section) (2001) The School We'd Like, 5 June.

Harber, Clive (1997) International Developments and the Rise of Education for Democracy, *Compare*, 27, pp. 171-191.

PART ONE

Pupil and Student Voice

This section of the book begins with the voices of pupils and students themselves. The voices represent a variety of levels of the education system – primary and secondary pupils from Birmingham in the United Kingdom and teacher education students from The Gambia. The pupils and students open the book by stressing the importance of democratic participation, mediation and discussion in education.

In her chapter, Lynn Davies shows how the importance of pupil voice and democratic participation is recognised and taken very seriously in a range of European countries – Denmark, Germany, the Netherlands and Sweden. Pupil participation in education is reinforced by national legislation and funding. Within this promising context for democratic education, the chapter asks pertinent questions about the purposes of pupil participation and the degree of actual power sharing. The outcomes of such official support for democratic education are articulate and confident learners.

Pupil voice again features strongly in Michael Fielding & Marcia Prieto's chapter on Chile, which discusses a project designed to explore pupils' knowledge and understanding of democracy, together with their perceptions of their school experiences through which they live it. An interesting and unusual aspect of this project is the inclusion of pupils as co-researchers. The project used two schools and involved the pupils in shaping the goals and nature of the project, and students, teachers and researchers in developing ways of working by which democratic principles were put into practice on a daily basis. A key outcome of the project noted by the authors is the enhanced sense of agency felt and practised by the learners.

Gerison Lansdown's discussion of human rights and learning provides an analytical framework for understanding the rights of children *to* education and *in* education. The United Nations Convention on the Rights of the Child has been signed by 191 governments – a record. She argues that the Convention emphasises pupil voice – the right of children to participate fully in their education, to express their views and have them taken seriously. However, unfortunately, this is not the actual model of schooling that predominates in most countries throughout the world. The chapter makes a strong case for increasing pupil voice by promoting human rights education in schools and closing the gap between the official policy agreed to by the majority of governments in signing the Convention and the authoritarian reality of current educational provision.

Student Voices on Democracy

EDITED BY MICHELE SCHWEISFURTH

Students from primary, secondary and tertiary education in Birmingham and The Gambia were asked a variety of questions relating to student participation and democracy. The following are excerpts from their replies, with a minimum of editorial comment and intervention.

The Birmingham students come from local schools with whom CIER at the School of Education has links. These relationships have developed out of the interesting and innovative activities taking place in the two schools in the area of democracy and citizenship. Groups from both schools were plenary speakers at the conference, slots which proved to be among the highlights of the event. CIER also has a CfBT (Centre for British Teachers)-funded project in Education and Democracy at The Gambia College; it is through this connection that the views of students there were solicited.

Nansen Primary School, Birmingham

Nansen's approach to pupil representation, and the innovative and successful mediation scheme, make it an excellent example of a school trying to give pupils voice. Pupils were asked how they felt about being a School Council representative:

> *I like being on the School Council because I like discussing issues like the canteen. (Ataf, year 5)*

> *I like being on the School Council because I like going to conferences and making presentations about our school. (Namra, year 4)*

> *I like being on the School Council because I like playing games and choosing ideas about how we can improve our school. (Zeinab, year 2)*

> *I like being on the School Council because I like meeting new people who enjoy listening to what the School Council has to say. (Zeinab, year 6)*

> *I like being on the School Council because I like changing things about the school. (Mediha, year 3)*

> *I like being on the School Council because I like talking about and trying to solve problems. (Sehar, year 4)*

> *I like being on the School Council because I am secretary and although it's hard it's an important job and I enjoy it. (Anam, year 5)*

> *I like being on the School Council because I most enjoy being the secretary when Anam is away. I like the responsibility of writing the minutes. (Madiha, year 4)*

> *I like being on the School Council because it is fun and very interesting and we do important things. (Haider, year 3)*

> *I like being on the School Council because I get to have responsibilities and also I get to miss my lessons. (Junaid, year 6)*

Also at Nansen, a peer mediation scheme operates. According to the school student newspaper:

> *Mediation is an effective way of helping people to sort out their differences and disagreements. Children in Nansen and other local schools have for years been using Mediation to settle playground disputes. A group of children are trained as Mediators, and are available every day to help other pupils to resolve their differences.*

Children were asked to write poems about the scheme, using the letters in the words 'mediation' and 'mediator'. Here are two of them:

> *Mediators want to help you.*
> *Everyone can be friends.*
> *Discussions about what we can do to help you.*
> *In every playground, there are mediators ready for you.*
> *A hat, a yellow bib and a badge is what we wear.*
> *Trained mediators are ready to help.*
> *Our aim is to help you sort out your problems.*
> *Really good games for you to play.*

Smiles are what we like to see.
(By Reema Akhtar)

Make people happy.
Encourage them to speak.
Discuss with the children.
Interact with all children.
Always remember you can discuss with us anything you want.
Try to forward your ideas.
Important to discuss.
Open all your thoughts.
Never be afraid to come and talk to the mediators.
(By Mareen Bi)

Hillcrest Secondary School, Birmingham

Students at Hillcrest Secondary School in Birmingham, who participate in the 'Let's Talk' programme, were asked to write about their experiences. These are extracts from their writing.

The programme was represented at the BAICE conference by two students, who talked about the project. This project, which has been running since 1998, originates in Northern Ireland, and includes groups from Ireland and Britain. It facilitates exchanged learning among students on themes of conflict resolution, and development and peace education.

We were asked to speak at the BAICE Conference. Jenny spoke about her experiences at the World Water Forum at The Hague. She was one of a group of five students from Hillcrest who made a Power Point presentation to the Youth Conference about water as a conflict issue. The chosen topic was the Ilisu Dam project in Turkey. It was pretty nerve racking but an amazing opportunity to meet people from all over the world ... I spoke about my experience with 'Let's Talk' in the Irish Republic. Our conference brought together students from Birmingham and both parts of Ireland. I didn't know much about Irish issues when I went, but I am much more aware now ... I think this highlights a key strength of 'Let's Talk' – its ability to involve and persuade those involved to learn about new ideas and opinions and incorporate them into their own way of thinking ... The most endearing quality of 'Let's Talk', to us, was the opportunities it gave young people to travel and meet new people who were previously just stereotypes to us and to listen to what their opinions, influences and values were. Also, 'Let's Talk' is surely unique in the importance and acceptance it places on the views of its young members no matter how challenging or unorthodox. (By Gina Hinsley and Jenny Shipway)

A 'Let's Talk' conference was held in Bray in November 2000 ... Issues discussed in the conference included Australia. Many real-life stories were told about how Aborigines had suffered, living in Australia ... By listening to these real-life stories and by looking at photographs, it made the problems more real ... Stereotypes were also a main point of discussion ... As people generalise an image they have seen of one person from a particular group, they see others of the same group in the same way and this is where problems can start. The conference was a very valuable experience ... people's negative views and attitudes can be influenced to change. (By Danielle Tosh)

The Gambia College

Members of the Student Union of The Gambia College, Brikama, The Gambia, West Africa were asked for their views on democracy. The following are some of the comments they made during the discussion.
On defining 'participation':

Participation is receiving by giving ... You are the architect of your own objective or dream, not just a naive recipient. (Lamin)

Through participation you express what you think, your own feelings; if that is not right, it needs to be modified. (Baboucarr)

To me, participation is necessary in any democratic relationship. But before you participate, you must be aware. You must be conscious; there must be a basis for that participation. There must not be domination. People must be clear on their intentions, not with ulterior motives. (Saine)

Participation is give and take. (Lamin)

We are talking of learning ... When a person is imparting knowledge you respond; the giver of knowledge also learns, creating an interaction. (Ann-Therese)

On the benefits of having a Student Union:

The whole thing started in putting up a group of people to represent us, and who should be there for us. When the administration is making decisions, it is not something imposed. Whatever happens, whether success or failure, everyone shares the responsibility. It is not possible for everyone to come together; what the subset does is a reflection of the majority representation. (Lamin)

On what is needed for democratic education:

It needs to run through the whole education system.

I want to differentiate between literacy and education. It is not just knowing the ABC.

Not everyone is well equipped.

We need to know our responsibilities as citizens, not only those who are doing Civics and Government.

People need to know what they are entitled to.

Knowledge that is linked to action is not enough.

There is a push and pull between Western leaders and our own leaders. We need to understand African democracy.

When one begins to listen to students' voices, it is striking how the themes they raise cut across age and national divides.

The Central Place of Student Voice in Democratic Renewal: a Chilean case study

MICHAEL FIELDING & MARCIA PRIETO

Introduction

The democratic government of Chile is having to face the legacy of the previous authoritarian regime, part of which consists of a loss of democratic values and a diminishing level of participation, especially amongst young people. One particular, powerful way of countering this negative trend is through the development of educational communities committed to developing education in and for democratic citizenship. In our view, this should not be a matter of choice, but rather, a matter of both legislative and cultural expectation.

The current situation in Chile is a long way from either of these desiderata. Whilst most of the countries in the world are reinforcing citizenship education, in Chile, civic education has effectively been abolished. Its nearest equivalent is now the Traverse Objectives in Secondary Education, which is subject to the uncertainties of teacher motivation, capacity, time management and the equally uncertain availability of resources.

In this situation, it seems incumbent on those who wish democracy in schools to be taken seriously to develop special measures and to implement additional initiatives that highlight, promote and develop participation in general and democratic practice in particular. Despite the fact that contemporary Chilean society largely ignores what young people know and think about democracy, a research and developmental project, funded by Fondecyt, officially called *Education for Democracy in Schools: myth or reality?* but renamed *VOICES* by the students, is under way. Central to this initiative is students' knowledge and understanding of democracy together with their perceptions about their school experiences through which they live it.

One of the distinctive features of this project is the inclusion of students as co-researchers. Although we regard it as fundamentally important to stimulate the expression of student voices and to know what they think about these matters, we also regard it as crucial for student perceptions and recommendations to be acted on, not merely treated as minor footnotes in an unaltered adult text. Despite its considerable potential, the practice of including students as co-investigators has been very restricted in the educational field. On the occasions when it has been used, too often students have operated as assistants, responsible for the realisation of relatively minor tasks. Their participation has been partial because they have been linked to the project only at its surface and have had no control over what is investigated. Students are more often than not the mere objects of the investigation. Their alleged inability to represent their perspectives properly; their difficulties in distinguishing what is important from what is not; their uncertain responsibility when they are assigned tasks; their inability to think properly; their limited linguistic capacity and a multitude of other failures which are constitutive of 'the ideology of immaturity' (Grace, mentioned by Rudduck et al, 1997) all conspire to keep students out of the investigative process altogether or assign them roles of minor significance.

1. Understanding the Necessity of Student Voice in Democratic Renewal

Searching for Students' Voices

In contrast to the approaches and dispositions just mentioned, the *VOICES* project has students at the heart of the research process. The decision to work in this way was born partly from a positive belief in the capacities of young people to see the world differently and become agents of their own and each other's transformation. It was also born of a mistrust in adults' capacities to speak authentically on behalf of young people.

We have become too used to speaking on behalf of others or about others in research. This has been particularly recurrent in the case of research that deals with aspects or problems related to students. We underrate the right and necessity of students speaking for themselves systematically. Their voices have remained separated from the problems that they themselves suffer from. Juan Bautista Martínez affirms that:

> *we ignore what pupils think and say because we do not listen to them. They are continually expressing themselves and narrating their experiences in a natural way. However, we*

> *don't listen to what they say. We don't use approaches or*
> *strategic forms to help us decode the insights they are*
> *expressing and we end up ignoring its significance for*
> *pedagogic relationships. (Martinez 1998, p. 56)*

It is important to remember that voice often articulates people's deep meanings and perspectives and, in the case of students, it often reveals and reflects their own understandings about the school world and the reality that they are living. Their voice, in consequence, constitutes a reflection of the realities they face and their efforts to define for themselves what they think, experience and expect. However, there remain problems of interpretation and representation in which there are real dangers of unwitting distortion and pseudo-translation. As Linda Alcoff reminds us:

> *In both the practices of speaking for as well as the practice of*
> *speaking about others I am engaging in the act of representing*
> *the other's needs, goals, situation, and in fact, who they are. I*
> *am representing them as such and such, or, in post-*
> *structuralist terms, I am participating in the construction of*
> *their subject positions. (Alcoff, 1991/92, p. 9)*

What right do we have to attribute to ourselves the role of translators of students' opinions? To do so with an untroubled alacrity too often constitutes an indefensible arrogance. We are in a very precarious position to penetrate and to fully understand the world of young people properly. The kind of sensitivities and negotiations that Schutz (1993) underscores in his account of interpersonal knowledge are an appropriate corrective to the sort of arrogance to which we are objecting.

In our daily life with others, including the young, we persist in believing and acting in ways which imply that interactions are mechanical and decoding processes are linear. We know from authors and from our own experience, firstly, the difficulty that adults have in understanding young people's voices, and, secondly, the fact that our cognitive and affective categories do not mesh with those of the young, with the result that misunderstandings often arise. Problems emerge because adults dominate the world and, in consequence, they seek to maintain their own form of seeing the world, of discovering it, of giving meaning to it.

Yet, as we know, there is no one way of understanding or interpreting the world. The necessity of dialogue remains absolute. All attempts to interpret the voices of young people or to propose solutions to their problems are suspect because, as Jean Rudduck et al say, 'young people's frameworks for making sense of the world are not yet standardised on the adult norm' (Rudduck et al, 1997, p. 3) or, as Fielding says:

> *We can only hesitantly speak on behalf of the others*
> *significantly unlike ourselves because we lack, not only*
> *understanding, but the means to understand those whose*
> *interests and causes we would represent. (Fielding, 1998, p. 5)*

Confronting Issues of Power in Researching with Students

The problem of power and the dangers of making decisions on behalf of students have been rarely studied. Saken (1989, citing Gough 1987) affirms that problems of power and valuing their personal importance represent two of the basic necessities for students. Regrettably, these two concerns remain largely ignored or unacknowledged in the research context. Too often adult versions of student perspectives serve to bind them into the status quo rather than provide an occasion for authentic dialogue and fresh thinking. As Giroux says:

> *voice and student experience are reduced to a mere thing*
> *when they are only turned into useful data; they become a*
> *thing that can be measured, administered, registered and*
> *controlled. Their distinctive character, their lively quality, all*
> *of them are aspects that are dissolved under an ideology of*
> *control and management. (Giroux, 1993, p. 188)*

There are now signs that the situation is gradually beginning to change and there is a growing interest in incorporating students in the research process. In some cases, they can contribute towards its voice and on occasions can support and analyse aspects of the investigation process (Hartman et al, 1994; Pearson & Santa, 1995; Stucky, 1995). Nevertheless, as Gitlin says, 'these changes in educational research methods have done little to alter the alienating relationships between the researcher and those studied' (Gitlin, 1995, p. 443). In fact, and especially in the case of studies related with school, researchers have operated under the assumption that investigators are alone responsible for constructing knowledge and have ignored students' capacities and left them outside the decision-making process.

However, a growing number of studies are incorporating students with the power to decide and to act not only for their own benefit, but also on behalf of their peers. Collaborative projects have been designed to encourage the expression of their voices so as to take them into account, to make them conscious of their right to choose, to take initiatives and to act on the matters that affect their school life; they have also been granted the possibility of operating and solving their own problems. These new approaches imply, among other things, that researchers are beginning to change from capturers of information to facilitators that empower students so that they can become social actors with the capacity to express their concerns and act on what has been researched. In other words, these studies empower students to become agents of their own historical transformation (Soo Hoo, 1993; Atweh & Burton, 1995; Oldfather, 1995; Fielding, 1999).

Collaborative Action Research

Our view is that a collaborative action research approach (Carr & Kemmis, 1988) lends itself particularly well to issues of students' agency mentioned above. An action research approach to school experiences with values conflicts and complex interactions among different people assumes differential understandings among those who make up the school community. It is not possible to think of automatic understanding. On the contrary, a fluid exchange process is needed to develop joint understandings and common meanings. Student approaches, often significantly different from those of adults, constitute a fundamental contribution to explain and understand the world from a more comprehensive perspective. What is in students' best interest in not necessarily a matter of solely adult judgement. Student participation and the expression of their voices are fundamental if we want to jointly build a better world. As Lincoln reminds us:

> *Because they do not necessarily reflect a dominant majority view of the world, such voices have the power to criticise the dominant power structures, to question 'how things are', what is meant by good, and even to provide new theories of how the world might be ordered. (Lincoln, 1995, p. 90)*

In our approach to collaborative action research with students, we felt it was important to establish a sense of equality among all the investigators as a way of ensuring the inclusion of all visions and voices in both the analysis and construction of new knowledge. Student researchers provide a bridge between the realities of school and the external world which outsider researchers often have difficulty traversing. Taking joint account of each other's perspectives promotes a sense of moral responsibility in the construction of knowledge and diversity; preferences and daily life are valued and respected.

The Central Role of Students in Researching Democracy

Taking student perspectives seriously is important. However, it is not enough. The intention of this project is not just to incorporate what we take student voices to be saying. Rather, it is to involve students as fully fledged members of the research and development team whose brief is to design and realise an educational programme for democracy that takes into consideration their understandings and proposals.

Since the topic of the research and development is democracy, it is fundamentally important to practise it, to live it in reality. Dewey (1972) defines democracy not only as a type of government, but also as a form of social coexistence, and as a way of enabling communication of combined experiences. He affirms that in democratically run organisations, individuals understand each other as part of a community in which problems are solved by collective deliberation and a shared concern for the common good, where the 'habit of intelligence' is one which is used to confronting and solving problems through reflexive inquiry, collective deliberation and rational debate.

The role of students in developing the democratic 'habit of intelligence' is as important for adults in the research team as it is for the students. One of the objectives of the project is to know the conceptions that the young people have about democracy. Given the difficulties that adults often have in understanding what students really mean, it was important to truly know from students themselves the aspects of the topic that they identified as important by respecting and appreciating the validity of their perspectives and contributions. This is integrally bound up with issues of language. As Juan Bautista Martínez reminds us, 'Students do not use adults' social or political vocabulary ... They use an everyday, colloquial language that incorporates intense experience' (Martínez, 1998, p. 59). We also agree with Rodríguez when he says that democracy supposes that those who communicate have something of their own to communicate, 'something personal ... something that is presented as an option ... That is to say, he/she is an autonomous being' (Rodríguez, 1996, p. 116) and to respect that autonomy more fully necessitates different approaches and different aspirations.

2. Developing Student Research Capacity

Initial Steps

To carry out the project, it was necessary to find two educational establishments willing to participate in the two stages of the project of (a) students gathering research data and (b) later on, students developing an educational programme designed by them to address challenges of democratic values and practices. We contacted several schools and eventually established a partnership with Colegio Guillermo Brown, a subsidised private school and the Liceo Francisco Vergara, a municipality school, both at Viña del Mar. In selecting the schools, we were keen to have mixed schools, schools that were subsidised and from the municipality, and schools that were within reasonable reach of the university campus to enable participants to attend meetings. In selecting students, we went for the second and third secondary year, given the 3-year time-span of the project and the necessity that at least second years could participate during the whole duration of the project. We also looked for a certain level of commitment and sympathy with the topic, a willingness to accept and share responsibility for agreed tasks, and a good disposition to work in a team and with staff at the university. The students also had to have the permission of their parents. Since it was necessary to select students, and the teachers were the only ones that knew them, we sought their help. Having been selected, our main mode of communication was with students directly.

As a way of developing the research team, we had a 2-day session at the University in which all researchers and the international consultant, Michael Fielding, participated. This work was intended to serve multiple purposes: it gave us the opportunity to become a team; it allowed us to reach agreement about a number of key issues; and lastly, it provided the student researchers with the skills to carry out interviews as the process of data gathering.

Establishing Shared Values and Mutual Understandings

One of the requirements of developing the process of the investigative action in a rigorous way entails the search for and identification of a common frame of values and understandings between all the investigators. Another requirement of a team composed of teachers and students involves respect for difference as well as the inclusion of diverse cultural concerns and of varied situational contexts. In our view, adults do not possess the monopoly of expertise over these matters. Similarly, we do not have privileged ethical standpoints by virtue of our adulthood alone, even less so in the context of an investigative action. Thus, we were not entitled to decide, in a peremptory and unquestionable way, the frame for operating in a mixed group with the variety of the one we had just constituted.

We also think that a team that is studying democracy should practise it. Thus, it was necessary to create an environment for practising freedom and the free expression of ideas. The values and principles that inform actions, that shape the life of groups, are not necessarily the same in all cases, just as there is no one way of living democracy. A legitimation of agreement is needed on the basis of a systematic reflection and dialogue resulting in consensus. This combined reflection stimulates, in turn, the generation of positions that go far beyond individual thoughts and become collective decisions for action and change.

The necessity of the construction of a base of common understanding in the group is not only a methodological demand. It is also a recognition of a social-constructivist perspective that considers that the source of knowledge and of the development of people is neither in the person nor in the object, but rather, in the interactive relationship among them.

With this in mind, the first activity related to the establishment of this common base. It would allow us to decide later on what we wished to do and how we wished to do it. We formed two groups among all the investigators and we undertook a reflective exercise to identify common meanings and from these to understand the collective process of definition and demarcation of the problem to investigate and to solve. We agreed, in general terms, that the bases of our work would be those that correspond to the central values of democracy: freedom to really express what our opinions and feelings were; equality, that is to say, we all had to feel equally valued; and lastly community, that is to say, we would take care and we would help each other, as a group of brothers and sisters that wanted to build a better world.

In specific terms, we concluded that we would respect and listen to what each one had to say in order to try to understand the points of view of others; we all considered ourselves as both teachers and learners thus constituting a society of equals. To work in this way required both humility and generosity; it was the only way to develop the courage and trust to ask about what we did not understand. We were aware that we had the right and the duty to express our opinions with freedom, trust, autonomy and authenticity. The recognition and valuation of our differences constituted part of the richness of the group.

Developing Shared Expectations

We went on to work on the expectations that each group – of students and university researchers – had about what they could contribute to the group as a whole. Even though we worked in separate groups of students and teachers, there was substantial agreement about what was expected from each group.

Students' own perception of their contribution was that they would be motivated and enthusiastic to enable the project to succeed. Their commitment would ensure the project was engaging and interesting. They would gather information rigorously; would become protagonists on behalf of students' voices and would find out what the other students thought about democracy. Starting from their own opinions, they would create an engaging programme. They would feel able to express their doubts, and would pay attention and try to learn to contribute to our emerging knowledge in ways which enhance unity and respect.

Regarding the university researchers, the students hoped we had a permanent disposition to support them and value everyone in a climate of trust already demonstrated in the project; we should also contribute our knowledge and encourage the expression of their voices; we should recognise them as equals; create opportunities for us to relate to each other and be able to address doubts and uncertainties. Finally, we should also be able to give answers to technical questions and be able to welcome their proposals genuinely.

What We Want to Achieve

A third phase of the training moved from agreement about aims and purposes to more substantive exploration of what we wanted to accomplish. There was a shared sense that what we were trying to do was substantial and significant and that each of the contributory tasks was possible if we lived our value aspirations. In general terms, the students wanted to improve the relationships between teachers and students in their school; they wanted to translate alienating and confusing terms into the language of young people; and they wanted to get to know their rights and duties. They also wanted to develop a shared commitment to the expression of their views, to learn from each other, and to offer their learning to their schools. They wanted to learn how to live democracy and develop and flourish as persons. They wanted a society in which every one was committed to living with rights, duties and responsibilities.

Learning How to Gather Data

A fourth phase of the training focused more directly on learning how to gather information in the form of interviews. The students were given a short exercise designed to help them foresee some of the obstacles and opportunities encountered in the interviewing process. What came through particularly strongly was the importance of trying to capture what the interviewee was saying, regardless of whether or not the interviewer agreed with it; descriptions and interpretations are not the same thing. Other issues that emerged in discussion covered the full range of considerations and concerns appropriate to interviewing as a form of data gathering. What was significant, however, was the manner of their emergence. That is to say, these issues became real and problematic through the students themselves being involved in active, reflecting interviewing, not listening to university staff telling them how to do it.

Explaining the Project to Fellow Students at School

A very important issue, which we faced towards the end of the training, concerned what the students were going to say to their peers in schools about the project. As a result of further work and reflection, the students suggested:

*We want to study what we think about democracy and how we
experience it. This activity is being developed for the benefit of
all young people and that is why we need to know what they
think about their own rights, what they think democracy is
and about the values implied in it so that everybody can know
about them. We want them to discover all this through
engaging, original processes designed by ourselves. This is an
activity carried out by young people, for young people.*

3. Learning to Live Democracy through Collaborative Research

A number of lessons emerged from our initial work together. In general
terms, we concluded that the process of joint reflection constituted a real
discovery for all involved. On the one hand, the teachers recognised the
maturity and creativity of the students' capacity for work; on the other,
the students felt that the invitation to participate as researchers in the
project was a sign of trust in their potential and they welcomed the
opportunity that we had given them of working jointly with us. As they
themselves said, 'university researchers worked with us as equals and
they gave us a lot of trust so that we were confident enough to say what
we knew and thought'.

Growing Together

The students are accustomed to working in the school in a hierarchical
and rigid atmosphere. Thus, working in a flexible learning structure was
completely different to the one they experienced daily. In addition to
learning research skills, this allowed them to come to the view that
learning is a dialogic and interactive process that goes beyond a passive
process controlled by adults. They understood it and they experienced it:
'they [referring to university researchers] allowed us to say what we
thought and in this way the cold teacher-student relationship
disappeared'.

This form of flexible work allowed them to confront their usual
ways of working with something quite different that they discovered
from group discussions. This was the satisfaction of ways of working that
go beyond a simple process of adding individual contributions to each
other. What happened was a cross-fertilisation of their individual
capacities. A student commented that 'together we work better and this
way we support each other'. This mutual support resulted in a body of
different knowledge that contained the individual contributions of all the
members of the team but integrated in a wider whole. The experience
seemed to provide a cohesion and identity that it would have been
difficult to achieve from individual practices. It provided a more

substantial group sense. They felt supported and confident that they would be able to respond to their own expectations because they were not alone in the task. As they themselves said:

> *As student researchers, we want this project to be successful and feel proud, because with our work, opinions and commitment we will be able to revalue democracy and thus we will grow as people.*

This approach has also allowed students to live the experience of learning how to manage their emotions. The conduct of arguments, having to respect the other's ideas, learning how to listen, to not dismiss others as stupid or worthless, to not feel personally attacked when someone has a different opinion – these were all important aspects of learning how to live with others, and, more specifically, learning how to be prepared for life in democratic society. One student, referring to the group work she had experienced, said, 'with the kind of work we have done the pattern related to "the one that knows speaks" and "the one that doesn't only listens" has been broken'. Another admitted that:

> *it is not necessary to try and demonstrate that you are better than the other person, or to put yourself in an advantaged position in front of the other person. On the contrary, one should rather be open and humble.*

It is particularly interesting to highlight the positions of the students regarding how they should interview. Discovering how to gather information in a rigorous way and developing their individual capacity to pose questions allowed them to discover by themselves the need to be faithful in the transcription of everybody's voices so as to understand and truly represent their own understandings. We strongly believe that learning the technical aspects of data gathering is not enough. The process must allow all those working to have the sense of becoming cooperating persons within a supportive community. As Benjamín Barber reminds us:

> *Democracy depends on the capacity to ask questions and on the faculty for independent thought and action, but democratic communities can be corroded by unending scepticism and undermined by forms of independence that recognise no mutuality. (Barber, 1992, p. 108)*

A confluence of each one of the individual efforts took place, promoting, in turn, the development of each one. All were compelled to contribute to the search for answers to the agreed problems. The discovery that it is possible to build new knowledge starting from the activity and effort of each one, but used and understood by all, represented a critical contribution for their research approaches and for the discovery of their own potential. They discovered the value of cooperating in a community of equals that had agreed on a series of values and understandings. In John Dayton's words, 'Education in democratic principles can lead to the exhilaration of discovery and the promise of hope for a better community' (Dayton, 1995, p. 137).

Living Democracy

The joint work developed by all helped us to be conscious that democracy is constructed by living it and practising it daily. Democracy is a human invention and therefore requires considerable effort and a renewed practice to learn it. This takes place when it is lived within a community committed to the destinies of those that comprise it. In all communities, people have different ages and outlooks. Therefore, learning how to live democratically requires the commitment of constant effort that will take everyone through the path of discovery of the other's potentialities. It is precisely with that other, the one that is by our side, be they young or adult, that we have to participate and learn how to relate to successfully. A student, highlighting her learning in the sessions, said, 'when we shared our thoughts we were able to reach agreements'.

Traditionally, adults have enjoyed a privileged situation with regard to young people that has authorised them to exert power over them. In this project, we wanted to use what privilege and power we had to promote the growth and development of democratic community. We were aware that adults have an obligation to provide students with experiences and opportunities so that they can know and practise democracy and work hard to achieve it. We were pleased that from the standpoint of at least one student, 'We discovered new ways of working. People have helped us to give our opinions and learn how to relate with adults'.

As adults, we cannot avoid the responsibility of creating, forging and promoting structures and relationships that encourage open dialogue, the expression of genuine voices and initiatives and the taking of decisions. In this way, we are working towards the construction of a society of equals in which teachers and student researchers learn together and negotiate agreement. We are mindful of both the wisdom and difficulty of John Dayton's observations about the responsibility of different generations in the developing of democracy:

> *The perpetuation of democratic community depends on an*
> *intergenerational commitment that recognises both rights and*
> *responsibilities as inseparably linked. Those that currently*
> *occupy the democracy must recognise their responsibility*
> *towards those in the past that created and sustained*
> *democracy for their benefit, and must also recognise the duty*

to maintain and transfer the democracy to future generations.
(Dayton, 1995, p. 153)

Students agreed that nothing was imposed. They were able to identify, analyse, and discuss with everyone to reach conclusions. Yvonna Lincoln is right when she says, 'Children and adults combine power and create new forms of wisdom when they explore learning together' (Lincoln, 1995, p. 89). But to achieve this, we had to do a great deal more than talk about students' participation; spaces, opportunities and possibilities were necessary so that they could intervene in the whole process of the research and not only in minor activities. Only in that way could students verify that they were being recognised as competent to make decisions and support actions they consider important.

Lessons for University Researchers

First, we have genuinely understood the dangers and the difficulties that make speaking for others so hazardous. Our sensibilities are different. Students have taught us that instead of discrediting their knowledge as trivial or lacking in seriousness, we should recognise that we are not expert about young people, that our understandings of their world are incomplete and sometimes distorted. We have to consider them as persons able to handle ideas, that have developed points of view and have forged convictions. Students send us messages that we would do well to hear. Thus, one of our student researchers observed:

> *A person can suddenly start talking at great speed without respecting what other people have to say. It is important to let people speak for themselves without putting words into their mouths by force. There are people who cover up your voice because they think they know more than you do and that is wrong, because we do have convictions.*

In the end, if we truly want to translate the message, we need to understand that they are telling us that we would benefit from their knowledge and intuitions. If we work at incorporating and encouraging participation and constant expression of students' voices, a richer awareness will be achieved with regard to future possibilities and the students' own abilities. This is confirmed by Pearson & Santa (1995), who worked with secondary students who investigated their own learning styles and discovered study strategies corresponding to these styles. It is also confirmed by the work of Oldfather (1995) involving students directly in the investigation of their own motivations and learning methods.

Secondly, they have taught us that passive strategies and directed routines do not allow students to express all that they are thinking and, consequently, they cannot be the real protagonist of their own learning. A student expressed this overtly when referring to the experience of the day: 'I thought that we would work by filling forms and not as we have worked here, that is by practising and giving our opinions'. They were also aware of the meaning and practice of being silenced. A student said that 'when teachers enter into the classroom they decide how and where everything should be organised, so they say "put this thing this way and in this place" and we have to do exactly as they say. That is to say, we cannot give our opinions'. It was evident that they did not like that kind of regime and wanted us to know that.

Thirdly, these experiences cannot leave us unaltered. They remind us of the necessity of treating them and respecting them not only as equals, but also as people that have something different and important to offer. We can no longer think of students as empty vessels or blank minds. On the contrary, their minds are already active with all that they have lived and are living. They have developed ways of seeing things, have learned how to solve their daily problems, have positions, ideas and suggestions coming from their continuous exchanges with the environment. They are able to build up knowledge if they are given the opportunity to reflect and their practical knowledge is taken into account. This was exemplified in their observation:

> *We thought that Michael [meaning the international consultant] was giving us a class and so we thought we should have to take notes, but it was not like that. Here nobody taught us anything and we built every thing by ourselves.*

Listening to their voices requires not only that we give them the opportunity to express themselves, but that we have a certain sensibility to identify the beliefs underlying their reflections.

Our experience working with student researchers meets all the requirements set by Gitlin's (1995) citation of Cold (1981) for a real investigation with students. Students have been involved voluntarily in this project. They feel they have the power to decide they are going to research something important because they are studying something they see as a necessity and they are being offered the possibility and the challenge of solving it. Both their peers and the school community are seeing their activity as of value and they feel that they are creating something new. We suspect that these factors have contributed significantly to their commitment to the project. They have attended all the meetings, often on not very convenient days, as most of the sessions have been carried out in vacations and on Saturdays. However, their desire to participate and their commitment have not faltered. As one student said, 'we are completely aware that all of us are responsible for the research'. When the students perceive that they have achieved their right to talk, that their voices are taken into account and their contributions valued, they become motivated to make critical reflections and do not consider themselves simple objects of experiments but reflexive, autonomous and with a common interest.

Fourthly, we are aware that we created a community in which all voices are to be respected, valued not only in inclusive terms but also in critical terms. Students have become conscious that they have the primary responsibility for their development processes. They realise that they have capacities to participate actively in the research. They have been able to take control of what they want to do and thus they perceive a sense of a better future. The motto for the project proposed by them confirms this: 'With democracy and our voices we will be able to construct a better world'. We hope this joint project reflects the optimism, commitment and idealism they show.

Students' Agency

The experience of working with students as researchers has gone far beyond anything we expected. It does not mean that we did not have faith or confidence in their abilities or commitment; rather, they have imposed their own pace and needs on our work together. When we started working with them, we had a sort of preliminary itinerary that covered small group sessions and general ones. These last ones were meant to take place according to the different stages of the research. We planned the training session to be followed by the students interviewing their classmates, before meeting again as a research team by the end of November to analyse data. However, once they started their interviews, the students proposed an additional session, this time with one of the students giving us a talk about democracy. We decided to organise a conference but the students were to be in charge of the academic aspects and practicalities associated with it, e.g. having transparencies, an overhead projector, pacing, and dealing with discussion. Despite the fact that the student who was to lead the session had to attend the funeral of an uncle, he managed to be there to deliver his talk. Such a high level of commitment demonstrates how responsible students can be as long as they feel they are involved in meaningful activities and are given the opportunity to shape and contribute to their development.

During the talk about democracy, the group explored a problem that the students from one of the schools were currently experiencing. The students at this particular school wanted to have a voice in organising a school day on which they had traditionally been allowed to do activities outside the normal curriculum. Customarily, staff would organise and decide the activities in which the students were supposed to engage and have a good time. However, the students were tired of trying to have fun with activities that had no meaning for them. It was time for them to have a say. Even though they talked to the headteacher and shared their hopes and enthusiasms with him, he would not listen to them. So, they approached the Student Council and proposed a strike.

Within a few days, they told us that the strike had been successful, that every single student has remained sitting in the yard for two and a half hours. What is more, the teachers gave them silent support as none of them tried or insisted in taking them into the classrooms. The students recognised that at least two of the teachers could have exerted their power over some of the classes and students would have, for sure, gone into the classrooms. Finally, the students got half of what they requested.

Two weeks later, the students asked for another session, this time to be trained in managing focus groups. We ran the session and the students worked very hard until they finally decided that they had mastered the procedure. The following week, the groups of students from the school not involved in the strike asked for another session in order to learn in detail about the processes that their peers from the other school had lived through. We, the staff, decided that this session was a good opportunity for teaching them within a meaningful context how to deal with and solve conflicts peacefully.

It is clear from these and other examples that our students have developed a certain sense of agency. They created a flow of events that we had not anticipated at all. We were tempted to let them pursue their initiatives without forcing situations or turning them into a discussion about key issues. However, we remembered that when we first met as a team and explored our mutual expectations, the students strongly expressed an expectation that we guide them and give them the information they needed to *grow as persons*. Our strategy, therefore, was to combine their initiatives with discussions and strongly connect to their own interests.

4. On the Necessity of a Better Future Now

The experience of the project thus far has helped us to understand that the creation of a community of work necessarily requires conditions that allow the development of a true and fraternal dialogue that includes all participants and can inspire a sense of moral responsibility in the construction of knowledge. This insistence on inclusion is a necessary condition for the success of this project, given the alienating nature of the great majority of the school experiences of the students. If we really believe that democracy should be understood as a critical contribution for the realisation of free, authentic and committed people, we teachers have to act in the belief that the research process is a joint construction and that in consequence we are all responsible for its results.

We believe that democracy is fundamental in the life of all people, especially students. Yet, too often it is parodied through the surface mechanisms of ritualised elections and voting. The present experience lived with students has allowed us to understand that it is necessary to develop and generate conditions for the flourishing of a true democratic culture that goes far beyond a merely formal participation in some decisions. It is about developing students' analytic and critical abilities that facilitate the expression of their reflections on decisions and actions they consider important in a community context of mutual support.

It is also important to report that the processes and experiences the project has entailed have developed in students a capacity to act, to intervene and to engage positively in changing their world together with others who care about its future. In fact, they have started acting by themselves. Their initiatives to promote activities that spring from their needs, their responsiveness in attending sessions on Saturdays, plus the weekly ones when they discussed the process of interviewing, reveal their deep engagement in a process of learning that cannot be stopped. They want to know more and would drag us into this stream of activities, propositions, initiatives and expectations.

We are amazed and utterly surprised. We never anticipated the immediacy of this kind of impact. We know we have a long road left to walk. But we are inspired by the students with whom we had the privilege to work. Voluntarily, they committed themselves to working for the well-being of their peers and for improvement of the school communities to which they belong. They are proud of creating something new and they expect that, with their dedication and our support, they will build a better world. We cannot disappoint them.

Acknowledgements

We would like to warmly acknowledge financial support from Fondecyt that has made and continues to make this project (Proyecto 1990634) possible.

References

Alcoff, L. (1991/92) The Problem of Speaking for Others, *Cultural Critique*, 20, pp. 5-32.

Atweh, B. & Burton, L. (1995) Students as Researchers: rationale and critique, *British Educational Research Journal*, 21, pp. 561-574.

Barber, B. (1992) *An Aristocracy of Everyone.* New York: Oxford University Press.

Carr, W. & Kemmis, S. (1988) *Critical Theory of Teaching.* Barcelona: Editorial Martínez Roca.

Dayton, J. (1995) Democracy, Public Schools and the Politics of Education, *Review Journal of Philosophy of Social and Science*, XX, pp. 135-156.

Dewey, J. (1972) *Educacion y Democracia.* Buenos Aires: Paidos.

Fielding, M. (1998) Students as Researchers: from data source to significant voice, paper presented to the 11th International Congress for School Effectiveness and Improvement, University of Manchester, January.

Fielding, M. (1999) Students as Researchers. Talk, Catholic University of Valparaíso, Julio.

Giroux, H. (1993) *La escuela y la Lucha por la Ciudadania*. Madrid: XXI Century.

Gitlin, A. (1995) Educative Research, Voice, and School Change, *Harvard Educational Review*, 60, pp. 443-465.

Hartman, J., DeCicco, E. & Griffin, G. (1994) Urban Students as Independent Researchers, *Educational Leadership*, 52, pp. 46-47.

Lincoln, Y. (1995) In Search of Students' Voices, *Theory into Practice*, 34, pp. 88-93.

Martínez, J.B. (1998) The Voice of the Pupil. Temporary Absence of Citizenship, *Notebooks of Pedagogy*, 275, December.

Oldfather, P. (1995) Songs 'Come Back Most to Them': students' experience as researchers, *Theory into Practice*, 34, pp. 131-137.

Pearson, J. & Santa, C. (1995) Students as Researchers of Their Own Learning, *Journal of Reading*, 38, pp. 462-469.

Rodriguez, M. (1996) Transversalidad y Democracia en el Contexto Europeo, *Revista de Educacion*, 309, pp. 95-126.

Rudduck, J., Wallace, G. & Day, J. (1997) Students' Voices: what can they tell us as partners in change? in K. Scott & V.N. Trafford (Eds) *Partners in Change: shaping the future*. London: Middlesex University Press.

Saken, D. (1989) Due Process and Democracy, *Urban Education*, 23, pp. 323-347.

Schutz, A. (1993) *La Construcción Significativa del Mundo Social*. Buenos Aires: Paidos.

Soo Hoo, S. (1993) Students as Partners in Research and Restructuring Schools, *Educational Forum*, 57, pp. 386-393.

Stucky, N. (1995) Performing Oral History: storytelling and pedagogy, *Communication – Education*, 44, pp. 1-14.

Pupil Voice in Europe

LYNN DAVIES

Democracy is adapting society ... You learn to stretch, bend down to the majority ... To respect the laws of the community you live in, written and unwritten responsibility for fellow citizens, neighbours ... you are part of society ... You have freedom to choose, to demonstrate, to tell how you feel if you don't agree. (Danish Efterskole pupils, 16)

Kalle: We're not allowed to eat sweets or chew chewing gum in class. I think that's stupid, I mean it's not as if we're eating them with the teachers' teeth. (Skolverket, 2000, p. 48)

Introduction

This chapter arises out of a funded research project, the 'Euridem' project, which explored pupil democracy in four countries of Europe (Denmark, Germany, the Netherlands and Sweden), in comparison with England. The project was instigated by the Children's Rights Alliance in London and jointly funded by Gulbenkian and the National Society for the Prevention of Cruelty to Children (NSPCC). This is an interesting coalition of interests; it is indicative that those known as child 'protection' agencies are now covering the whole spectrum of contexts in which children's rights and humanity have the potential to be abused – including formal education. The initial context was the awareness by those working in the area of rights and democracy in the United Kingdom that some European countries have more advanced systems for pupil voice. Increasing numbers of schools in the United Kingdom, of course, have school councils, class councils or circle time and there are some exciting initiatives involving regional councils, youth parliaments and shadow G8 conferences. Yet, these are projects from individual schools or local authorities: there is no national legislation that pupils must have representation in their schools or on national educational forums. While the new citizenship education guidelines recommend structures such as school councils, these are not compulsory. There appears to be resistance to such obligation because of the English grand tradition of liberalism (and in spite of a centralised and obligatory National Curriculum). Some European countries, in contrast, have firmer legislation on pupil representation and more autonomy for regions or schools on curriculum. We were interested in the history, extent and effect of such legislation, in order to make concrete recommendations for practice in the United Kingdom.

The research involved examining legal and other official documentation from each country, interviewing policy-makers and stakeholders in Ministries of Education and visiting schools to talk to pupils, teachers, parents and principals. The full report is found in Davies & Kirkpatrick (2000); this chapter highlights the issue of pupil voice, tracing, in the four countries, the contexts and styles in which pupils are able to make themselves heard. Such contexts are true of other countries as well, of course – we are not saying that Europe is unique. School student councils have a long tradition in Tanzania, and other countries in transition (for example, Chile, in this volume, South Africa, Namibia) have recognised the need to involve pupils in decision-making and start to give them some ownership of the educational process. Yet, the United Kingdom Government does not have a tradition of learning from developing countries, and – if it looks anywhere at all – looks to developed countries and/or those who seem to do better on international tests of mathematics achievement. It is important to demonstrate that firm national systems for pupil voice are neither part of some Stalinist state nor only associated with transitional economies; they are part of a mature democracy that ensures rights and responsibilities for all its citizens and subjects of whatever age.

This chapter firstly describes five contexts in which pupil voice could be heard: councils, curriculum negotiation, school committees, regional councils and pupil unions. These do not all derive directly from legislation, but I would argue that the legislation and its associated traditions provide a climate in which it becomes 'normal' to involve young people in decisions that affect them (as specified in Article 12 of the Convention on the Rights of the Child). The chapter then discusses some of the issues and dilemmas involved in enabling pupil voice.

Contexts for Voice

Councils

Councils involving pupils naturally have different names in different countries; the Netherlands, for example, uses the term 'participation council' and Germany refers to a 'Schulkonferenz'. The common form of participation is that of class councils or class times for discussing issues for representatives to take to the next level or whole school council, bringing back the results in various ways. The divergences between countries were the ages at which pupils should be represented in different arenas, and the balance in committees or councils between pupils, parents and teachers (parental voice is also taken seriously in Europe, with formal representation built in at class and school level).

For the participation council (half teachers, half parents/pupils) in V college in the Netherlands, for example, the pupils and liaison teacher came together before the meeting, to read through the materials and discuss them. Pupils could put items on the agenda directly. Constituting one-quarter of the body, pupils have a significant voice, even if outnumbered by adults: 'They are listened to, although they are not always at ease'.

The council can provide a forum – and a budget line – for responsibility. The head in P college in Sweden had a '24 hour repair' policy. Any breakage or disfigurement of the environment had to be fixed within 24 hours. This meant that pupils were not faced daily with the spectre of broken lockers or graffiti on walls. If the pupils were responsible for the damage, then the money for repair was taken out of the pupil council budget. This left less for activities and visits. The result was a pleasant and conducive setting, where pupils felt ownership of it, and felt that the head cared about the environment in which they worked.

Curriculum and Teaching

What is striking compared to the United Kingdom is the extent to which pupils have a voice in curriculum and teaching/learning. In NordRhein Westfalen (NRW), for example, secondary schools must have a 'Fachkonferenz' (subject committee) for each subject, the committee including elected parents and pupils as well as the subject teachers. The committee meets to decide the framework for subject method work and evaluation of performance, and discusses teaching methods and resources. From such formal structures, each school can then develop further pupil participation in the curriculum. S school has as its philosophy 'self-responsible behaviour' and spells out in its School Programme all the layers of participation set out in the law. Pupils have 2 free hours a week for project work and decide as a year group, in consultation with their teacher, on what and how to work. Every year, pupils reflect on their work at an away weekend for pupils, parents and teachers. The aims are that besides the leadership of the class council, pupils should be strengthened, supported and trained to lead single lessons for themselves, and that parents and older pupils should become motivated to offer development and spread their competences to others.

In Denmark, following a tradition of teacher and pupil discussing learning throughout their school life, teachers and pupils in upper secondary schools must discuss teaching regularly and undertake continual internal assessment of it. The purpose is to heighten pupils' awareness of their own joint responsibility for benefiting from the teaching. What is being assessed is not the teacher or students individually, but the teaching, i.e. the 'work-related interaction'. One *Handelskole* in Denmark had evolved a complex but student-centred option system. Unusually for a secondary school, teachers had a group with which they often spent a large part of the day, on interdisciplinary work, which may or may not be in the teacher's specialism. Pupils and teachers learned together, pupils often using the Web and training the teachers. During the option periods, specialist teachers were available in specific rooms for help, and students could choose their teachers (as also found in Sweden and the Netherlands).

In Sweden too, pupils must by law be involved in curriculum planning, both at class level and at school level. At this point, it should be acknowledged that this may be one of the most difficult areas to implement fully. In 1993, Persson quoted a National Agency report which was then discouraging:

> *Pupils should have influence on classroom instruction. This was established by the School Act as well as by the National Curriculum, but according to the evaluation, this is seldom the case. Even more striking is perhaps just what pupils feel that they can exert influence on. They have the most influence when deciding where to go on school journeys or who to work with in a workgroup. They have the least influence when it comes to text-books, home-work and tests.*

The Swedish National Agency has been making strenuous efforts to increase pupil influence, and the situation is changing. It has to be said that choices that we saw in all four countries were more to do with broad topic or project themes for the class, rather than textbooks. The latter would present resource problems. Danish pupils said firmly though: 'We can negotiate decisions on homework with our teachers'.

Committee Work

We also saw examples of pupils being involved in a number of important committees – for example, the discipline committee that looked at pupil exclusions, the complaints committee or the safety committee, all of which are regulatory bodies. I shall return to the question of whether this is a Foucauldian 'surveillance' later on. In all Danish upper secondary schools, the scope of influence of pupils' councils has been increased by offering members a seat on almost all the existing committees they cared to join. 'Already, by virtue of this, pupils have been endowed with powers which presumably reach further than is the case in most other countries' (Paludin & Prinds, 1999). Interestingly, in the 'private' school visited in Denmark, similar structures existed, although the legislation did not always cover these. What seemed to occur was a national acceptance by teachers and parents that such involvement was important.

Of great significance was participation in appointments committees. There is growing recognition of the importance of the pupil view in deciding who is, or will make, a good teacher or headteacher. Pupils are becoming more involved in the appointment of staff in England, both at primary and secondary level (Davies, 1999). Interesting examples were also found in Europe: at de B college in the Netherlands, pupils were involved in the appointment of the new director, reading all the application forms. An equally critical part of their work was in the evaluation of probationary teachers. Teachers are appointed for 2 years, and must have their contract agreed before continuing. In this school, a task group of 15 year-olds formulated a questionnaire, distributed it to pupils in a range of classes taught by the teacher, analysed the results by computer and presented a report to the main appointments committee. The pupil voice counted for one-third of the final judgement. The questionnaire asked about whether the teacher explained things, was punctual, marked homework and kept to the same rules as had been agreed for all members of the school (such as smoking or eating in class).

The interesting link with budgets in terms of teacher appointments/retention is the delegated budgets to schools. Schools in the Netherlands who do not wish to keep on a teacher after 2 years' probation have to demonstrate that the teacher has had a chance to improve and that they have had a mentor. The financial risks are 'enormous'. Involving pupils in decisions on teacher retention helps those decisions, and enables the right teachers to be retained. As one head commented, 'We haven't kept anyone we didn't want'.

Local, Regional and National Councils

Pupil voice is not something to be confined to the school level. A striking contrast to the United Kingdom was the extent of recognition of the need to consult pupils within broader frameworks of decision-making. Denmark's Folkeskole Council is a national body which decides the policy for the 7 years of compulsory education. This has representation of pupils and parents. It would be unthinkable in Denmark to instigate new laws or guidelines without consulting all various bodies, and while pupils would have a small voice on such national bodies, it is significant that they are there. The Netherlands has Primary and Secondary Consultative Committees where the Minister and representatives of teachers', heads' pupils' and employers' organisations meet. In contrast, if one looks down the list of consultative bodies for Department for Education and Employment documents, pupils are conspicuous by their absence. One problem is that there are no systematic regional or national structures for pupil voice and representation that the Government could consult, even if it wanted to.

Nordrhein Westfalen probably had the most extensive layers of representation. This happened at four levels: the school, the district, the region and the *Land*; the Land then chose representatives for the national or *Bund* level. This was set out in a clear diagram of the roles of representatives and link teachers and how each level elected representatives into the next level. The Land Board is supported by a permanent and paid management. These pupil committees or unions are very active, in production of materials, mounting conferences and training. The Land Board produces handbooks on legislation for school and regional representation as well as information pamphlets, such as on 'The extreme right in our schools'.

There was, however, at least one view that there were too many levels, with it not being clear what should be discussed at each level, and with difficulties of travel for pupils. What seemed to be most effective was the coordination to promote big events or conferences, such as on large-scale political themes of anti-fascism or women and sexuality. With a pyramidal structure of ever-smaller representation, the top seems a long way from the bottom, and the room for decision-making or even advice is small. With a large congress, anyone can attend and perhaps have their voice heard. The local levels of representation, next to the schools, are also effective; one in NRW discussed the current thorny political issue of types of selective/comprehensive school, as well as talking of rights and duties, and the pupils felt this was very useful.

Unions

While most countries would have student unions at higher education and further education level, not all have them at school level (or, as in the United Kingdom, they have struggled and failed to continue). We were impressed by the contribution of the pupil unions in Europe, coordinated by OBESSU (the Organising Bureau of School Students Unions) based in the Netherlands. In its explanation of its European School Students' Rights Charter, OBESSU (1995) begins:

> *In a truly democratic system every part of society is*
> *represented in legislative and decision-making bodies,*
> *including those who do not have the right to vote because they*
> *have not passed the age of consent.*

OBESSU works on the principle that pupils are able and critical enough to evaluate their own school and their own education; it was indicative of official support for this line that for us to talk with the union representatives, they were invited to the relevant Ministry, where they seemed at home and indeed may have received funding. It was a genuine partnership to deliver training and to provide opportunities for young people to meet together with teachers' or parents' unions.

In Sweden, there are two types of pupil 'union'. The *Elevorganisationen* (pupil union) for pupils aged 14-18 has individual members or membership by local unions, and the *Sveriges Elevrads Samarbetsorganisation* (SVEA) is a federation of school councils at the upper secondary school level. The latter receives funds from the National Youth Council, although the representatives felt that this was not sufficient, and that funds should come from the Government or from the National Agency. It has a well worked out set of aims and philosophies based on nine key words: improve, educate, develop, inspire, cooperate, engage, inform, communicate and influence. These words interact, for example, in 'educate' and 'cooperate': SVEA can educate school councils, but they also educate each other and share common problems. (SVEA's view on councils was that although they are compulsory, not all schools schedule them properly, and the law should be tightened to say that they should be made to work, not just that they should be there.) A network, project database, a magazine which goes to all schools seven times a year, a web site, and various conferences, meetings and projects means a mass of communication possibilities. SVEA conducts its own research, sending questionnaires to pupils and teachers on what sorts of influence they want, and visiting schools as well as meeting government representatives. It would also give support in an area of conflict or pupil strikes.

In the schools themselves, there were sometimes mixed reactions to the unions. In Sweden, there was awareness of the different political stances of the two unions. In NRW, the problem was that the union was dominated by *gymnasium* (grammar school type) pupils; the vocational schools had tried to establish their own association at the level of the Land, but were not successful. Pupil representatives in the gymnasium were very scornful of the regional school organisations, and did not attend meetings, seeing them as hard left activist.

In the Netherlands, however, there seemed universal support for LAKS, which is described as a pupil 'national action committee' on the promotion of youth participation in schools. LAKS stimulates the setting up of pupils' councils in schools. It has prepared legislation on this subject, which was ratified by Parliament. It has produced a Secondary School Guide for parents and pupils which lists 16 questions which should be asked about a school with regard to 'having a say in what goes on'.

One of the key roles of the Danish pupil union was to take part in consultations. As indicated earlier, they were routinely consulted by the Ministry at all stages of educational change. In their magazines and information for pupils, they can include the political work that they do, and explain what is happening in the Ministry. Their magazine is financed with advertising, and a copy goes to every school in Denmark (30,000 copies). The whole union is supported by the Government, with sources from two different foundations and from the lottery. As with SVEA, they visit as many schools as possible, to tell them about the organisation, encourage individual or school membership and give training and advice. Their view is that 'it is not difficult to get influence if you really want'. Denmark is probably unique in the degree to which the unions really feel the pupil voice is heard in the Ministry, that they can 'represent' pupils in government. They would always want a greater say, or feel that they could be listened to more when new laws are made, but there is, nonetheless, an appreciation that they do have a direct channel of communication.

Issues in Pupil 'Voice'

Three central questions will be seen to emerge from the above descriptions: what and whom the voice is for, what decisions can be made and who makes them. Much has been written on 'empowerment', whether of women, ethnic minorities or pupils (Troyna, 1994; Davies, 1994). Some of the critiques of the notion relate to its vagueness, that is, whether it stays at the level of 'raising awareness' or 'giving a voice' or whether it really means such awareness and voices creating change.

What is Pupil Voice For?

It can be argued that simply giving pupils a voice is counterproductive if such voices are ignored or incorporated into structures where they lose ownership or the impact is not felt (see Fielding in this volume). It has to be very clear to participants what their powers and decision-making capacities are. Lower down the levels, councils may be advisory only, or deal with what are sometimes seen as 'minor' issues to do with playgrounds, trips, parties or vending machines. Degrees of power are linked to whether the council has a budget of its own, and/or participates in budget and resource decisions of the school. Further up the levels, greater questions of whole school budgets occur, or, as we saw, even in some cases, the appointment or retention of teachers. There are dilemmas here: pupil representatives on school boards where the major concern of the teachers is, say, teachers' conditions of service, or the timetable, reported feelings of being bored or unable to contribute. Yet, if pupil contributions are restricted only to immediate concerns of pupils, then their voice can be viewed as peripheral. This came out too in Davies's (1999) study of school councils in England.

As always, the political question is whether involvement of pupils in councils and committees is just a more subtle form of policing, a contribution to 'surveillance' (Foucault, 1977). Just as with the old prefects and monitors, children are better controlled if their peers do the controlling, or if decisions are seen to be made by those who are nearest to their interests. Pupils may be unable to move or see outside the traditional regulatory frameworks. The downside to democracy has always to be reckoned with, that of living with inappropriate decisions. An example in Saarland was of the class committee who decided to expel a pupil for truancy.

My view is that the benefits of formal pupil involvement outweigh their possible abuse or misuse by those in power, and that pupils generally see through or subvert ritualistic representation or overdomination by 'trusties'. There is, nonetheless, an issue about the evaluation of children when it comes to democracy and participation. Ziehe (1998, quoted in Skolverket, 2000) warns us of the consequences of assessment of the 'whole child'. He maintains that students have the right to protection against further expansion of the 'pedagogical calculation', however well intentioned it is. Students are entitled to a certain degree of opacity in their student world; they have a right to assessment-free zones in their everyday life at school. 'We might talk of the right not to succeed'. The challenge will be to find a way of finding out whether democracy is working in schools without placing the burden on individual children –or teachers – to demonstrate 'competence' in it.

What Decisions Can Be Made?

Even if the pupil voice is there to make decisions rather than just to advise or represent, then the linked question is the nature of decisions they can make. Democratisation would imply a sharing or redistribution of power; yet, so much depends on the amount of power the school itself has to make rulings and control its finances. If the school itself, as in Germany, cannot choose or appoint its own teachers or principals, nor fully decide curriculum, then there is not much power for a head to delegate or mandate – to teachers or parents, let alone to pupils.

Conversely, there is the question of whether pupils can have 'too much' power and voice, a fear expressed by many teachers. In P school in Sweden, pupils were unhappy with a teacher of Swedish. She did not, as specified in the regulations, consult with pupils about the course and its content; she yelled at them, she insulted them, she broke down and started crying in class, she 'didn't want to listen'. Having failed to convince her of their point of view, the pupils went to the Director of Studies to complain. A series of meetings between the Director of Studies and the pupils ensued, the first without the teacher present, and then five more with her there. She then did change her behaviour. The pupils seemed to take a very mature line: 'Now she listens and we are listening to her, giving her respect. Most still don't like her, but they are giving her respect'. Yet, on recounting this to a United Kingdom teacher, he was of the view that this episode was reminiscent of a Chinese communist state, with an 'exposure' of the teacher and a re-education ensuing. Is this a function of pupil voice?

Who Makes the Decisions?

There remains the perennial problem of representative democracy: that those elected into positions of class or school councillors will enjoy and benefit from school democracy, while the bulk of pupils may remain unconcerned or apathetic. This would be true of any political regime, where, unless voting is compulsory (as in Australia) large segments of the population may choose not to vote in elections or take part in local politics or community life. There is no reason why schools should have solved this problem, but it was certainly a concern for many in our research. They had provided as many avenues as possible for a pupil voice to be heard, yet not all pupils used these avenues, either because they were satisfied with school life or because they saw the councils as not being able to achieve a great deal.

In the Netherlands, it was felt in some schools that the more autonomous the school gets, the more the agenda of the participation council is dominated by aspects concerning school staff and their status as employees. An obvious problem was that democratic structures of decision-making and consultation take much time, and the temptation to short cut these, especially in declining resources, is ever present. We were told that even pupils get questionnaire fatigue if they are asked their opinion too often. In Sweden, a gymnasium pupil representative pointed out that, ironically, with a very open and democratic set of relationships, not all pupils will see the need to be on the school council, as they can talk to a teacher or the head at any time anyway. They see council meetings and activities as time-consuming, and want to *learn* something in school. When asked about what was necessary to make pupil participation and pupil councils effective, the view of one Swedish pupil councillor in Malmo was that, firstly, you need a head and teachers who push for it, and secondly, you need a 'burning issue' which would galvanise the pupils into activity. Can schools be too happy for democracy?

Schools were concerned about providing pupil motivation and rewards for participation, and there was some experimentation with giving 'credits' for being a member of the school council or other forms of participation.

P school in Sweden was so concerned that it had set up a dedicated 'pupil participation committee' of teachers and pupils to look at how to involve everyone. What then evolved was a parallel structure to the council/committee structure called 'workteams'. Fifteen different workteams with 8-10 teachers and 180 pupils designed curriculum projects which enabled pupils and teachers to work together in innovative and integrated ways. The head felt this was more powerful for pupil involvement than the council, as all have an investment in their own learning; for the pupils interviewed, both were equally important, and none wanted to abandon the council structure, as it fulfilled important functions.

Other schools were experimenting with special periods where all pupils were to participate in various committees and task groups; but as always, those pupils who were keen to take part found an interesting avenue; those who were not took the opportunity to 'sleep'. More successful, as indicated earlier, were periods set aside for pupils to choose their own curriculum activities, negotiating with teachers about attending extra mathematics classes or doing project work. The message seems to be to try to find a way for all pupils to take some control over the direction of their personal learning, *together with* the formal structures which generally direct such teaching and learning.

Linked to the question of whether the democracy is representative or participative is that of who represents or participates. There would be questions of gender, ethnicity and 'ability' here. Many schools in the four countries said that girls tended to be 'more active' in councils and committees than boys. Boys apparently considered such things 'not interesting' and girls 'saw more sides to a question than boys'. This raises interesting questions about gender divisions, and the nature of political involvement in schools. Pupil councils may be seen as associated with the 'caring' and stereotypically female side of involvement, rather than the public image traditionally associated with wider politics. Denmark mentioned the lack of research into gender participation in democracy generally and in schools, but knew that women participated more in the voluntary sector than did men, and voted differently. More research certainly seems needed in this area, as Sweden too was concerned about boys' underachievement and the possible link with a sense of identification with the school. A study there found that gender differences in school performance were not limited to traditional school subject tasks, but that girls performed better than boys also when it came to complex cross-curricular competencies such as creativity and the ability to consciously adopt ethical standpoints.

With regard to ethnicity, there was little in the laws of the countries about ethnic minority participation, and the link with ethnicity came more from the role of pupil groups in anti-racism campaigns or in challenging school policy. In some European countries, there is a shorter tradition of immigration than in the United Kingdom, and they will still talk of the 'problems of immigrants' in ways that would be unacceptable in Britain. There were still discussions in S college in the Netherlands about whether Muslim girls should be allowed to wear headscarves. Similarly, in V college, the school had planned to ban the wearing of headscarves, but students and the pupil council had protested. All students started putting scarves around their heads, to show that learning could still take place, and they won their case. The school was worried about its image outside, and whether white parents would send their children there, but pupils 'had to explain to the head' the importance of acceptance of different dress codes. This was a good and important example of pupil power, of young people working for the rights of others in the face of a neo-liberal agenda of markets and publicity image.

We did not find any examples of specific legislation on the representation of pupils with special needs, presumably as this is seen to be included in rights to participation for all children. Yet, it might well become an issue in terms of who actually becomes elected to positions of responsibility – often the highly articulate, the confident academically, those able to travel to meetings – groups traditionally underrepresented among those designated with special needs. This is another reason why pupil voice should not be restricted to the micro-political level of councils and committees but should be there at the curriculum and teaching level for all children. In some ways, this is there in the growing trend for individual negotiated learning plans for children with learning difficulties, and there is interesting research on self-advocacy by those with profound and multiple learning difficulties by Tilstone & Barry (1998).

My view would be that there should be national legislation to provide a framework for the participation rights for all children, but that decisions about quotas or targets for who participates in the representative arena should be left to individual schools – in negotiation with pupils of course. There are huge problems of continuity, for, unlike politicians, pupils do not want to remain in power where they are, and by definition, move on to new lives.

Discussion

Particularly impressive was how articulate and confident the pupils were that we met in the four countries. Mostly working in a second language, they were able to define democracy, to talk of its tensions or dilemmas as well as its benefits and to describe how it impinged on their lives. In group discussions with teachers and pupils, many small dialogues with teachers opened up in front of us as we posed our questions. There were disagreements and points of contestation about reality or policy. Yet, these were invariably conducted in a spirit of calm, of respect, of tolerance. We saw no aggressiveness, and few pupils 'showing off' or 'making statements' in their stance towards adults.

It is difficult to assess how much of this confidence and expressiveness stems from the overall culture of a country which values young people and their views, and how much would come from the formal structures which demand that pupils articulate what they want and need. In the end, the question is perhaps not that of voice but of rights. Unlike in England, in European schools we found pupils seen as having indisputable rights to be involved in matters such as curriculum, teaching, exclusions, dress and discipline, and to have charters and formal procedures for grievance. In England, these have more the spirit of being in the 'gift' of the school. A significant message is that of funding: in European countries, pupil voice is seen as important enough to receive funding at national, regional and school level, with pupils given permanent meeting rooms, travel expenses for meetings, funding for conferences and rooms allocated in schools for the school council (sometimes equipped with telephone, fax and computer); indirect funds come through the appointment of liaison teachers and teachers being given time to work with pupil representative structures. This may be out of the range of many countries, but this chapter has indicated some 'cost-free' examples of innovative ways in which pupil voice and pupil rights can be taken seriously. If national democracy is to develop, in the end they are not an optional extra.

References

Davies, L. (1994) Can Students Make a Difference? *International Studies in Sociology of Education*, 4, pp. 43-56.

Davies, L. (1999) *School Councils and Pupil Exclusions.* London: School Councils UK.

Davies, L. & Kirkpatrick, G. (2000) *The EURIDEM Project: a review of pupil democracy in Europe.* London: Children's Rights Alliance.

Foucault, M. (1977) *Discipline and Punish.* London: Allen Lane.

Organising Bureau of School Students Unions (OBESSU) (1995) *European School Students Rights Charter.* Amsterdam: Organising Bureau of European School Student Unions.

Paludin, P. & Prinds, E. (1999) *Evaluation of Education in Citizenship and Moral Judgement: an introduction to the SICI conference in Copenhagen.* Copenhagen: Danish Ministry of Education.

Persson, B. (1993) Children: decision-makers in Swedish schools – reality or another paper tiger? Paper provided by the Swedish National Agency.

Skolverket (2000) *A Good Enough School: a study of life at school and school's role in life.* Stockholm: National Agency for Education.

Tilstone, T. & Barry, C. (1998) Advocacy and Empowerment: what does it mean for pupils and people with PMLD? in P. Lacey & C. Ouvry (Eds)

Interdisciplinary Work with People with Profound and Multiple Learning Disabilities: a collaborative approach to meeting complex needs. London: David Fulton.

Troyna, B. (1994) Blind Faith? Empowerment and Educational Research, *International Studies in Sociology of Education,* 4, pp. 3-24.

Human Rights and Learning

GERISON LANSDOWN

Education is a universal human right, indispensable as a means of realising other rights.[1] This principle has long been recognised in the international arena. The right to education for all was included in the 1948 Universal Declaration of Human Rights. It was extended in the International Covenant on Social, Cultural and Economic Rights, and reasserted as a specific right for all children in the UN Convention on the Rights of the Child. However, education rights extend beyond the basic provision of education. The Convention on the Rights of the Child places three key obligations on governments with regard to education:

to recognise education as a human right for all children;
to respect the human rights of children within the education system; and
to provide education for human rights.

There are significant political, economic and cultural barriers to be overcome before those rights begin to be respected for all children. Behind the rights rhetoric, there are many competing agendas in the provision of education systems. Education is both a right of individuals and a necessity for society. For governments, there are two major goals in funding education – to develop the economic workforce and potential wealth of the future and to promote social cohesion and integration. Education is crucial to both. For parents, too, there are two demands on the education system. Most parents want to see their children achieve an education which will equip them for a successful future life. They also look to schools to transmit their values, culture, language – in other words, they seek in the education system the reinforcement and promotion of their own beliefs. There is recognition in international law of the right of parents to educate their children according to their beliefs.[2] It reflects the need to introduce boundaries on the exercise of power by a state to impose its political and religious agenda on children.

The UN Convention on the Rights of the Child introduces an additional perspective. It imposes boundaries not only on the state but also on parents. It insists that children's best interests must be a primary consideration in all matters affecting them, that their views must be given serious consideration and that respect must be given to the child's evolving capacities.[3] In other words, the Convention diminishes the parental prerogative – parental rights to determine their children's education are never absolute and are seen to recede as children grow older.[4]

There are, then, significant and often competing demands on the education system – from governments who are providing the legal and administrative framework and funding, from parents responsible for their children's upbringing, and children themselves as the consumers of education. In considering the relationship between human rights and learning, it is important to bear in mind these political and social realities and the inevitable tensions that they produce.

Education as a Human Right

Article 28 of the Convention on the Rights of the Child sets out the basic principle of entitlement to education, stressing the need for states to make primary education compulsory and available free to all children on the basis of equality of opportunity, and to encourage the development of secondary education for all children. In promoting the realisation of the right to education, governments must make it *available* to all children through adequate provision, *accessible* without discrimination to all children, *acceptable* in providing quality education appropriate to the cultural needs of all children, and *adaptable* to the changing and different needs of children.[5]

A total of 191 governments have ratified the Convention on the Rights of the Child – a record unparalleled by any other human rights treaty. The commitment undertaken by governments in so doing represents a unique and important opportunity to raise awareness of the education rights of children on the national and international political agenda. Nevertheless, progress remains profoundly disappointing. The reality is that too many promises made on the world stage by governments in ratifying the Convention, as well as many international conferences on education, have failed to materialise. These promises are not merely a matter of good will. They are underpinned by clear human rights obligations on the part of governments. Many governments in the developing world have failed to 'undertake measures to the maximum extent of their available resources' to ensure the right to education is realised for all children.[6] Furthermore, the right to education is a shared responsibility, and too many of the richer nations are in breach of their human rights obligations to promote international cooperation in education 'with a view to contributing to the elimination of ignorance and illiteracy throughout the world and facilitating access to scientific and technical knowledge and modern teaching methods'.[7]

The grim facts are that more than 130 million children of school age still have no access to any kind of basic education and 855 million people are functionally illiterate.[8] Some 150 million children enter the education system but fail to complete the basic programmes they start.[9] Millions more are experiencing substandard provision where little learning takes place. And behind the statistics lies the corrosive impact of the failure to provide education: higher mortality rates (a 10% increase in girl's primary enrolment can decrease infant mortality rates by over four deaths per thousand [10]), restricted employability, limited capacity to promote healthy living, impeded progress towards democracy.

Obviously, many of the poorest countries in the world experience profound difficulties in finding the resources to provide adequately for children's education. Crippling debt and the imposition of structural adjustment policies have forced governments to divert resources away from education. In Zambia, for example, whereas 2.5% of annual spending was on education, 10% was spent on debt-servicing.[11] Yet, accumulated evidence demonstrates that increased investment in education is of critical importance in the struggle for sustainable development.[12] Countries cannot afford *not* to invest in education. However, it is not just a question of resources, but also a matter of political commitment. Remarkable progress has been made by many developing countries in providing access to basic education. For example, amongst countries with per capita gross national products below $300, Bangladesh, Kenya, Malawi and Vietnam have rates of enrolment of over 80%, about 20% above what could be expected at their income level. In a similar income range, Haiti, Ethiopia, Mali and Niger enrol less than 30% of children.[13] In other words, it is possible to make significant progress towards the realisation of the right to basic education even in the poorest of countries where the political will exists.

Equality of Access

The problem of the right to education, however, is not merely one of national availability of resources. It also reflects how those resources are distributed. The requirement in Article 28 to provide education on the basis of equality of opportunity needs to be read alongside Article 2, which insists that all rights in the Convention apply to all children without discrimination on any grounds. The only discrimination permitted would be positive discrimination to ensure greater educational opportunities to groups of children traditionally denied access. But there are many groups of children who remain excluded from education – girls, rural children, disabled children, children from many minority or indigenous groups or children caught in armed conflicts. This chapter will discuss the implications of minority groups' right to education.

Minority Groups

Article 30 places obligations on governments to respect the rights of minority and indigenous groups to enjoy their own language, culture and religion. Most societies in the world include such communities – Australian Aborigines, the Catholics in Northern Ireland, the Palestinians in Israel. They usually have a separate language and culture which isolates them from the mainstream education system. This poses three profound challenges to governments in implementing the Convention. How are their rights to education to be secured? How will governments ensure that in providing that education, their right to respect for language, culture and religion is protected? And finally, in protecting those rights, how will they ensure that children's access to the mainstream culture is secured in order that they are not excluded from opportunities to participate in employment, training and higher education?

Efforts to protect the rights of minorities to education, whilst preserving their cultural rights, have prompted considerable debate about the alternatives of segregated or integrated provision. In respect of segregated education, it can be argued that it provides opportunities for children to be educated in their own language, and in accordance with their parents' own philosophical beliefs. For example, in Northern Ireland, almost all schools remain segregated on religious grounds. The Committee on the Rights of the Child recommended that the United Kingdom Government provide greater support to promote integrated schools.[14] Little progress has been made to date and this reflects, in part, the resistance on behalf of much of the population to integrated education policies, where there is mistrust that it would serve to undermine the integrity of the separate communities. However, segregation can also serve the cause of inequality and perpetuation of prejudice and stereotypes. The segregated schools of minority groups are too often characterised by poorer teaching and less resources. In South Africa, the separate education systems sustained and perpetuated the apartheid system. In Israel, where there have been two educational strategies – integration for all Jews of whatever ethnic origin, and separate education for Arabs – one outcome has been significant inequality for the Arab community. Its education is chronically underfunded, children have become disadvantaged with regard to jobs and higher education because of their weak command of Hebrew, and Arab teachers are often inadequately trained.[15]

On the other hand, integration brings its own problems. It often serves as a strategy by the dominant culture to impose its values on children, as a weapon in cultural repression. By forcing children to learn in the national language, and adopt its political and social values, it can erode either deliberately or by default, the culture of minority communities. Children in many countries are required to learn in schools which disregard their history, language, religion and culture. In Kosovo, for example, education in the Albanian language was not allocated any state funds, teaching aids in Albanian were not published and the curriculum and approach of teachers in the mainstream Serbian schools was highly politicised in favour of the dominant culture.[16] Similarly, in Turkey, Kurds are punished for using their language in schools and teachers dismissed for permitting it to be spoken.[17] In the United Kingdom, state schools are required by law to hold religious assemblies which must be wholly or mainly of a Christian character.[18] The religious syllabus, too, must reflect the fact that religious traditions are mainly of a Christian nature, despite the fact that in some schools, as many as 95% of the children might come from Muslim families.

In recent years, there has been a growing recognition that policies of assimilation which seek to impose a presumption of the desirability of cultural homogeneity are neither morally acceptable nor ultimately effective. In some countries – for example, Italy, France and India – there has been an insistence on secular education in which priority is given to no individual set of beliefs. Others have sought to introduce multicultural education, although this is often met with criticism both from the establishment – suspicious that it is being used to water down the dominant culture – and minority groups themselves, who often perceive it as a top-down initiative simply focusing on minority culture as an object of study.

Protecting the human right of minorities to education is a complex and challenging task. There are 5000 languages in the world, posing logistical problems with enormous resource implications if the right of all minorities to be taught in their own language were to be respected. Greater emphasis is needed to promote pluralist policies which allow for the preservation of distinct cultures whilst seeking to create equal opportunities to education for all children. International human rights law provides us with a framework for addressing these issues, but offers no easy solutions. It requires that governments evolve education systems which both seek to promote social integration whilst respecting diversity of culture. It requires that children are recognised as being themselves subjects of rights and that their wishes and feelings with regard to education must be given consideration. There are no simple solutions, but some of the changes that could be explored to promote appropriate education for minority children include:

curriculum adaptation to make it more meaningful for minority children;
bilingual teaching;

after school or weekend classes to help minority children keep pace with peers;

improvements in teacher training to reduce prejudice towards minority cultures;

recruitment and training of minority and indigenous teachers;

decentralisation of education structures to allow more local say over management and educational content;

involvement and participation of minority parents and children in the decision-making in schools.

Children in Western Countries

The right to education is, in principle, fulfilled to a much greater degree in developed countries where statutory entitlement to full-time education exists at both primary and secondary levels. However, these countries cannot afford to be complacent. Growing problems of truancy and exclusion from school are emerging in many European countries. In England, for example, there has been a significant increase in the numbers of children permanently excluded from school during the 1990s, from around 2000 a year at the beginning of the decade to 13,000 by the end.[19] Many children, once excluded, fail to re-enter the education system with the consequent loss of qualifications, and increased risk of unemployment, involvement in criminal activity, poverty and poorer health. Furthermore, the patterns of exclusion indicate discrimination against some groups of children in its use as a sanction. Afro-Caribbean boys in England, for example are up to four times more likely to be excluded than their white counterparts, and children in the care of the local authority and those with special educational needs are also significantly overrepresented amongst those excluded.[20]

To date then, the right to education is far from being fulfilled for all children. The four essential elements of accessibility, availability, acceptability and adaptability remain for too many an unattainable dream. Implementation of rights to education requires more than a legal framework of entitlement. It requires policies for translating the law into practice on the ground, diversion of resources to implement the legislation, and clear strategies for ensuring that vulnerable children, whether through poverty, gender, ethnicity or disability or any other status, achieve equal access. It also requires global action and practical commitment from the governments of the developed world, the international finance institutions and the relevant United Nations agencies. Then and only then, can the right to education for all become an achievable goal.

Respect for Human Rights in the Educational System

The Convention formulates a philosophy which promotes respect for children as individuals and recognises each child as unique in characteristics, interests and needs.[21] This philosophy needs to be reflected in the organisation, structure and ethos of educational provision. It is implicit in a number of principles in the Convention: the right of children to express their views and have them taken seriously, the right to freedom of expression, thought, conscience and religion, to information, the obligation to administer school discipline in a manner consistent with children's dignity, to promote the child's best interests and to aim to fulfil the child's potential.

The spirit of the Convention suggests the creation of schools which are child-friendly and in which children are encouraged to be curious, to argue, to challenge, to be creative, to explore and find out, to be listened to and respected. The Committee on the Rights of the Child has consistently recommended that governments take further steps to encourage greater participation by children in schools.[22] The Convention also stresses that as children begin to develop the ability to take decisions for themselves, they should be encouraged and enabled to do so. It recognises the important role that parents and others with responsibility for children have in providing them with direction and guidance but expects them to do so in ways which respect that, as children grow older, they become more capable of taking responsibility for themselves. In other words, children should be given every opportunity to be involved in matters of concern to them and as they acquire the understanding and maturity necessary to take decisions for themselves, they should be encouraged to do so.

But this philosophy is significantly at odds with the cultural traditions of education in most countries throughout the world where schools are characterised by authoritarianism, with the child constructed as the passive recipient of adult wisdom and expertise. It is still the case that in too many schools children sit in rows, learning by rote, and are punished by beating or other forms of humiliation for minor misdemeanours or difficulties in learning.

These challenging demands of the Convention on educational orthodoxy bring most sharply into relief the tensions described earlier between the goals of governments, parents and children in the provision of education. If governments are concerned to promote social cohesion, then isn't the traditional approach to education more likely to be effective in suppressing conflict and challenges to the status quo? If parents want children to acquire greater understanding of and respect for their cultural traditions, then surely legitimating the right to question those values may threaten that process?

Nevertheless, there are both principled and pragmatic arguments in favour of developing a more child-centred approach. It is clearly right that children are treated with respect in schools and that governments fulfil the obligations they have voluntarily undertaken in ratifying the Convention. But ultimately, its implementation in schools will be of practical benefit not only to the individual but to the wider society as a whole, for example, through the following.

Through enhancing the skills necessary for the world of work. It is through learning to question, to express views and having opinions taken seriously, that children will acquire the skills and competence to develop their thinking and to exercise judgement in the myriad issues that will confront them as they approach adulthood. And respecting these rights of individual children is entirely consistent with the broader agenda of governments to produce an economically viable workforce. In a world where the skills needed at work are increasingly those of communication, conflict resolution and negotiation, schools must provide children with the opportunities to develop those competencies. The ethos and environment of the school needs to create opportunities for active involvement of pupils. The world of business increasingly recognises the benefits of creating more democratic workplace environments. But it is a lesson not yet fully learned either by politicians or the teaching profession.

For promoting democracy. In both well-established and newly formed democracies, the education system must play a part in helping children understand the principles and practice of democratic decision-making. And as so many countries face heightened internal tensions which threaten democracy, such awareness takes on an even greater significance. Children need to learn through experience what their rights and duties are, and how their freedom is limited by the rights and freedoms of others. They need opportunities to participate in democratic decision-making processes within school, and learn to abide by subsequent decisions that are made. Only by experiencing respect for their views will they acquire the capacity and willingness to listen to others and so begin to understand the processes and value of democracy.

For creating effective schools. There is a significant body of evidence which indicates that schools which do involve children and introduce more democratic structures are likely to be more harmonious, have better staff-pupil relationships and a more effective learning environment.[23] Children who feel valued, feel that there are systems for dealing with injustices, who are consulted over the development of school policies are far more likely to respect the school environment. If the devastating drop-out rate of pupils in so many countries in the world is to be stemmed, schools must become places where children want to be, where they experience respect and engagement with their concerns. If they are to experience some ownership of the school, and develop a sense of commitment and responsibility towards it, then they need opportunities to be involved in the decisions, policies and structures of the school that affect them on a daily basis.

Despite these compelling arguments in favour of a commitment to a more participative model of education, many countries have not yet begun to address the changes necessary for compliance with the philosophy of the Convention. This is not surprising. Children generally are not viewed as individuals with rights to express themselves and be taken seriously. Prevailing cultural attitudes towards children throughout the world persist in constructing them as the property of the adults with responsibility for them. Children are discouraged from asking questions and expressing curiosity. Education is seen as a one-way process of passively receiving information and knowledge, rather than an interactive process. And in non-democratic countries and those with governments reluctant to face criticism, there are difficulties in making the case for respecting children's participation when the price will inevitably be a more challenging and articulate young generation.

There are exciting and imaginative initiatives being developed throughout the world – school councils which give children a genuine say in the running of the school, peer counselling where children are trained as mediators to help other children resolve problems, teaching styles rooted in respect for children and their abilities.[24] However, they are far from widespread or mainstream. The process of ratification of the Convention has begun to open up debate internationally on these issues. It is increasingly recognised that it is not sufficient to discuss the *scope and uptake* of educational provision but that governments must also address the *nature* of that provision. There is an urgent need not only to disseminate examples of working more collaboratively with children, but to undertake evaluation of such approaches in order to accumulate the evidence of their potential benefits.

Of equal importance in promoting respect for the human rights of children in schools is the need to challenge the use of corporal punishment and other forms of humiliating treatment. The Convention demands not only that children are protected from all forms of violence, but also that school discipline is administered in a manner consistent with the child's dignity.[25] The Committee on the Rights of the Child has consistently challenged the use of violence as a form of discipline in schools.[26] Yet, corporal punishment continues to be condoned in schools throughout many countries in the world and too few governments have taken measures against its use. Teachers throughout the world also continue to humiliate and bully children. However, change is accelerating in the context of the Convention and the Committee's recommendations. All European countries have now banned corporal punishment in schools. In the United Kingom, it was, until recently, still lawful to beat children in private schools, a fact that was strongly criticised by the Committee on the Rights of the Child when the United Kingdom Government appeared before it in 1995.[27] However, legislation passed in 1998 has finally outlawed this practice.[28] Other countries, such as Namibia, South Africa, Ethiopia and Korea, are also addressing these issues seriously by banning all use of corporal punishment and seeking to construct a more positive approach to discipline in schools.

Physical discipline by teachers against pupils is not the only expression of violence that arises in schools. Much violence is perpetrated by children against children, behaviour which it is equally important to challenge. Bullying is widespread in schools throughout Europe. In the United Kingdom, for example, research in 1994 revealed that of over 700 children interviewed, 43% of secondary pupils reported having been bullied, 33% were upset by the experience, and 29% commented that it had made them less able to concentrate at school.[29] Even more worrying is the evidence that as many as 50% do not report the bullying, believing that school staff will fail to take any action. Schools must make active commitments to non-violent conflict resolution through whole school policies in which everyone takes responsibility for prevention.[30] Such policies might include circle time, peer counselling, clear sanctions, increased playground supervision and redesigning playgrounds, which have all proved effective in tackling bullying. Additionally, an explicit message from teachers, communicated through their own behaviour and attitudes towards non-violence, is crucial.

Explicit recognition of the human rights of children within school has added significance in view of the compulsory nature of education. Children do not have the freedom to opt out if their rights are violated. It is, therefore, imperative that their rights are explicitly recognised, embodied in legislation and clearly promoted and enforced within the school.

Education to Promote Human Rights

Respect for children's rights in schools is clearly closely linked with the obligation to provide human rights education. Article 29 asserts the need for education rooted in a commitment to the development of the child's potential, promotion of respect for fundamental human rights, respect for parents, one's own and other cultures, for diversity and equality of sexes. The importance of imparting these values could not be greater. In a world facing growing evidence of ethnic conflict and violence, there is an overwhelming imperative to educate children in tolerance, respect for others and for peace and democracy.

The Committee on the Rights of the Child consistently presses governments to incorporate human rights education in the school curriculum. Yet, the failure to do so is evident in reading its concluding observations – Belgium, Columbia, Finland, Guatemala, Iceland, Italy, Nicaragua, Lebanon, Norway, Portugal, Ukraine and the United Kingdom are amongst those which have been criticised for failing to teach human rights.[31] But its introduction into the curriculum cannot happen in a vacuum. At present, there are a number of barriers impeding progress, which need to be addressed before human rights education becomes a reality.

> Promoting respect for human rights is not a matter simply or even primarily of the curriculum. Democracy cannot be taught in an undemocratic environment. The principles must also permeate the ethos of the school. Children need to be included as participants in school decision-making processes – for example, curriculum, behaviour codes, teaching methods, school policies.
>
> Human rights need to be incorporated throughout the curriculum. It is not a discrete subject, but can be addressed, for example, in geography, to explore the issue of unequal access to resources, in biology, to consider issues relating to genetic testing and the right to life of disabled babies, in chemistry, to examine the impact of environmental pollution and the right to health. There is a need for the development of materials and tools to help teachers in this work.
>
> Teachers need training on human rights and help in learning how to teach about rights. This will also involve learning to understand that their behaviour must to be consistent, with respect for the rights being taught. Abusive and violent attitudes towards children cannot be accepted in a school seeking to promote tolerance, understanding and respect for others.

These changes involve a profound reconsideration of the way education is provided in most countries in the world. But if we are committed to promoting democracy, respect and tolerance of all peoples, as well as the fulfilment of children's potential, they are changes which must be made to happen.

Conclusion

Near universal ratification of the UN Convention on the Rights of the Child constitutes a huge leap forward for children. The commitments made at the World Summit for Children, the 1990 World Conference for Education for All and at the World Education Forum in 2000 by international institutions and individual governments to respecting the education rights of children are important. But paper commitments are not enough. This brief overview of the current state of children's education rights highlights how far we have to go. The Convention provides us with a tool, a philosophy and a framework of standards against which to monitor progress. The challenge is to use it to develop concrete plans of action to implement its principles on the ground for all children. Right now, many schools fall far below its standards. Too often, teachers are poorly paid, badly educated and inadequately trained. The curriculum is irrelevant, boring or inappropriate. The material conditions of both buildings and equipment is poor. The authoritarian ethos is inimical to respect for human rights. Violence is endemic. Parents and local communities are excluded from the life of the school. Huge numbers of children are excluded altogether from the education system.

Clearly, poverty and inequality in many countries serves as a brake on the potential for progress. But the goal of universal access to education is not a pipedream. The cost of putting every child in school by the year 2000 is estimated at $60 billion dollars. Compare that with the $800 billion dollars spent annually on weapons, or indeed, the $100 billion spent on the Gulf War.[32] What is needed is a massive shift in political priorities at national and international level. But those priorities should not be directed solely at raising enrolment and reducing drop-out. They must also address the equally fundamental principles embodied in the Convention demanding respect for the dignity of children. So doing will be ultimately beneficial not only to individual children but also to the needs of the wider society. Children will become less disaffected if the curriculum is relevant to their needs. They will learn more effectively if they are valued as individuals. They will become socially responsible if they learn respect for human rights through their own treatment in school. The traditional nineteenth century model of education is no longer either appropriate or desirable if we are to meet the needs of our children in the twenty-first century. Indeed, the whole approach to school needs to be rethought in the light of social, economic and technological change. School is not synonymous with education. There is a great deal to change, it will take time and will require more resources. But the outcome is win-win. There can be no excuse for failing to make an active commitment to the fullest possible implementation of the Convention. We owe it to the world's children.

Notes

[1] General Comment No. 13, 21st Session, 1999, Committee on Economic, Social and Cultural Rights.

[2] For example, Article 26(3) of the Universal Declaration of Human Rights, Article 18(4) of the International Covenant on Civil and Political Rights, and Article 2 of Protocol No.1 to the European Convention on Human Rights.

[3] Article 3, the best interests of children, Article 12, the right to express views and have them taken seriously, Article 5, respect for the evolving capacities of children.

[4] Douglas Hodgson (1996) The international human right to education *and* education concerning human rights, *International Journal of Children's Rights*, 4, pp. 237-262; 1996 Report to the Commission on Human Rights by the Special Rapporteur on the Right to Education (E/CN.4/1999/49, para. 50).

[5] Report to the Commission on Human Rights by the Special Rapporteur on the Right to Education (E/CN.4/1999/49, para. 50).

[6] Article 4, Convention on the Rights of the Child.

[7] Article 28.3, Convention on the Rights of the Child.

[8] UNICEF (1998) *Facts and Figures*. New York: UNICEF.

[9] UNICEF (1998) *State of the World's Children*. New York: UNICEF.

[10] For details, see UNICEF (1999) *State of the World's Children*. New York: UNICEF.

[11] Oxfam International (2000) *Education Now: break the cycle of poverty*. London: Oxfam International.

[12] Frank Dall (1995) Children's Right to Education: reaching the unreached, in James Himes (Ed.) *Implementing the UN Convention on the Rights of the Child: resource mobilization in low-income countries*. New York: UNICEF.

[13] UNICEF (1997) *Progress of Nations*. New York: UNICEF.

[14] Concluding observations of the Committee on the Rights of the Child: United Kingdom of Great Britain and Northern Ireland, CRC/C/1 S/Add.34, February 1995.

[15] Sarah Graham Brown (1994) *The Role of the Curriculum, Education Rights of Minorities*. Florence:UNICEF/MRG.

[16] Educational policies and ethnic divisions (unpublished paper by Innocenti Research Centre, UNICEF, 1998).

[17] See note 16.

[18] Section 386(2), Education Act 1996.

[19] Carl Parsons (1996) Permanent Exclusions from Schools in England in the 1990s: trends, causes and responses, *Children and Society*, 10.

[20] Commission for Racial Equality (1996) Exclusion from School: the public cost. London: Commission for Racial Equality.

[21] Thomas Hammarberg (1997) *A School for Children with Rights*. Florence: UNICEF.

[22] See Article 12, in R. Hodgkin & P. Newell (1998) *Implementation Handbook, for the UN Convention on the Rights of the Child*. New York: UNICEF.

[23] See, for example, studies cited in G. Lansdown (1995) *Taking Part: children's participation in* decision-making. London: Institute for Public Policy Research.

[24] See, for example, L. Davies & G. Kirkpatrick (2000) *The Euridem Project: a review of pupil democracy in Europe.* London: Children's Rights Alliance for England; and UNICEF (1999) *State of the World's Children.* New York: UNICEF.

[25] Articles 19 and 28.

[26] See Article 28, in R. Hodgkin & P. Newell (1998) *Implementation Handbook, for the UN Convention on the Rights of the Child.* New York: UNICEF.

[27] United Kingdom Initial report concluding observations, Add.34, para. 16, and Summary record, 206, para. 5.

[28] School Standards and Framework Act 1998.

[29] S. Sharp & P. Smith (1994) Bullying in UK Schools: the DES Bullying Project, *Early Childhood Development and Care,* 77, pp. 47-55, and paper delivered to British Psychological Society, 13 July 1994.

[30] See, for example, *Checkpoints for Promoting Non-violent Schools* (1998) London: Forum for Children and Violence.

[31] See Article 29, in R. Hodgkin & P. Newell (1998) *Implementation Handbook, for the UN Convention on the Rights of the Child.* New York: UNICEF.

[32] Frank Dall (1995) Children's Right to Education: reaching the unreached, in James Himes (Ed.) *Implementing the UN Convention on the Rights of the Child: resource mobilization in low-income countries.* New York: UNICEF.

PART TWO

Identities and Contexts for Democracy and Citizenship

This part of the book opens with Lore Arthur's chapter about the identities of two types of foreign language teacher – those who are expatriates who live in another country, bringing their original language and culture with them, and those who are nationals but who have studied a foreign language and culture. The chapter is based on interviews with 12 German and British teachers and explores their sense of national and cultural identity, the biographical contexts shaping their identity, their concept of citizenship and their attitudes to teaching and learning.

Julia Preece's chapter focuses specifically on gender identity in relation to citizenship and governance. It draws on post-structuralist literature which looks at the relationship between power and discourse to analyse the gendered nature of citizenship in the context of Europe. The chapter also discusses implications for civic education and how people learn to be active citizens in a democracy.

The next chapter, by George Hudson & Wang Meifang, explores the question of citizenship identity in two very different national and political contexts – China and England. The chapter both analyses citizenship curricular documents from the two countries and discusses the result of a survey questionnaire administered to Chinese and English students on initial teacher training programmes. The questionnaire responses from the two sets of students are compared in terms of knowledge, attitudes and levels of citizenship activity and participation. A key finding of the research is that teaching citizenship as a designated course is more effective in enhancing students' knowledge but does not determine attitudes or participation in the community. This finding has negative implications for the introduction of compulsory citizenship education for democracy in English secondary schools from September 2002.

In the final chapter of the section, a UNESCO view of civic education and learning of democracy is provided by Svend Poulsen-

Hansen – the invited *Compare* speaker. This contribution spells out 14 key pointers about civic education internationally but also emphasises its contextuality – that the aims and nature of civic education vary greatly, even among countries which describe themselves as democratic.

Intercultural Communication and Identities: foreign language teachers' perceptions of culture and citizenship

LORE ARTHUR

Teachers of a second/foreign language are by nature comparativists, perhaps more so than most teachers of other subjects. By constantly interacting with the language and culture of the target country, they think and often act 'comparatively' without, in most instances, articulating their views in a formal manner. Their knowledge and understanding is challenged on an almost daily basis, not only by the subject matter and teaching materials but also by learners, friends, family – not to mention the media. Newspaper headlines, for example, often serve to reinforce stereotypic images such as 'Britons work harder, Greeks smoke too much and Finns are suicidal' (*Independent*, 15 October 1999). Anti-German or anti-English prejudice, of relevance here, is nothing new. In British literature, and over the centuries, Germans often were, and continue to be, perceived in a negative light or at least as being different (Althaus & Mog, 1992; Blaicher, 1992). The *Sun*'s headline, 'The Sun meets the Hun', following the Ridley affair in July 1990, has, it seems, been raised to levels of a 'cause célèbre' in Anglo-German relationships (Cullingford & Husemann, 1995; Kielinger, 1996). Incidents such as these touch upon controversial debates about national characteristics, stereotyping and perceptions in, and across, a number of academic disciplines (Mallison, 1975; Peabody, 1985). They also raise questions about normative values and tasks for those in education, where one of the aims is to break down barriers, broaden the mind and combat ethnocentrism for the sake of society as a whole – values which are implicit in the teaching of foreign languages and citizenship.

The research project presented here aims to look at some of the underlying issues in second language teaching. It concerns university language teachers, who can be grouped into two broad categories: they are expatriates who live in a country other than their country of origin and who bring their original culture with them as 'native speakers'; or they are nationals who have studied a foreign culture, usually involving a period of extended residence abroad, and who now transmit this knowledge. In each case, their own sense of identity is likely to affect their judgements concerning not only culture and intercultural communication but also their sense of being 'agents' of another culture.

It is the relationship and interaction between the various elements of language teaching and the language teacher which prompted possible research questions. For example, do native speakers of, let us say, French or German, have different attitudes towards their own and the other culture than native speakers of English who teach the other language? To what extent do personal biographies influence their sense of 'mission' in the classroom? What aspects of the other country or countries are particularly important to them in terms of knowledge and understanding? Or, quite simply, what made them become language teachers in the first instance? Seen from the 'purist' comparative perspective, such phenomenological interpretations present additional complexities since they are considered, at least by some, to be utterly incompatible with any form of comparative research (Epstein, in Schriewer & Holmes, 1992, p. 11). However, they do make this kind of project all the more challenging since it is about feelings and attitudes of individuals who are in one way or another 'bicultural' in its broadest sense.

The Research Project: an overview

The research project described here was initially undertaken jointly with my colleague, Hugh Starkey, also from the Open University. It is based on semi-structured, individual, hour-long interviews with Open University tutors of languages. These interviews involved 24 tutors of French and German, equal numbers of native and non-native speakers as well as men and women.

The purpose of these interviews was to explore with the interviewees those factors which may influence their approach to language teaching. These include the following.

Personal details (age, gender, nationality, country of birth).
Biography: what caused interviewees to become language teachers; influences at home and school; first experiences; evolution of teaching approach; aims and ethos of the interviewee's approach to language teaching.
Sense of national/cultural identity: personal, professional experiences in relation to the home country and the country of other language; being a citizen in another country; representing another culture at

home; involvement in local community activities, political activities; understanding of and attitudes towards citizenship and culture.

Professional context: negative and positive factors which may have arisen out of a bicultural context; the most important aspects to be conveyed about the other country; the role of cultural stereotyping; cultural differences and similarities; to what extent the interviewees consider themselves to be an 'agent of change'.

Our aim was to pursue in-depth, qualitative research undertaken with a relatively small number of tutors. It was assumed that the researcher would go beyond the 'cut-and-dried' character of the limited survey interview and thus open the door to a more genuinely human relationship between the participants. In such an interview, according to Massarik (in Reason & Rowan, 1997, p. 203), the level of rapport is significantly elevated and the interviewer is genuinely concerned with the interviewee as a person, going beyond the search for delimited information input. In turn, the interviewee sufficiently reciprocates this feeling, valuing the interviewer's motives and seeking to respond in appropriate depth. Though still limited, the time frame is not tightly constrained, and the interviewee in turn may ask questions of the interviewer, exploring intent, seeking clarification and otherwise actively participating in the process of seeking understanding. Furthermore, we accept that the researcher, by adopting an *emic* position, constructs a form of new meaning out of his or her own situation and mediates that meaning to others in the spirit of mutuality and cooperation.

Provisional Findings

The findings presented here are based on 12 interviews of Open University teachers of German which, for comparative purposes, have been divided into two groups.

> Group A: consists of six German native speakers, who were educated in Germany and who, for a number of different personal and professional reasons, are now teaching their mother tongue to Open University students in Britain.
>
> Group B: consists of six English native speakers who followed, in the main, a conventional career pattern by having studied German at university, spent some time in the country and now teach the language to Open University students.

Tutors of both groups are engaged on a part-time, hourly-paid basis by the Open University. Most also teach in a variety of other educational sectors, e.g. in schools and higher education on specialist and non-specialist German courses, adult and further education and/or industry and commerce. Open University students of German and French are mature students, most of whom are aged between 40 and 50. Open University modern language courses are offered up to diploma level (120 credit points). What follows is a summary of a few key issues which have emerged in the course of the research.

Biographical Details

Interviewees were asked, 'What caused you to become a language teacher?' Studies have shown that people become teachers of foreign languages for a number of different reasons. Nott (1992), for example, examined factors which contribute to the supply and demand of modern language teachers in secondary schools and higher education. He noted disparate, even conflicting factors, such as the public perception of teaching as a profession, the attractiveness of other career options, government policies towards modern languages, and the status of modern languages in the curriculum. In the context of this study, however, we were interested in the less obvious and more intrinsic aspects of initial motivation.

Almost all interviewees referred to a sense of having been good at languages at school, to the love for the other country or countries, which developed during their teenage years particularly. Some had wanted to become teachers as long as they could remember while others drifted into teaching later on in life. It is perhaps not surprising but, nevertheless, noteworthy that just under half of all of those interviewed come from families with strong teaching traditions. Furthermore, while most members of Group A referred to their love of English as a foreign language (rather than any other language), those of Group B were often torn between either French or German as the main language of study and teaching. Unlike those in Group A, all respondents in Group B have had experience of teaching in Germany, either in schools or in higher education as language assistants, where they usually taught English to Germans rather than German, the language of their study.

These early influences relate to:

a desire to learn another language and experience another culture;
a desire to become a 'teacher' per se, irrespective of the subject; and
the environment, such as parental influences, good teaching at school, pen friends with someone in the other country, prolonged visits to the country.

The study does not point to marked differences between both groups, as the following interview excerpts indicate.

Group A (native speakers of German)

I always wanted to be a teacher of German for foreigners. I don't know why but I wanted to do this.

I wanted to be a teacher from when I was very little. But originally I thought that I would be a primary school teacher of German, then my favourite subject at school.

My second favourite subject was English ... I have always loved foreign languages and have done English, French and Latin ... The only reason why I didn't become a French teacher was that I preferred the English teacher.

Yes, both my parents are teachers; ... there were some inspiring teachers at school ... I was always interested in English as the language and the country.

I come from a teaching family, my father is a teacher, my mother trained as a teacher although she did not work as a teacher, an aunt of mine is a teacher, and I always wanted to do something different ... but ...

I came here for an English course when I was 15 and we stayed in Hastings and I think probably it was the first time that I was away for a few weeks on my own from home and I just loved it. We came to London on a day trip and I fell in love with London then.

And from someone who had not set out to become a teacher:

This was a total fluke. Because the only thing I was interested in as a youngster was sport, so I was determined to do something that had to do with sport, and because in Germany teachers in the secondary area have to have a second subject at least, because I thought it might be useful to know a bit of English to speak to people of other countries ... I enrolled to become a teacher of sport and English.

Group B (native speakers of English)

I was very keen on languages ... For A-level I studied English, French and German ... I come from a family of teachers. My father is very strong. He became a primary headmaster, a very dedicated teacher.

I had a good German teacher. Actually, looking back on this, I don't think he was particularly good but I liked his methodology in getting German across, so he inspired me.

> *I was very academic at school and I was very good at languages, I think I just drifted into doing a degree in languages, I was more interested in the language and literature rather than in a career in teaching ... My mother had studied languages, French and German at university.*

Sense of National/Cultural Identity

Central to the study were questions about national, regional and cultural identity. All have their own centrifugal and centripetal forces which cross numerous boundaries and time spans. Past experiences influence meaning, which in turn affects subsequent meaning, and so on. According to Hall (in Hall et al, 1992, p. 275), the postmodern subject has no fixed, essential or permanent identity. Identity becomes movable, formed and transformed continuously in relation to the ways we are presented or addressed in the cultural systems which surround us. Identity, therefore, is historically and not biologically defined.

Predictably, each interviewee raised a number of different 'movable' points, which makes a summary of these difficult at this stage of the research. It should not be surprising that those who now live in another country have been challenged by their personal circumstances, perhaps more so than others who have never left the home environment. However, all interviewees had experiences of another culture. They had thought a great deal about issues of cultural identity, in relation to their country of origin and to the other country or countries, often over many years. Furthermore, they responded to issues raised with considerable sensitivity and reflexivity; the topic on hand seemed almost too complex to handle for some of them; many became very emotionally involved in the course of the interviews. Some stated that while they had thought about such issues, they had never been 'forced' to articulate them in the course of an in-depth discussion conducted over a lengthy period of time. Most had to come to terms with crude forms of stereotyping, particularly those in Group A, the German group, though no one seems to have experienced more serious forms of prejudice on a personal level. The media is frequently blamed. Interviewees in this group seem to be almost apologetic for being German and very conscious of so-called national characteristics they are keen to reject. For those in Group B, the English group, the fact that foreigners seemed unable to understand cultural differences between the English, Scots, or Welsh, all labelled 'English', caused irritation to some. It is, however, interesting to note that almost all statements made in relation to cultural identity by respondents in both groups relate to Germany in one way or another, as if there was simply less to say about 'England' and 'Englishness'. Members in the 'non-native' speakers group, the English group, seemed to be much less critically reflective and perhaps less aware of their own cultural identity than those in Group A, the 'German' group. The answers that follow are illustrative examples.

Group A (native speakers of German)

It's very difficult to say ... I don't think I have got these German attributes of always baking cakes and keeping the house really, really tidy.

The English are much more relaxed. .... Whenever I go to Germany, I notice that. For example, people always ask me, 'What do you do?' and 'What are your prospects?' Nobody over here asks me what are the prospects ... Also they come out with all these things: the weather in England is horrible, the food is awful, the English are so strange, and the English hate the Germans.

It's a difficult thing to define where is home because I live here and I am at home here, but sometimes it does not feel quite like at home as I don't quite fit in and when I go back to Germany I still don't quite fit in there, so it's very difficult to say where I am at home.

My in-law family here, for example, Roger's grandmother, whenever we came to see her, she would say to everyone: this is Roger and he married a German girl, so this must have been a big thing for her ... It's all to do with the Third Reich, Nazis, and you feel uncomfortable about it ... You reject being seen as a German ... When I hear other people speaking German I cringe a bit.

[In school teaching] we have always got this problem that as a subject we need to be seen as fun and positive, which is good, but in Germany teachers do not have the onus that they have got to be also liked; you know, it is quite a tough task as well.

Group B (native speakers of English)

I would say I was British because I have just come back from three days in Wales, another of my cultural homes ... I would probably say I was European because of how I peddle myself round and about really.

> When I am abroad, I have a stronger feeling of being a
> Londoner, than of being British.

> In West Germany, you were an English visitor and people
> identified your Englishness in your sometimes cold humour
> and in your politeness and your dirty fingernails ... It was the
> kind of thing I was not aware of.

> ... in general social behaviour, the Germans and the British
> have more in common than the French and the British. Maybe
> in the end it's just a question of linguistic skills but I find it
> much harder work to get on with the French people than with
> Germans.

And with reference to a prolonged stay in the former East Germany:

> In Dresden [before unification], I was a rarity. It was a
> different thing. I was feted as a Westerner, it did not matter
> whether I was English or not.

Concept of Citizenship

Interviewees were asked what the concept of citizenship meant to them
and to what extent they were actively involved in community life or
political organisations. The word 'citizenship', in the current language of
the European Union, implies a holistic concept, which includes legal,
political and social elements as well as working critically with a
foundation of diverse and overlapping values and identities. It is the very
complexity and fluidity that enables the maintenance of a negotiated
social integration (European Commission, 1998, pp. 11-12). Concepts of
citizenship here are intertwined with education for democracy, notions
which have been particularly pertinent to the history of post-war
Germany. It is not surprising, therefore, that almost all interviewees in
both groups referred to an impression gained that Germans seemed to be
politically more aware and sensitive to potential dangers to democracy
than their counterparts in Britain. Terms such as 'responsibility' and
'obligations' were mentioned in the German context, much more so than
in the British one, where the emphasis was more on 'being involved in a
community'. The question of age in relation to domestic responsibilities
was also raised; those with schoolchildren were much more likely to be
involved in local groups such as parent-teacher associations or the
Church. None of the interviewees was actively involved in party politics,
though some had belonged to the Labour Party at one time in their lives
and all tended to vote for a party on the left of the political spectrum.
The answers can be grouped into two categories:

personal attitude: what citizenship meant to individual interviewees; and
important matters to convey: what citizenship means in terms of teaching either schoolchildren or adults in this country.

Personal attitudes – Group A (native speakers of German)

Citizenship means where you get your passport and where you vote. I don't really mind where I vote, in Germany or this country. If I vote in this country, it would be better because I have a direct say. As long as I vote somewhere.

We have had always much more responsibility for our own learning ... This comes across as this typical German pushiness that the Germans exhibit. Always louder and more dominating and some even more aggressive and critical ... this is stereotyping again.

I almost feel like I have been a little bit disenfranchised. What I have come to realise is that in Germany you are never allowed to be unpolitical. Everything you read, literature from centuries ago, electing a school speaker or going to the headmaster and tackling injustices, ... we have always had this drummed into us that being unaware isn't a way out.

Being part of a society. [As a German] the English word citizenship has two meanings for me. Sense of nationality. Member of that society that carries with it certain rights and obligations, such as the right to vote. You can't escape the personal responsibility when you have those obligations.

I think the English are not really aware at all. They are so comfortable with their system. Things like – in Germany we worry about if one of the right wing parties gets, say, 8% of the votes, we start worrying that we could have another dictatorship. People here, I don't think, the idea that democracy could ever collapse ever occurs to them.

Group B (native speakers of English)

I am nearest to the Green in colour. I was a member of the Labour Party ... when we were younger it was fashionable to be left wing.

*I find that really difficult to answer, actually I would really
have to think about that. I mean obviously social
responsibility, perhaps citizenship in the smaller framework,
being available to help people, fulfilling responsibility in
society ... I am really stumped by that, I have a vague idea that
I try to be a responsible citizen.*

*For me it's a very vague concept. A concept of belonging
somewhere. Where you were born and, therefore, grew up with
a certain set of values about the way of doing things and
acting and dealing with other people.*

*I think Germans are politically wiser and more active but also
politically more fearful because of their history. I also found
that they looked upon Old England, as they called it, as a
symbol for security. [In Germany] that was one of the things I
found quite uplifting, the participation of students. I do not
know if it was because their teacher was so good ... their
knowledge of their responsibilities, their citizenship and so on.*

Important Things to Convey When Teaching a Second Language

Byram (1988; Byram & Risager, 1999) and others have promoted methods
and approaches to cultural studies in foreign/second language pedagogy.
The cultural dimension, it is argued, involves not only factual knowledge
about the target country or countries but also about how people in
different countries collectively and individually understand matters in
relation to themselves and the rest of the world. Cultural awareness, it is
proposed, should make learners both ethnographers and informants,
allowing them to gain a perspective through comparison which is neither
entirely one nor the other. In the process of comparison from two points
of view, Byram (1988, p. 143) argues, lies the possibility of attaining an
Archimedean leverage to both cultures and thereby acquiring new
schemata and intercultural competence. Byram, however, writes in the
context of initial education. Adults learning German, on the other hand,
usually have experience of that country and generally very positive
attitudes. Furthermore, in the context of the Open University, many
adult-oriented cultural issues are dealt with extensively in the course
materials. Since there are relatively few face-to-face tutorials, there is
relatively little scope or a perceived need to act as 'agents of change'. The
answers given by interviewees, therefore, reflect their wide range of
teaching experiences in different educational settings. Those who teach
or have taught in schools have a very different sense of 'mission' to those
who mainly interact with adults. In higher education, too, the age range

of students matters. Young undergraduates have much less experience and knowledge of German culture, for example, than mature students. In the course of the interviews, no noticeable differences between either the German or the English group emerged; instead, differences in the type of educational institution and student body were marked indeed, as the following examples indicate.

> *An understanding why Germans are the way they are – to do with history, and having to make sure that things like that don't happen again and putting things into context on the news, Neo-Nazis for example, I always try to put these into context. (School context)*

> *Well, I think the thing that frustrates me most about England and the English, rather than Britain and the British, is this complete monolingual outlook and I guess I see that I have a role to play there. (School context)*

> *We start too late in this country. There is not enough urgency. Pressure. (School context)*

> *The people in my classes (all adults) generally quite like Germany. I get the impression that most Germans generally like England, too ... how we celebrate Christmas, which I found quite different in the South compared to the North of Germany. We have different traditions, we get up earlier, you work until 5 o'clock, and you don't stay a minute longer. (Adult education/Open University)*

> *Really, I just want to give them the tools to be able to find out for themselves. In the end I think this is what language teaching is all about. If a person takes up German than I guess he or she must be pro German in his or her attitude. (Adult education/Open University)*

> *Here in Britain I welcome the opportunity to teach politics because I am actually teaching English politics [when teaching German]. The students are so naive and lacking in knowledge about their own system that you can do interesting things like the division of power. Federal, they do not really know what federal means ... I had to try and explain the whole logic and complexes of the rise of the Second World War and the rise of a dictator to power. (Higher education, 18-22 year-olds)*

Concluding Remarks

Embedded in this project are numerous comparative questions which have not yet been explored. There are, between both groups, shared similarities and some obvious differences, though even these might best be described as differences-within-similarities. Many issues relate to time and space distantiation, to locality, age, environment, personal circumstances and personalities, all of which have not been taken into account; indeed, some of these may well be outside the scope of this study. However, some conclusion can be drawn, even at this early stage: all interviewees, British and German, expressed a strong love for the German language and culture, and a marked sense of commitment to teaching, particularly to teaching adults in the Open University context. Most had developed a love for learning another language and for teaching in their formative years. Most had been influenced by their home and school environment at a crucial point in time. Biographical accounts point to many similarities rather than differences between 'native' and 'non-native' speakers of German. Marked differences between both groups, however, appear in relation to cultural identity and the understanding of citizenship. As previously stated, the interviewees in the German Group A were much more self-conscious and critical about their own cultural background than were the British in Group B. Both groups noted a stronger sense of political awareness and engagement in German society, which was seen to be much more developed in Germany than in Britain. It seems that, even today, Germans still find it hard to be German, sentiments which are supported by research undertaken in the European Community. Here seven out of ten European Union citizens are proud of their own nationality and country. Some 81% of British people are, it seems, very proud of their own cultural heritage compared to 45% of Germans. Even here, 35% explicitly state that they are not proud to be Germans (Eurobarometer 42, 1995).

It is not surprising, therefore, that many teachers of German, irrespective of their own culture and country of birth, see themselves as 'agents of change' with a strong sense of mission. There seems to have been a deep sense of a common bond and shared values in both groups. Differences which did emerge in the evaluation of these interviews can be related to the type of students teachers have; these may be adults, young undergraduates or schoolchildren. Tutors of adults, for example, and this is borne out by theories in adult learning, see themselves much more as facilitators rather than pedagogues; they are aware of the knowledge and experience adults bring into the learning situation. The need to change attitudes is, therefore, much less pronounced in the context of adult education when compared to teaching schoolchildren or even young undergraduates.

Perhaps the most striking aspect of doing this kind of in-depth study relates to the feelings expressed by interviewees about the process itself. Many stated that although they had often thought about their own cultural identities in relation to the other country and reflected on their bicultural experiences, these somewhat eclectic thoughts usually remained locked into their own private space; they are rarely talked about, let alone analysed and evaluated within the context of an hour-long interview. Furthermore, in the course of the interviews, some became aware that their own views and attitudes had become bounded in a particular time frame linked to experiences they had perhaps many years ago. Others constantly reconstruct their personal meaning scheme, which evolves out of the environment in which they find themselves. These meaning schemes are not predetermined but they are part of 'an everyday process involving a myriad of spontaneous, responsive, practical, unselfconscious, but contested interactions, we unknowingly shape or construct between ourselves' (Shotter, 1993, p. 21).

Discussions about cultural identity and meaning are laden with complexities. Indeed, the deeper one probes, the more complex matters seem to be. Both questions and answers are rich in diversity, thoughtfulness and sensitivity. Inevitably, they lead to many more questions which in themselves are perhaps more meaningful than their possible answers. Challenges indeed.

References

Althaus, H. & Mog, P. (Eds) (1992) *Die Deutschen in ihrer Welt. Tübinger Modell einer intergrativen Landeskunde*. Berlin: Langenscheidt.

Blaicher, G. (1992) *Das Deutschlandbild in der englischen Literatur*. Darmstadt: Wissenschaftliche Buchgesellschaft.

Byram, M. (1988) *Cultural Studies in Foreign Language Teaching*. Clevedon: Multilingual Matters.

Byram, M. & Risager, K. (1999) *Language Teachers, Politics and Cultures*. Clevedon: Multilingual Matters.

Cullingford, C. & Huseman, H. (1995) *Anglo-German Attitudes*. Aldershot: Avebury.

Eurobarometer, 42 (1995). Brussels: European Commission.

European Commission (1998) *Education and Active Citizenship in the European Union*. Luxembourg: Office for Official Publications of the European Community.

Hall, S., Held, D. & McGrew, T. (Eds) (1992) *Modernity and its Futures*. Milton Keynes: Open University.

Kielinger, T. (1996) *Die Kreuzung und der Kreisverkehr. Deutsche und Briten im Zentrum der europäischen Geschichte*. Bonn: Bouvier Verlag.

Mallison, V. (1975) *An Introduction to the Study of Comparative Education*, 4th edn. London: Heinemann; first published 1957.

Nott, D. (1992) Modern Language Teachers: supply and demands, *Language Learning Journal*, September 1999, No. 6.

Peabody, D. (1985) *National Characteristics*. Cambridge: Cambridge University Press.

Reason, P. & Rowan, J. (Eds) (1997) *Human Inquiry. A Sourcebook of New Paradigm Research*. Chichester: John Wiley.

Schriewer, J. & Holmes, B. (Eds) (1992) *Theories and Methods in Comparative Education*. Frankfurt: Peter Lang.

Shotter, J. (1993) *Conversational Realities. Constructing Life through Language*. London: Sage.

The Learning of Citizenship and Governance: a gender perspective

JULIA PREECE

Pupils' attitudes to active citizenship are influenced quite as much by schools as by many factors other than schooling: by family, the immediate environment, the media and the example of those in public life. (Kerr, 1999, p. 281)

There is virtually no literature which addresses the issue of governance and gender. There is an increasing body of literature concerning gender and citizenship (for example, Ackers, 1998; Werbner & Yuval Davis, 1999). This chapter therefore represents a critical appraisal of concepts of citizenship in relation to gender and suggests some consequent implications for governance. It draws particularly on post-structuralist literature which looks at the relationship between power and discourse. This perspective provides an analytical tool for exploring how gender has been understood in the construction of citizenship and governance values in Europe. I start with the hypothesis that the concept of citizenship is gendered. This means that the way men and women learn what is valued in terms of active citizenship determines their identity as citizens, their perceived entitlements as members of a given society and their perceived role within society. Whilst the focus of this discussion will be gender, the implications of this analysis for disability and race will also be highlighted. I argue for a broader, more inclusive, ethical definition of active citizenship that, in turn, will influence how people learn to be citizens and take part in governance.

Feminist theories are used to deconstruct some normative assumptions about citizenship. These address issues of identity, agency, difference and power relations for both men and women and between different social groups within the categories of men and women. A selected literature identifies different ways in which citizenship is portrayed and learned through texts, schooling, family and social behaviours and traditions. The changing European and globalisation contexts provide additional commentary on the demands for new forms of citizenship. Particular attention is paid to the concept of active citizenship with some recent interpretations of the dichotomy between private (family) and public (political) domains in relation to citizenship and gender.

Feminisms

There is no one feminist position, although all share a commitment to understanding and challenging what has caused women's subordination to men. Weiner (1994) and Grant (1993) identify three broad strands of feminist thought: liberal, radical and socialist. A fourth strand is often called post-structuralist or postmodern (Snick & de Munter, 1999).

Liberal feminism is generally associated with a concern over equal, democratic, rights with men and free choice within existing social structures. It differs from other feminisms in that it does not challenge relationships of domination. Its emphasis is on campaigning for a level playing field of access within a legal framework.

Radical feminism identifies the specific historical role of male domination over women. It defends the essential qualities of femaleness – in other words, valuing women differently. As such, it defends female ways of being but does not challenge the categories of gender power differentials (Preece, 1999).

Socialist feminism brings in an awareness of differences between women but primarily explores the ways in which gender is socially, rather than biologically, constructed throughout history. It allows for an understanding of different sources of oppression on women. Weedon (1987) argues, however, that this form of feminism does not help us understand how social relationships between men and women create different effects. In other words, socialist feminism is still unable to explain how patriarchy exists in the first place.

The postmodern or post-structuralist debate shifts the focus of difference onto the relationship between language and power. This analysis explores how women (and therefore other social groups) are positioned in different ways as a result of shifting identities and meanings – how individuals are caught between acting as knowing 'subjects' and acting unconsciously as individuals who are socially conditioned (Jones, 1997). This enables us to identify different interest groups and different forms of oppression across all groups. As the analysis is based on understanding power relationships, it also enables us to see how individuals might act as their own agents of power and challenge normative assumptions and expectations for themselves. The life history experiences of individuals can help us understand how those processes have come into play and shaped people's behaviour as citizens.

The literature on gender and citizenship concerns reflects these different feminist positions. Whilst these perspectives are touched on briefly, the main focus is on a postmodernist analysis which takes account of pluralism and change:

> *There is no gender but only women, men and genders*
> *constructed through particular historical struggles ... over*
> *which races, classes, ... sexes etc. ... will have access to*
> *resources and power. (Harding, 1991, p. 151)*

In summary, the generic features of a gender perspective in relationship to citizenship include the following.

Consideration of power relations, manifested through use of language, behaviour, structural systems and the internalised meanings behind those manifestations (*discourses*); for example, who makes decisions in organisations, who controls economic decision-making, how those decisions are made, how words are 'gender-blind'.

The experience of being a woman, as described by women – how women perceive their social reality and how they construct their self-image based on their perception of their relationship to others (*identities and subjectivities*).

The way people create multiple meanings from their interpretation of conflicting discourses. From these individual interpretations, people develop their own sense of *agency* or independent action (Scott, 1992). The degree to which people feel able to develop their capacity for agency depends, however, on the multiple experiences and discourses and power differentials which influence their lives.

The way society constructs images of women, men, racial difference, sexuality, disability etc. through text, the media, social behaviour. The impact of these constructions influences people's opportunity to participate and be heard in different social and political contexts.

The need to look beyond what appears normal and common sense in order to expose inconsistencies in explanations for citizenship and governance.

An analytical framework which sees *experience* as an interpretation that has to be read according to our understanding of context. All knowledge is subjective, situated in time and place, and therefore value laden (Harding, 1991). The goal of understanding people's social reality in the research process therefore involves reflecting back our own analysis of people's experiences with them.

The way people are perceived as active citizens also impacts on the part they are enabled to play in governance.

Governance

The notion of governance, as opposed to government, is a relatively recent concept. Whilst there is some confusion as to what the term means, there is a sense that governance is an attempt to develop a bottom-up model of governing, based on participatory decision-making: 'The role of the state is to empower stakeholders and facilitate cooperation among them, therefore a "steering" role rather than a "rowing" role' (Holford & Edirisingha, 2000, p. 8). Whilst Holford & Edirisingha explore this term more fully, a partial explanation for the current popularity of governance is the acknowledgement that we are living in an increasingly heterogeneous and complex world, where decision-making networks cross states and societies. The link between governance and citizenship, then, in simplified form, is through the way citizens participate in the available decision-making processes of society and whether their actions have any influence on state procedure.

Citizenship and the Historical Legacy through Texts

The feminist critique of citizenship literature claims that citizenship has been presented as a universalist concept. This means that the issue of gender and related class, race and disability positions have been rendered invisible in the explanation of citizen values. The concept of citizenship is distinctly male and predicated on an idealist notion of the white, middle-class, able-bodied man. Historical origins have helped perpetuate this view. Brindle & Arnot (1999) identify English texts associated with citizenship education between 1940 and 1960. The ideal citizen was portrayed as male and citizenship as a man's duty: 'Women's duty went undiscussed' (p. 103). Brindle & Arnot explore three approaches to gender in texts dealing with citizenship education. The majority are designated as exclusionary of women, with the exception of some recognition of women's caring activity in the home or private sphere. Text examples include stories of boys growing up and talking to father about the world. Women's citizenship is reduced to the question of suffrage (obtaining the right to vote), with the assumption that inequality ends with this right. Where later texts do address potentially wider rights and responsibilities for women (for example, Borer, 1962), this is in the context that equality means women do the home chores plus go out to work. Brindle & Arnot find few examples of texts that do challenge attitudes to women and their historically and culturally constituted roles. Even in these examples, the social system itself remains unchallenged, since responsibility for the home remains with the woman. From these texts, people learn their contribution to citizenship values: 'Texts of citizenship education reflect the range of opinion that is deemed legitimate enough to be provided for children' (Brindle & Arnot, 1999, p. 119).

A primary source of criticism with regard to the legacy of today's version of citizenship originates from T.H. Marshall's (1952) classic exposition of a universal citizenship. This consisted of civil (property, personal freedom), political (voting) and social (economic welfare) rights. Marshall described the evolution of citizenship chronologically through these phases from the eighteenth century through to the twentieth century. Vogel (1991), Walby (1994) and Torres (1998), however, point out how women had no political rights in terms of suffrage or ownership of property until 1928. And even then, women's political rights came before their rights to personal independence. Indeed, the legislation to ensure women's right to tax equality did not take place until 1988. Vogel (1991), Lister (1997) and others point to a number of anomalies in the characteristics which define citizenship in a male image, even where women's tasks may be quite similar. Vogel points out, for example, that the primary feature of citizenship was defined by the man's capacity to bear arms – but also to perform a soldier's services to the community, contributing to the common good, such as working in hospitals. Vogel points out this is 'nothing but what women do anyway' (p. 69). Pateman (1992) too claims that 'Women's political standing rests on a major paradox; they have been excluded and included on the basis of the very same capacities and attributes' (p. 19).

The most commonly cited way in which women are excluded from the public world of citizenship is through the duty of motherhood – specifically, the procreation of tomorrow's citizens. The private world of motherhood itself is not regarded as a (public) citizenship activity. From this private/public divide emerges a range of discourses that are associated with valued masculine characteristics (reason, disinterest, impartiality, independence) and non-valued, female characteristics (emotion, interest, partiality, dependence) – the more personal values required for caring and motherhood. Partiality, for example, is portrayed as apolitical because the public role of working for the 'common good' requires a less involved perspective, one that ignores difference. Difference has 'merely private significance' (James, 1992, p. 51).

Associated with impartiality is the notion of independence. Again, James comments that 'the conditions of independence have been interpreted so as to exclude women' (p. 55). Power differentials within the family, along with pay differentials in terms of work prospects, all impact on the connection between gender and independence – as they do for different racial groups and people with disabilities.

Attempts to incorporate women into the citizenship fold mean that women are often targeted in public policy as a unitary whole. For example, the affluent can afford various forms of economic independence from men, such as childcare assistance. McRobbie (2000) points out, however, that these measures of inclusion benefit only the affluent and ignore problems imposed by the social structure of society. They can also still leave the responsibility for care with women.

The context of the family is significant for two reasons: firstly, because it is largely ignored with regard to its location for citizenship activity, but also because it has been ignored in terms of a locus for citizenship rights for women. Isin & Wood (1999) show how citizenship rights were developed in non-domestic, public spaces, whereas the family became a space of responsibility for the man to govern. Women have traditionally been encouraged into the private spaces of home duties. Where they had access to public workspaces, these would frequently be for lower wages and limited job choices. Such dichotomies perpetuate the way citizenship activities are learned and valued. Isin & Wood follow a now common argument amongst feminist writers that the public/private divide for citizenship ignores the complexity of people's lives, particularly in the context of today's postmodern world, the influence of globalisation on time and space boundaries and the increasing mobility of individuals. These changes are reconfiguring identities and forms of governance on a global scale. Such changes also impact on how the home space is used as a public (work) and private (family) domain.

European Citizenship

The additional prospect of European enlargement and incorporation of countries with different histories of democracy raises public consciousness of the reality of diversity and difference within the desire for a common European identity. Oommen (1997) explores the relationship between citizenship and national identity. She posits that where the nation might mean the homeland, inclusive of language and territory, nationality takes on its own collective identity. Citizenship, however, traditionally has implied the belonging to a political, collective identity (Oommen, 1997; Alfonsi, 1997). These tensions are played out through the government of Europe. Osler & Starkey (1999) argue that there is no single concept of Europe. European identities will run alongside other national identities, with implications for democracy, cooperation, participation in decision-making and community involvement. Perhaps as a consequence of these changes, Ackers (1998) suggests that the status of European citizenship is increasingly being determined by employment, rather than legal identity. For women, the disadvantages of migration may mean they suffer a dual dependency rather than citizenship independence. Their access to paid work is often determined by migration theory, which still assumes the man is the breadwinner. In addition, the woman may be caring for dependants in the homeland as well as in the immediate migration context. Furthermore, for ethnic minorities in the United Kingdom, the state offers contradictory legislation in terms of citizen rights, so that we see the coexistence of anti-racist legislation and racist immigration laws (Yuval Davis, 1997). Citizenship status, therefore, is a contested concept – with implications for how people act as citizens and how they learn to become active citizens.

Another factor affecting the relationship between the state and the individual is the increasing influence of neo-liberalist notions that the state is overprotective. Its goal is to diminish state reliance by placing a strong emphasis on the relationship between paid (public) work and citizenship status. Sawer (1996) expresses concern that there is an association of state 'public' care with 'feminine', whereas the new ethical purpose of the state is construed as protecting personal freedom. This, in effect, protects the haves from the have-nots and assumes that dependence and reliance on the state run counter to citizen autonomy. This notion of self-reliance, she argues, conceals the interdependence of the family (p. 120) and, by implication, the relationship between family activity and citizenship rights and responsibilities:

> *The conflation of the individual and the family serves as a vanishing trick whereby women and their non market work disappear behind supposedly self-reliant market men ... [wives] do not really share in the characteristics required of citizens of the minimal state. (p. 122)*

Citizenship, therefore, will be learned differently by different social groups according to their assumed status in society and according to how policy decisions privilege certain qualities of the good citizen above others. Even where women are not constrained by family commitments, their role and status within society are already internalised and embedded in social structures that define women normatively according to their gender. Their opportunity to act as a citizen and play a part in governance must be seen in this context.

Today's Civic Education Values

Whilst many of the above arguments reflect the informal ways in which gendered notions of citizenship are absorbed in everyday life, there are indications that formal schooling has an influence on political attitudes. Hahn (1999) explored interpretations of civic education across six countries. She identified differing patterns of attitude and levels of interest in politics by students according to the climate in which citizenship values were addressed in school. Whilst the survey did not explore gender differences, it was clear that those countries which allowed democratic exploration of controversial issues in the classroom (USA, Denmark) produced higher interest in voting and desire to influence public policy. This suggests that formal education has the potential to raise awareness of the above issues.

This then leads to the question, is the opportunity well used? A recent initiative in the United Kingdom on education for citizenship in schools (Qualifications and Curriculum Authority, 1998) addresses the relationship between school and community, citizens' life in a global context and individual participation in politics and society. The aims of this initiative are to develop:

> *Knowledge, skills and values relevant to the nature and*
> *practices of participative democracy; the duties,*
> *responsibilities, rights and development of pupils into citizens*
> *... [resulting in] improvement in the local and wider*
> *community ... awareness of economic realities of adult life.*
> *(Kerr, 1999, p. 277)*

Whilst the report (1998) addresses the issue of equal opportunities and gender equality, the commitment is to 'active citizenship' associated with 'public life', implying a liberal, rather than radical, interpretation of gender. That is, it is assumed that gender differences can be addressed by claiming equality of opportunity within existing definitions and social structures – rather than questioning the power relationships which determine those very exclusionary definitions and social structures. The concern remains that whilst awareness of diversity may increase along with potentially enhanced interest in political life, the structures and systems which perpetuate inequality will remain unexplored. These issues inevitably have implications for how women are enabled to participate in forms of governance.

A New Interpretation of Citizenship?

A number of writers argue that there is a need to look beyond liberal, radical or socialist definitions of citizenship, particularly in relation to the new emphasis on citizenship obligations for paid work. This emphasis leaves unaddressed the status of care as work or active citizenship and the balance between rights and responsibilities or the power relations which determine who has access to those rights and responsibilities (Lister, 1997). The demand is to critique the public/private divide in terms of understanding citizenship and its associated connection with a universalist 'good citizen' who works for the common good. A more pluralistic approach is called for in which political activities are more broadly defined, where 'society' includes 'family' and in which:

> *Conceptualisation of the political and of citizenship [is] no*
> *longer rooted in the experiences of men and divorced from*
> *those of women. When the perspectives of women and of*

> *minority groups are written into the equation, the outcome is a*
> *broader, more inclusive, portrayal of what participatory*
> *political citizenship can mean in a large-scale complex*
> *society. This less rigid conceptualisation, which includes the*
> *struggles of members of oppressed groups and the everyday*
> *politics of community organisations, invokes the spirit of a*
> *gendered political theory that redefines and enlarges the scope*
> *of politics. (Lister, 1997, p. 31)*

In defence of this position, Lister specifically identifies aspects of citizenship that need to be analysed in the context of women's lives. Some key words are: agency, identity and independence.

Agency, Lister argues, is associated with autonomous decision-makers. Feminist agency is constituted from a sense of self and its power relationship with context, experience and discourses (the meaning given to language and behaviour at any point in time). Whilst this form of agency can potentially change the world, the relational self needs to be nurtured and allowed to have space:

> *To act as a Citizen requires first a sense of agency, the belief*
> *that one can act ... agency is not simply about the capacity to*
> *choose and act but it is also about a conscious capacity which*
> *is important to the individual's self identity. (Lister, 1997,*
> *p. 38)*

Lister (1997) interprets a positive sense of self as emotional independence – 'a stable sense of one's own separate identity and confidence that one is worthy to participate in political life' (p. 39). James (1992) also argues that self-esteem and a secure identity are necessary features for agency. The experiences in the private domain influence the individual's potential to play a part in the public.

Lister argues that individual agency needs to be translated into collective action if it is to have citizenship value. In other words, agency needs to be able to challenge legal structures if they are exclusionary. She suggests that whilst neighbourhood action should be seen as active citizenship and political, on its own this form of participation is not enough to create an inclusive concept of citizenship. Women's activity should also be located in formal democratic structures so that the notion of rights is reconceptualised to take account of difference. She acknowledges the ongoing tension between feminist desires for difference and equality but suggests that independence (rights, autonomy) and interdependence (care) should be seen as complementary rather than mutually exclusive. In other words, we need a multilayered concept of citizenship with a 'broader understanding of the significance of difference' (p. 197).

Vogel (1991) supports the proposal that the concept of citizenship for women should not address women's issues in isolation. She highlights the issue of autonomy, stating that citizen access to 'resources of participation', such as money, knowledge, work and time are linked to how women's independence is constructed. For women's voices to be heard in the political arena, their status needs to be redefined in mutual dependence with others, not as a gendered notion of individual dependence.

Pateman (1992), too, argues that the struggle for citizenship is not just about the rights of men to be extended to women. In acknowledging difference, however, motherhood needs to be included as a citizen category but not in an exclusionary way. In other words, if the political meaning of sexual difference is to change, so must the power relations change between men and women. She, too, argues that women's difference needs legitimation in public as well as private spaces. The public/private divide is questioned for its value in identifying men and women's spaces since it ignores the complexity of people's lives (Isin & Wood, 1999). Lister (1993) includes in this issue the need to recognise the value of unpaid work as well as enhancing the possibilities for women to engage in formal politics by providing childcare support, encouraging family sharing of care responsibilities, and addressing power differentials in public and private spheres.

Yuval Davis (1997) develops this latter point. She suggests that by including the private (family) sphere in the state and civil domains, this will influence the systems of welfare, power and political organisation. Otherwise, even where women have received state support for domestic commitments, the loci of control in public spaces are still with men. She broadens the debate to show how being different denies other groups their right to citizen status. Being an active citizen must include different standpoints for activity. For instance, disabled people cannot carry out normative citizen duties if they are defined by such criteria as the ability to die for your country: 'Different social attributes construct the specific position of people within and across communities in certain social categories' (Yuval Davis, 1997, p. 91).

All these arguments have implications for the concept of governance. The modern notion of governance includes accountability and responsibility through a range of institutions and relationships involved in the process of governing. The identification of those institutions and relationships is crucial to how much access women and minority groups have to the status of government. So, for example, groups associated with single issues such as disability rights or ecological concerns may have more or less influence in terms of governance, depending on their political status. The role women or other individuals play in those organisations depends on the values attached to their ability to act and make decisions according to their social circumstances and beliefs.

The Potential to Address the Gender Perspective

A new kind of citizenship is proposed. Snick & de Munter (1999) call this an ethical social practice which acknowledges power differentials. An ethical education for citizenship would allow the voices of different groups to be heard, encouraging a pedagogical approach which explores a wide range of perspectives. It might be argued that education systems claim to do this already. But the indications are that this is within a liberal, rather than postmodern, framework. Prokhovnik's (1998) ethical dimension includes a redefinition of the public/private distinction. This means recognising citizenship practice in the private realm and a diversity of citizenship practices. Indeed, it is argued that women and men already work in both private and public arenas:

> *It is* not *that women need to be liberated from the* private *realm, in order to take part in the public realm as equal citizens, but that women – and men – already undertake responsibilities of citizenship in both the public and the private realms. (Prokhovnik, 1998, p. 84)*

But the ethical dimension gives greater significance to marginalised ideas and experiences. By highlighting social, rather than civil, citizenship (and, by implication, 'governance'), we enhance the moral relationship between citizens, which requires involving more women actively in the formal political process, improving conditions for women in work and revising the state's responsiveness to care roles. Citizenship should be seen as a broader concept 'than either "the political" or of socio-economic concerns' (Prokhovnik, 1998, p. 85). Private activities are not simply just the natural rhythms of biological necessity; they also have political implications (p. 86).

Prokhovnik argues that by taking citizenship beyond the political dimension, this means that the experience of political power is not itself a necessary part of the granting of full citizenship to women. In this respect, she differs from Lister but claims that feminist citizenship needs to take account of what citizenship means to differently situated women:

> *This conception must ... and in opposition to the liberal, unitary idea of what citizenship involves, allow for a notion of citizenship which recognises more fully that women make different choices, and that within that diversity of choices there is not only one which is valid. This conception must ... thus see a range of activities, in both public and private realms, as forms of citizenship which are relevant to different women's lives. And ... this conception must extend the understanding of men's gendered subjectivity too (Carver, 1996). (Prokhovnik, 1998, p. 96)*

91

Julia Preece

In doing so, she also claims space for opening up new definitions of masculinities and citizenship.

Implications for How People Learn to Be Active Citizens

From these debates, we can see that the concept of active citizenship is subjectively defined according to political or normative values at a given point in time. *How* people learn to be active citizens (the sources of learning) may be similar across most sectors of European society. The learning of citizenship *entitlement*, however, is defined both formally and informally through value systems and social expectations for different social groups. Women, men, different ethnic groups, etc. will learn to play certain roles which may or may not be understood in public documents as active citizenship. Their rights and responsibilities will be learned, at least in part, according to how they are positioned in society. The social structures of society will either facilitate or hinder their access to political decision-making and roles in governance.

In order to move towards the pluralistic, inclusive notion of citizenship, as recommended by the above writers, citizens will need to understand how the very systems of which they are part contribute to hegemonic practices or enable new possibilities for agency. It is hoped this chapter will enable readers to enhance their own critique of citizenship and governance across the different European agendas.

References

Ackers, L. (1998) *Shifting Spaces – women, citizenship and migration within the European Union.* Bristol: Policy Press.

Alfonsi, A. (1997) Citizenship and National Identity: the emerging stirrings in Western Europe, in T.K. Oommen (Ed.) *Citizenship and National Identity: from colonialism to globalism.* London: Sage.

Borer, M.C. (1962) *Citizenship – its rights and responsibilities.* London: Museum Press.

Brindle, P. & Arnot, M. (1999) England Expects Every Man to do his Duty: the gendering of the citizenship textbook, 1940-1966, *Oxford Review of Education*, 25, pp. 103-123.

Grant, J. (1993) *Fundamental Feminisms.* London: Routledge.

Hahn, C.L. (1999) Citizenship Education: an empirical study of policy, practices and outcomes, *Oxford Review of Education*, 25, pp. 231-250.

Harding, S. (1991) *Whose Science? Whose Knowledge? Thinking from Women's Lives.* Milton Keynes: Open University Press.

Holford, J. & Edirisingha, P. (2000) Citizenship and Governance Education in Europe: a critical review of the literature, Unpublished Framework 5 funded Project Report, Education and Training for Governance and Active Citizenship in Europe. Guildford: University of Surrey.

Isin, E.F. & Wood, P.K. (1999) *Citizenship and Identity.* London: Sage.

James, S. (1992) The Good Enough Citizen: citizenship and independence, in G. Bork & S. James (Eds) *Beyond Equality and Difference.* London: Routledge.

Jones, A. (1997) Teaching Post-structuralist Feminist theory in Education: student resistances, *Gender and Education,* 9, pp. 261-269.

Kerr, D. (1999) Changing the Political Culture: the advisory group on education for citizenship and the teaching of democracy in schools, *Oxford Review of Education,* 25, pp. 275-284.

Lister, R. (1993) Tracing the Contours of Women's Citizenship, *Policy and Politics,* 21, pp. 3-16.

Lister, R. (1997) *Citizenship: feminist perspectives.* Basingstoke: Macmillan.

Marshall, T.H. (1952) *Citizenship and Social Class.* Cambridge: Cambridge University Press.

McRobbie, A. (2000) Feminism and the Third Way, *Feminist Review,* 64, pp. 97-112.

Oommen, T.K. (Ed.) (1997) *Citizenship and National Identity: from colonialism to globalism.* London: Sage.

Osler, A. & Starkey, H. (1999) Rights, Identities and Inclusion: European action programmes as political education, *Oxford Review of Education,* 25, pp. 199-214.

Pateman, C. (1992) Equality, Difference Subordination: the politics of nationhood, in G. Bork & S. James (Eds) *Beyond Equality and Difference.* London: Routledge.

Preece, J. (1999) *Using Foucault and Feminist Theory to Explain why some Adults are Excluded from British University Education.* Ceredigion: Edwin Mellen Press.

Prokhovnik, R. (1998) Public and Private Citizenship: from gender invisibility to feminist inclusiveness, *Feminist Review,* 60, pp. 84-104.

Qualifications and Curriculum Authority (QCA) (1998) *Education for Citizenship and the Teaching of Democracy in Schools,* Final Report of the Advisory Group. London: QCA.

Sawer, M. (1996) Gender, Metaphor and the State, *Feminist Review,* 52, pp. 118-134.

Scott, J.W. (1992) Multiculturalism and the Politics of Identity, *October,* 61, pp. 12-19.

Snick, A. & De Munter, A. (1999) *Women in Educational Policy Making.* Leuven: Leuven University Press, Studia Paedagogica 24.

Torres, C.A. (1998) *Democracy, Education and Multiculturalism: dilemmas of citizenship in a global world.* Lanham: Rowman & Littlefield.

Vogel, U. (1991) Is Citizenship Gender-specific? in U. Vogel & M. Morgan *The Frontiers of Citizenship.* Basingstoke: Macmillan.

Walby, S. (1994) Is Citizenship Gendered? *Sociology,* 28, pp. 379-395.

Weedon, C. (1987) *Feminist Practice and Poststructuralist Theory.* Oxford: Blackwell.

Weiner, G. (1994) *Feminisms in Education: an introduction*. Milton Keynes: Open University Press.

Werbner, P. & Yuval Davis, N. (Eds) (1999) *Women, Citizenship and Difference*. London: Zed Books.

Yuval Davis, N. (1997) *Gender and Nation*. London: Sage.

An Anglo-Sino Study of Young People's Knowledge, Attitudes and Activities as they Relate to Citizenship

GEORGE HUDSON & WANG MEIFANG

Introduction

This chapter presents the findings of research on citizenship knowledge, attitudes and activities of 187 Chinese and 124 English students on initial teacher training programmes. The research was carried out at University College Worcester (UCW) and Shandong Teachers' University (STU), Jinan.[1] No claim is made that the findings typify young adults but their analysis does provide insights into the effects of two different modes of citizenship education.

The objectives of the research were (1) to analyse official citizenship curricular documents and the association between them, students' knowledge, attitudes and activities; and (2) to compare the differences in citizenship knowledge, attitudes and activities of teacher training students in the two higher education institutions.

Chinese and English societies are dissimilar economically, historically, culturally, politically and linguistically. Research between such dissimilar societies, however, requires a common means of collecting comparative data. This was achieved by a questionnaire that asked questions that had an equivalence of meaning for Chinese and English students. The major source of these questions was derived from a content analysis of Chinese and English curricular documents. These documents represent the ideals of politicians and policy-makers and their prescriptions for citizenship – the way it should be understood, accepted and practised by members of a society. The questionnaire was, therefore, divided into sections on knowledge, attitudes and values of citizenship.

The Social and Educational Context

Citizenship and moral education is a global issue and in recent years has been exercising the formulation of curricular policies around the world (Kerr, 1999a). In England, this policy-making has been variously signified by the publication of packs of school curricular materials by a number of non-governmental organisations (NGOs, e.g. Oxfam), the publication of the Crick Report, *Education for Citizenship and the Teaching of Democracy in Schools* (1998) and the Government's insistence that citizenship education should be a required subject in the revised National Curriculum.

Contemporary discussion of citizenship in Britain has been informed by Marshall's 1950 classic analysis, *Citizenship and Social Class*. The discussion of citizenship as a social and educational issue, however, has been inhibited by the historical force of British institutions, not least that of the monarchy. Evolutionary rather than revolutionary change of institutions, together with a relatively stable social order and the passive acceptance of 'subject' status, has meant the absence of the promotion of citizenship. Indeed, English curricular history has been more about maintaining the collective interests of dominant social classes rather than any universal promotion of citizenship rights and responsibilities. Only in the post-war years, with the rise of liberal education, so-called because of its spectrum of subjects, and the coming of the 'classless society', have elements of 'citizenship' in England been belatedly embedded in a national curriculum. Only since the publication of the cross-curriculum document, *Education for Citizenship* (National Curriculum Council, 1990) has it been expressed as an official educational discourse.

In China, radical economic and social change has caused central and provisional governments to revise the curriculum for moral and political education. School curricula have changed with political policies, although the framework and aims of moral education have more or less remained constant. The syllabus is based on the study of ideology, politics and ethics. Moral education is a compulsory study for school pupils and even for master's and doctoral students. Central government regards moral education as the basis for the construction of a 'socialist spiritual civilisation', i.e. the construction of individual conscientiousness and a guarantee for politically correct talent training and enhancing all-round development. Schools and colleges must take Marxism-Leninism, Mao Tsetung's Thoughts and Deng Xiaoping's Theories of Socialist Construction with Chinese characteristics as a guide to study. Mental health is a recent addition to the content. Approved guides such as students' textbooks and teachers' reference books are formulated by the Ministry of Education (Li, 1990).

The Research Design and Methodology

All political parties have an ideology, a sectarian system of ideas about how they would have society organised. A political party that becomes the party of governance will try to implement policies based upon its ideology. Ideology is manifested in the official discourse of government documents such as parliamentary acts, circulars, directives, reports, guidance literature and textbooks. In England, the ideological discourse of 'Education for Citizenship' has had an uncertain status. The implementation of the 1988 Education Act established the National Curriculum (NC) for state primary and secondary schools and from 1990, guidance was given on its incorporation into subjects as a cross-curricular theme. Kerr (1999b) has noted the catholic nature of 'citizenship education' and its various subject labels. In China, moral and political education has the equivalence to 'citizenship'. Unlike the diffused and embedded NC cross-curricular themes, it is a prescribed and distinctive subject, whose detailed discourse is published by the state publishers, the People's Education Press.

Whether prescribed or described, specific or diffused, the implementation of a national curriculum remains implicitly a top to bottom model. As we shall see, this simplistic model does not have much validity. The official discourse defines the ideal but the processes of policy implementation and delivery will inevitably change it. The amount of change depends on the journey of implementation through administrative controls that keep it on the straight and narrow of a government's political correctness. Even so, what is learned at 'the bottom' is the official received curriculum. But what students know as members of society, as citizens, is a dialectical product of the received curriculum with other wider and informal learning experiences.

The Student Sample

The student sample was selected to ensure that in the year of the research, 1999, the English students were likely to have had some citizenship education as published in the 1990 guidelines.[2] At UCW, the training programme also offered students a one-semester option course on Citizenship. Sixty-nine students in the sample took this option and should have had enhanced knowledge of citizenship education. These were designated an 'experimental' group. The remaining 55 students acted as the 'control' group against which any gain in knowledge could be measured.

All the Chinese students had been taught moral and political education but 81 students had also elected to study political and moral education as a specialist teaching subject. This subsample was analogous to the English experimental group whilst a further 106 students acted as the control group.

The Analysis of Documents

The content analysis of the curricular documents entailed searching their text for pre-defined categories (Silverman, 1993). These categories had been derived from reading the works of Marshall (1950) and Oliver (1994) to provide a generic definition of citizenship. The readings produced citizenship categories and definitions of the following.

Civil – forms of organisation and activities that are publicly known of as part of the society and community and made available because of universal or individual need. This is a very large category that would include the legal system and municipal services.

Ecological – the interaction of natural systems and human activities.

Economic – the production, distribution, consumption of goods and services and activities, collective or individual, organised around these.

Political – the governance, national and local, of society and community. The institutions of law-making, order and control. Included in this category would be the processes by which these institutions come into being and to which they are accountable.

Social – the interaction of the self with others, the space left between the other categories. The action of self and others is partially but not wholly determined. Culture, traditions and belief systems could be included.

Working independently, the five members of the research team used these categories to read and code both the Chinese and English curricular documents. This analysis produced a very high level of agreement between the researchers. It is important, at this stage, to note that no evidence of the Ecological category text was identified in the English documents (i.e. National Curriculum Council, 1990) and was barely present in the Chinese ones. The content of Chinese documents did produce a category concerned with the acquisition of individual moral qualities, e.g. to be honest, to keep oneself fit for the benefit of the community. This was labelled 'Self'. The initial analysis produced an extensive list of repetitive statements and when reduced by a secondary analysis, produced the following statements that described the content of each citizenship category (C and E indicates the emphasis given in Chinese and English documents).

Civil

Knowledge of the law. Observing and abiding by the law. Protection under the law. (C & E)
The individual in civil society. Duties, rights and responsibilities. (C & E)

The provision and use of municipal services. State, private and voluntary provision. Knowledge of the service sector (e.g. leisure and transport provision). (E)

Ecological

Appreciation and respect for the natural environment. (C)
To understand the use of resources and the need to protect the environment. (C)

Economic

Work. The appreciation of hard work of others. (C)
The values of individual hard work. (C)
Understanding wealth creation for society. (C & E)
Understanding wealth creation for the individual and the need to be frugal and not be wasteful. (C)
Knowledge of economic systems, economic modernisation and its effects. (C & E)

Political

Knowledge of different political systems. (E)
Knowledge of theory of political systems. (E)
Knowing members of political parties. (C)

Social

Pluralism, the recognition of group difference. (E)
Recognition of the value of their traditions. (C & E)
Collectivism and the importance of community and family. (C)
Individualism, to be open-minded and enterprising, able to reconcile the differences between individual and collective interests. (C & E)

Self

Integrity of self, honesty and regard for others. (C)
The constructive used of non-work time, responsibility for individual fitness and health, self as a community resource. (C)

The Survey Questionnaire

The content analysis statements were translated, after much debate, into a range of 32 questions on knowledge and four on activities plus 46 attitudinal statements with a Likert scale of possible responses. A pilot survey highlighted the need for modifications and these were incorporated into the main survey. With the consent of students, the survey was carried out during their classes at UCW and STU.

The Results of the Survey

(a) Knowledge

There were significant differences in the knowledge scores in almost every category between the Chinese control and experimental groups, but there were no significant differences between the two English groups. This indicated that the optional one-semester course had not enhanced the knowledge of the English experimental group. This finding meant that the research methodology comparing control and experimental groups could not be carried out. The findings presented below, therefore, only compare the Chinese and English students as two subsamples, i.e. data from the experimental and control groups were combined. The Chinese and English cumulative scores, expressed as percentages, compared all the categories except 'Self'. There was a highly significant difference between the Chinese and English students (p <0.001), the former with higher scores and a smaller standard deviation (SD= 2.49, SD=3.29). Chinese students scored more highly on all the five categories of civil, economic, ecological, political and social questions.

Given the differences between the curricula, this was not a surprising finding and strongly suggests that the Chinese education system is more effective in teaching knowledge of citizenship. The high level of Ecological knowledge scored by both the Chinese and English students was notable, despite the fact that this category was given low emphasis in the Chinese documents and none at all in the English.

(b) Attitudes: a methodological tale

Students' strength of attitudes to statements about their beliefs, opinions, attitudes or values was indicated on a Likert scale (Strongly Disagree, Disagree, Indifferent, Agree, Strongly Agree). These produced categorical data analysed by a chi-square test. For the analysis to be valid, it was necessary to combine the data into three categories, Disagree, Indifferent, Agree.[3] Chi-square tests produced very significant differences between Chinese and English students. This finding, however, was erroneous because of a very peculiar effect of the English students' tendency to choose the response 'Indifferent'. If this signified not only their indifference to a statement but an indifference to the questionnaire, it would jeopardise the research. A visual inspection of the data set allayed this concern and showed that they had responded strongly to some statements throughout the questionnaire, indicating that students had read the statements and made considered responses. They had not simply ticked the middle response of 'Indifferent'. The high average response rate of 'Indifferent' (27%) possibly means that they either had not reflected upon the nature of particular statements or these posed an irresolvable dilemma. In general, Chinese students avoided choosing 'Indifferent' (average response rate 9%), indicating they were able to resolve such statements. The nature of these data reoriented the analysis of attitudes and responses, and data for each subsample of students were visually examined for patterns based on the strength of a response rather than a response to a category. This revealed a pattern of five different clusters.[4] These were as follows.

1. Definitive. There was a high percentage of either Agree or Disagree positive responses with none or only a small number of other responses.
2. Affirmative. A relatively high percentage of positive responses but with some indication of other responses.
3. Bias. Relatively high responses to Indifferent but with a clear preference. (Some English responses of indifference reached over 50% but there was still a clear 2:1 preference for Agree or Disagree responses.)
4. English split. An almost equal division between Agree and Disagree responses, with high indifference.
5. Chinese split. An almost equal division between Agree and Disagree but with low indifference.

Cluster Commentary. (N.B. In the following discussion, the order of data given is Chinese and English and the three percentages refer to Agree, Indifferent, Disagree).

Almost without exception, individual Chinese students made positive responses even when they were collectively divided between Agree and Disagree, as in Cluster 5. Apart from responses in the 'Definitive' cluster, English students tended to have high numbers of 'Indifferent' responses. All the citizenship categories figured in the 'Definitive' cluster for both groups of students, with 20 (44%) Chinese and 12 (26%) English responses. The category of 'Self' did not feature in the English responses. The Ecological category did have the most definite responses, six Chinese and five English, mirroring the data of the knowledge scores.

There was a congruence between the Chinese and English students' responses as they tended to agree and disagree about the same statements but it is the strength and decisiveness of response that differentiates them. The highest Chinese response (98%) was to agree with the statement, 'You have a duty to know the law in order to protect yourself and others'. This also received a high English response (79%). The highest English response (96%) was 'Your joining the activities of the local community is a matter of individual choice', followed by 'Individuals should be free to live their lives as they choose' (75%). Both these statements appeared in the Chinese 'Affirmative' cluster (78% and 62% respectively). Other statements on the relationship of the individual to the community were also supported by the Chinese students, e.g. 'You should keep fit and live a healthy life to be of value to the community' (96%), 'Individuals should be involved in the activities of the local community' (72%) and 'Individual lifestyles should take account of the expectations of the community' (69%). The English students agreed that they should be involved in community activities but when this was coupled with a value to the community, they became collectively more ambivalent (40%, 26%, 34%). This was typical of their responses when a statement contained two elements.

Both nationalities supported the ideal of the law as protection for the self and others and they were definite in responses that their national governments should have strong commitment to environmental issues and that an individual's actions can help to protect the environment. They valued the worth of older workers and thought that national economic success is achieved by people working cooperatively. The Chinese students were prepared to be more frugal in their finances and more generous in helping others. Indeed, Chinese students were altogether more supportive of other cultural groups; for example, compare 85% for 'Cultural diversity enriches society and should be celebrated' with the English 62%.

English students were definite in their response that 'It is acceptable to have children outside marriage', with a marginal Chinese response of disagreement. Curiously, there were some counter responses to 'The traditional family best serves the interests of the children and should be supported'. English students' responses were 60% agree, 19% indifferent, 21% disagree, with the Chinese the exact inverse. The Chinese would definitely consult their parents when making important decisions whereas the English students marginally disagreed.

Even the Chinese 'Bias' cluster responses were more positive, with, 'You should obey the law no matter how it interferes with your personal ambitions'. The Chinese would not break the law for their individual advancement but agreed that it would 'sometimes be justified to disobey the law' (52%, 9%, 39%); the English responses were 27%, 42%, 31%.

The institutions of government and the law were supported by Chinese and English students but they were sceptical about the integrity of their functionaries, as they disagreed with 'It does not matter if an individual votes' (Chinese 68%, English, 67%) and 'Most politicians act in the best interests of the electorate' (Chinese 61%, English, 51%). Knowing the law should protect individuals but whether 'The law will protect the individual rights of the individual citizen' produced Chinese responses (47%, 5%, 48%) and English (22%, 30%, 48%).

Statements concerning personal commitment also elicited collective ambivalence but less so for the Chinese. Even responses to ecological statements make this point: 'Industry should be free to pursue its own interests with regard to the environment' (disagree 97% and 86%) and

'Good environment practice begins with care of the home, community and the workplace' (agree, 95% and 81%). Involvement, as in 'You have a duty to report any incidents which damage the environment' – Chinese responses (80%, 14%, 6%), English (48%, 45%, 7%) – weakened with 'A lower standard of living is a price worth paying to ensure limited ecological damage' (62%, 6%, 32% and 27%, 38%, 36%) and virtually disappeared with 'In order to have a decent standard of living it is acceptable to exploit finite resources' (49%, 5%, 46%) and (59%, 35%, 6%).

In the category 'Self', altruism was clearly supported when there was a specific need – 'You should donate whatever resources needed to help natural disaster victims' (Chinese 92%, English 62%) – but fell away with the non-specific statement, 'You should help others in trouble even at cost yourself' (Chinese 85%, English 52%, with 33% Indifferent). The rather weak censure of others' behaviour, as in, 'You should never turn a blind eye to wrongdoing no matter how minor' (Chinese 64%, 22%, 14%, English 42%, 32%, 26%) was given stronger support by 'Telling lies can never be morally justified', where the Chinese agreed (72%, 6%, 17%) but the English disagreed (17%, 41%, 50%). Maybe lie telling could not be justified but this was negated to a degree by the Chinese in disagreeing with 'You should never say one thing and mean another in any circumstances' (Chinese 28%, 13%, 59%), and although the English responses were in accord (15%, 54%, 31%), the high indifference was more indicative of students' shying away from moral decision-making. Chinese students seem to be able to reconcile individualism with commitment to community and family. This was not the case with the English students.

(c) Activities

Whatever the knowledge and 'attitudes' of citizens, it is the involvement in the processes of society that marks out the difference between being an active or passive citizen, and participation in a socially acceptable way should be the most important outcome of citizenship education. Citizenship knowledge and attitudes not translated into participation remain merely academic. The survey asked about political activities, remunerative and voluntary work and participation in college and community groups. This comparison was difficult because of radically different arrangements in China and England. Chinese students were more politically active, with 94% membership of the Youth League, one-time precursor for membership of the Chinese Communist Party, and still a vehicle for progression in a career. The Chinese students' union is an organisation representing academic arrangements whereas the English students have their membership paid for by the National Students Union and at local level, it is concerned with a range of academic, cultural and sports activities. Membership is virtually 100% and offers the benefits of discounts on goods and services.

Overall, English students had more experience of work, in secondary school, during holidays and during the college semester. These patterns of work are probably an effect of the abolition of student grants and the introduction of student tuition fees.

The results of a survey conducted by the National Foundation for Educational Research (National Forum for Values in Education and the Community, 1996) reported that 78% of secondary schools were engaged in charity fund raising but this activity did not figure in any of their English answers, but voluntary work, such as visiting and helping in retirement homes, was a Chinese feature. Chinese students' participation in various interest groups was 81% compared with English students' 67%. As with other activities, the Chinese responses were more focused upon a single activity whereas English responses indicated a core of students involved in range of activities. These data probably reflect the characteristics of the student sample, differences between the two academic institutions and access to community resources.

Discussion and Conclusions

The analysis of curricular documents showed the differences of emphasis for citizenship education. Some of these have already been noted, such as the prescriptive and explicit content of the Chinese documents for all levels of their education systems, in contrast to descriptive suggestions of the English cross-curricular document for primary and secondary schools. The category of ecology was virtually absent from the Chinese documents and totally absent from the English one. Ecological knowledge could have been acquired from other sources in their curricula but it was only a marginal second for both groups of students, behind political knowledge for the Chinese and social knowledge for the English. For both student samples, the ecological statements elicited some of the most strongly held attitudes.

To answer objective one, which was to analyse official citizenship curricular documents and the association between them, students' knowledge, attitudes and activities, it was found that there was a low association between the emphasis given to the citizenship categories in the curricular documents and students' knowledge and attitudes.

To answer objective two, which was to compare the differences in citizenship knowledge, attitudes and activities of teacher training students in the two higher education institutions, data demonstrated that Chinese students were more knowledgeable than their English counterparts in all the citizenship categories. The Chinese knew significantly more than their English counterparts, strongly supporting the argument that citizenship education as a prescribed subject is learned more effectively. The smaller variation in the Chinese knowledge scores supports this claim. All the English students' knowledge scores were 60% or above, the lowest being on economic, the highest on social questions.

Chinese documents	Knowledge scores	Attitude responses	English documents	Knowledge scores	Attitude reponses
Civil (40%)	Ecology	Ecology (6)	Social (38%)	Ecology	Ecology
Social (22%)	Economic	Economic (4)	Civil (28%)	Social	Civil
Political (13%)	Political	Political, Social & Self (3, 3, 3)	Economic & Political (17%, 17%)	Political	Economic, Political & Social
Economic (11%)	Social	Civil (1)	Ecological & Self (0%, 0%)	Civil	No Self
Ecology & Self (7%)	Civil				

% = emphasis given to a citizenship category
Number in parentheses = the number of positive student responses given to a citizenship category.

Table I. Ranking emphasis given to categories in school curricular documents, compared with knowledge scores and the positive attitudinal responses from 'Definitive' clusters.

Although the social category was emphasised most by the English *Education for Citizenship*, issues such as equality of opportunity, pluralism and multicultural education were also an integral part of the teacher training programme. Given the uncertain provision of citizenship education in English schools and the possible influence of the content of academic subjects, the acquisition of citizenship knowledge was probably more of the happenstance garnering rather than the deliberate policy of seeding and reaping of the Chinese.

The effects of citizenship curricula on the attitudes of both groups of students was problematic and there was only a loose relationship between students' knowledge and their 'attitudes'. There was no discernible relationship between knowledge and attitudes and students' participation in activities. The attitudes and activities of the students can perhaps be explained, not by the received curriculum, but by students' informal learning experiences in their wider social and material realities. In England, many community activities receive state funding but Chinese activities are more self-reliant, as indicated in the responses to 'Local community groups (e.g. cultural, recreational) should be self-funding and not rely on the state'. Some 67% of Chinese agreed but 61% of English disagreed. In both societies, pensions have been an issue; in China, it is the duty of sons and daughters to financially support their parents but this has not been so in Britain's welfare system. Pensions, however, have been eroded in value and the need for stakeholder pensions promoted. Hence, in the response to 'It's the state's duty to provides pensions', 75% of Chinese and 52% of English disagreed. Indeed, Chinese students supported subscribing to private pensions (59%) whereas the English students were more ambivalent (41%, 26%, 33%). Both agreed they should save for the future but 94% of Chinese were against 'paying out for good time and not to worry about future needs', while again the English students demonstrated their collective ambivalence with 33%, 43%, 24%. Chinese frugality is also an effect of the reality of community and family life into which China's modernisation programme and the policy of one child are beginning to intrude. The expectation that grown-up children will financially support the traditional family of 'working father, caring mother' could, in the near future, impose an increased financial burden on the individual young adult, a burden that has traditionally been shared by siblings.

English students' responses to statements concerning the worth of a pluralistic society and help for others were less positive than those of the Chinese students. This cannot be explained by the different nature of pluralism in the two societies or that the 56 'nationalities' of China are regionally located over a vast land mass and England's ethnic groups are largely urban. Although English students have had the benefit of a welfare state and liberal education, these have not generated particularly strong community values, as attitudes supporting individual freedom and choice were stronger. This could be described as individualism without commitment.

With its emphasis on community and family, the moral and political education of the Chinese curriculum still reflects the organisation of their society. English citizenship education, with its emphasis on pluralism and the rights of the individual, also reflects, in its organisation and content, not only the relativism but also the fragmentation of a postmodern society. This raises fundamental questions about the nature of citizenship, both as an individual as a member of society and whether such a society has core values around which membership can be organised. China too will face these questions when the development of a free market economy begins to fragment society.

Teaching citizenship as a designated course is more effective in enhancing students' knowledge but does not determine attitudes or participation in the community. The weaker the teaching and the more pluralistic, even fragmented, the society, the more invalid become educational policies to create an active citizen. What hope, then, for the Secretary of State, David Blunkett's statement:

This is also the first National Curriculum in England to include citizenship, from September 2002, as part of the statutory curriculum for secondary schools. Education in citizenship and democracy will provide coherence in the way in which all pupils are helped to develop a full understanding of their roles and responsibilities as citizens in modern democracy. (Introduction to the National Curriculum: Handbook for Primary Teachers in England. Citizenship: Key Stage 3-4, *Department for Education and Employment and Qualifications and Curriculum Authority, 2000)*

when it is intended to continue citizenship provision embedded across the National Curriculum (see Harber, in this volume).

Students' level of knowledge and their responses to attitudinal statements on ecological issues are indicative of 'educative' influences outside the Chinese and English education systems. These influences – socio-economic, technological and cultural – could dilute the education of a national citizen. Ecological problems have no national boundaries but concern about the environment brings optimism that individuals, such as in the student sample, will have some understanding of global issues rather seeing them as narrow national interests.

Acknowledgement

With thanks to Tony Bates of University College Worcester, United Kingdom for his interest and comments.

Notes

[1] The research was supported by a grant from the British Council, Beijing. The authors of the questionnaire were George Hudson, Kate Macdonald and Duncan Parsons of University College Worcester and Chen Yueru and Wang Meifang of Shandong Teachers' University. Wang Meifang translated the Chinese curricular documents.

[2] There is no evidence as to what, when and where any of the content of the guidelines was provided in schools. The teaching of citizenship education was, and remains, problematic in English schools although the returns to Fogelman's survey claims it was taught but mainly embedded in Personal and Social Education. In one survey, only 19% of schools reported teaching citizenship as a defined subject (Fogelman, 1991; Kerr, 1999a).

[3] Comparing the two samples along a 5-point scale produce a matrix of 10 cells. To be valid, a chi-square test needs a minimum of five responses in each cell. This was achieved by combing five types of responses into three.

[4] The clusters were produced from comparing the relative, but separate, strength of responses for the Chinese and English students. Hence, for example, the strength of some Chinese responses in the 'Affirmative' cluster were greater than those in the English 'Definitive' cluster.

References

Crick Report (1998) *Education for Citizenship and the Teaching of Democracy in Schools.* London: Qualifications and Curriculum Authority.

Department for Education and Employment and Qualifications and Curriculum Authority (2000) *The National Curriculum.* London: HMSO.

Department for Education and Employment and Qualifications and Curriculum Authority (2000) *Citizenship: Key Stage 3-4.* London: HMSO.

Fogelman, K. (1991) *Citizenship in Schools.* London: David Fulton.

Kerr, D. (1999a) *Re-examining Citizenship Education: the case of England.* Slough: National Foundation for Educational Research.

Kerr, D. (1999b) *Citizenship Education: an international comparison,* International Review of Curriculum and Assessment Frameworks, Paper 4. London: Qualifications and Curriculum Authority.

Li Maosen (1990) Moral Education in the People's Republic of China, *Journal of Moral Education,* 19, pp. 159-171.

Marshall, T. (1950) *Citizenship and Social Class.* Cambridge: Cambridge University Press.

National Curriculum Council (1990) *Cross Curricular Theme No. 8. Education for Citizenship.* York: National Curriculum Council.

National Forum for Values in Education and the Community (1996) *Values in Education and the Community. Final Report and Recommendations.* London: SCAA.

Oliver, D. (1994) *The Foundations of Citizenship.* London: Harvester Wheatsheaf.

Silverman, D. (1993) *Interpreting Qualitative Data: methods for analysing talk, text and interaction.* London: Sage.

Some Notes on Civic Education and Learning of Democracy: a perspective from UNESCO

SVEND POULSEN-HANSEN

He said:
Do you want to fight?
I said who?
He said you!
I said me?
He said yes!
I said no!

No, we do *not* want to fight. Neither did the eloquent 'Scarlet Pimpernel' quoted above. As you might know, the Scarlet Pimpernel operated during the French Revolution in the steady state of war between England and France at the end of the eighteenth century – with Denmark on the side of Napoleon, the British attacks on our navy in 1801 and the bombardment of Copenhagen in 1807. It is a long time ago.

It is a fair assumption that we want to live peacefully together, which means being able to solve our inevitable conflicts in a civilised manner. In order to do so, we have to learn citizenship – and to learn democracy.

In the following, I shall guide you through some insights into these processes, through the knowledge and understanding which we have obtained over the past 4-5 years in Denmark in collaboration with UNESCO. The text is not intended to be academic. It does not give references to general or specific theoretical knowledge or empirical facts and it does not drop names or use footnotes. On the top of that, some of the statements may easily be characterised as commonsensical or trivial. Often, however, it is my observation that we tend to overlook the obvious.

Background

At the twenty-eighth session of UNESCO's General Conference in 1995, the Member States adopted a resolution on support for *Reform and renewal of education in central and eastern Europe.*

In 1996, UNESCO invited the Danish National Commission for UNESCO to prepare a 1-week workshop for participants (mainly teachers, researchers and administrators/bureaucrats) from 15 selected central and eastern European countries on the theme 'exploring civic education'. The workshop took place in 1997 with 30 participants at Blaagaard Teacher Training College, Copenhagen. In the final report, some 25 pointers and recommendations are put forward with regard to content and methodology of civic education. It is evident that these pointers themselves are contextual, i.e. related to time and space. They are formulated to be relevant for societies in transition or transformation: from a centralised, bureaucratised political economy into a not so politically centralised and much more market-based economy. The workshop proved to be very productive in the sense that several following conferences, workshops and meetings of experts in this field took their point of departure from the conclusions of the Blaagaard workshop.

Denmark (i.e. the author) thus took part in the round table on civic education organised at the twenty-ninth session of UNESCO's General Conference in 1997, giving further momentum to the approach outlined at the workshop. In 1998, the ideas were presented by the author in Lithuania, Thailand, Australia, Belarus and Croatia, in 1999, in Estonia and Slovenia, in 2000, in Poland, and now, in the United Kingdom. The basic ideas have thus been modified, supplemented and corrected in at least eight different iterative processes.

The Danish National Commission's subcommittee on education has continued working with the subject, giving it a high priority, the latest under the heading *'learning active citizenship'.* This initiative is in line with the citizen education project of the European Council.

What is expressed in the following is not necessarily in line with official Danish policy formulations. It rather corresponds to some ideas we have been working with in the Danish National Commission for UNESCO. But first and foremost, it is the product of an interested and concerned sociologist.

Context

Let us start with the report from UNESCO's World Commission on Education in the Twenty-first Century, chaired by Jacques Delors. Its title is *Learning – the treasure within.* The report points out four central areas of learning, namely, 'learning to be', 'learning to know', 'learning to do' and finally, 'learning to live together'. The focus is on learning rather than teaching – on the learning person rather than on the teacher and the educational institution. The shift of focus is well accounted for, especially when we look at the fourth pillar, learning to live together.

Social learning goes on everywhere. It starts in the nuclear family, develops in the extended family, is modified in the local community, and so on. We live with others in different subcultures with related social norms and roles. The micro social world is a very meaningful observatory. Many processes and outcomes at that level do not in essence differ from what happens at higher levels. UNESCO has labelled the intended ways in which we are formed as social beings, able to participate in society, as 'civic education'. I will not go into a detailed conceptual analysis of what 'civic education' is, or how this concept differs from 'learning of citizenship'. Below I will treat the important, even paradigmatic shift in perspective from teaching to learning.

For quite a few years, we, i.e. Denmark and the other Nordic countries, have not paid special attention to precisely how we undertook civic education. It was well interwoven in the social norms and agendas for 'doing kindergarten', 'doing school' etc. A generation ago, in psychological/pedagogical circles we would speak of the *hidden agenda* and demonstrate its practical potential. It seems to me as if the agenda has become hidden once more. We have nearly forgotten the ways in which we created the low-tension welfare state society, where practically all conflicts were institutionalised. In our countries we have now been urged to look upon civic education anew, especially during the past 5-10 years. To a smaller or larger degree, we all face problems derived from the fact that *nationality and ethnicity have become a social and political issue within our own countries*. With growing prejudice, antagonism and even racism, we have to take a new look at living together on a multicultural basis, to see intercultural coexistence as a perfectly normal way of life, as a source of enrichment rather than a cause of confrontation. We also have to cope with the effects of too extreme individualism. We are thus forced to further develop and apply our knowledge on conflict prevention and conflict handling – underlining participatory democracy and human rights. In that light, civic education within our own countries has to have a new beginning.

Civic Education

Although there is no common unified concept of civic education in central and eastern Europe – nor in modern Western societies – common concepts like human rights, liberty, tolerance, democracy, participation, rule of law, international interdependence and global responsibility seem to constitute basic elements of the topic.

Civic education may have the form of a specific course or classes, like other subjects. It may take the form of bits and pieces of knowledge integrated in other subjects like social science or history or mother tongue. It may take the form of specific lessons aimed at constructing knowing and actively participating citizens. It may comprise knowledge of and discussion of values, norms and attitudes. It may treat conflict and prejudice, and train conflict resolution. It may treat behaviours and aim at the obtainment of specific desired skills. In some countries, these would be called cross-curricular competencies. Furthermore, civic education may be a uniformly prescribed activity or it may take different forms in different areas. We find no clear-cut model, but see many different approaches at the national and subnational levels in geographical Europe.

We will now turn to some pointers about civic education. These pointers are presented here in the form of a protocol statement. They vary in scope and level. The order of presentation might, of course, be discussed. The different aspects or modalities of civic education, however, are interwoven not only in their theoretical backgrounds but also in their practical implications.

1. *The full contextuality of civic education needs to be spelled out.* Any form of civic education must be seen in relation to time and space. As for *time,* it is obvious, I think, that the content of the subject or topic is likely to change over time. Society is dynamic and historic. So is the international community. It might be said that we do have – in some similar countries – some core elements of a philosophical nature, the 'isms', for example: liberalism, conservatism, socialism. Yet, not only the content but also the forms of teaching are likely to change over time. The full contextuality also comprises other subjects, topics or elements in the field. The main questions to be asked here are: *Where are we? Where were we? Where are we heading?*

2. *Civic education is a specific subject, not a universal one.* It is not possible (nor is it useful) to generate a civic education course which can be used across national borders. I know of some of the activities by the US-founded and funded CIVITAS in the former Soviet bloc or Soviet-dominated countries. They aspire to teach 'democracy' in these new nations but begin from the US version of democracy and would promote the values of the US constitution. Such an approach may fail to encompass the situation in the country in question. Being a specific subject implies that there is need for continuous production of educational material, which in itself is an answer to the demands posed by contextuality. In short, we cannot successfully export civic education.

3. *There is no simple answer as to whether civic education as a topic should be integrated in other subjects on the curriculum or be treated as a single subject.* This is the result of a comprehensive investigation made

by UNESCO at the beginning of the 1990s. Civic education may be treated independently, or integrated, or both. There is, likewise, no simple answer as to *when* on the curriculum. The general notion is that behaviour and skills (such as ability to listen and discuss) can be established early, whereas the 'theory' comes later. In fact, children can easily be taught and learn how to behave in a democratic manner before they actually can spell it or get to know what democracy is.

4. *The rights of minorities and the problems and possibilities of multiculturalism are particularly relevant for civic education.* This is a sort of an 'acid test' for the subject but also for the ways in which we organise educational systems and institutions. Civic education should enhance living together in a peaceful way, and the perceived differences are particularly productive.

5. *Civic education and human rights education differ only in point of departure.* This, of course, lends itself to discussion. My main point is that human rights education *without* human rights in the classroom and in society is so revolutionary that it is not likely to happen. Human rights education without reflection of the *where and how* of the situation is purely academic. It is the ways in which human rights are embedded and used in society that counts. And then we are back at civic education.

6. *Civic education is but one of the ways of 'making citizens'. Social learning goes on everywhere in society.* Educational institutions are not the sole providers. A significant context is the family and the local community, not to mention society at large. The micro-social unit of the family is probably the most powerful contributor to social learning. But also the local community, the sports club, the scout group or even the 'gang' serve as important influences by providing norms and rules. The main question is whether these three interlocking subsystems – school, family and local community – support one another or are conflicting. And which one is the strongest, as we move over time and space?

7. *In civic education, form and content cannot be separated. Form is the content and vice versa.* This is a strong formulation of a very important observation and 'theoretical fact'. To put it provocatively, we cannot beat democracy into the pupils or the students. The teaching style must mirror the subject or topic. Open teaching styles are vital to democratic civic education. I do not claim that an open or democratic approach is the best no matter what is to be taught. But I do claim that the way in which teaching of, for example, 'democracy' takes place must necessarily reflect the subject.

The authoritarian or perhaps the autocratic teacher has traditionally been the dominant. On the road away from this now 'politically incorrect' style with its many demands and directives to the pupils, some teachers have arrived at a 'laissez faire, laissez passer' attitude with corresponding behaviours – no demands, 'better wait and see' and 'do not interfere'. This orientation is not conducive to civic education. It supports unknowingly the construction of the law of the jungle. Since many of the teachers in the former Soviet bloc were trained towards an autocratic bent, the situation now requires a significant effort in training and retraining of teachers. If the 'system' demands the use of learner-centred educational material, this may accelerate the training of the teachers by the learners themselves.

8. *Learning takes place also without teaching. Education and teaching does not always result in learning.* Let us now take a closer look at these two central concepts, learning and teaching. Above I have stated that the so-called Delors report described a paradigmatic shift in the world of education from concentration on teaching aspects to focusing on the *learner*, a shift taking place around the turn of the century. I consider this notion highly relevant, not only in relation to civics but to many other subjects or topics as well. In the classic situation, teaching succeeds and learning occurs. But you also have to recognise that sometimes teaching fails, i.e. nothing is learned. It is in fact not only wasted teaching but also wasted learning. On the other hand, there is the huge area of learning which takes place in informal and non-institutionalised settings, without teaching as such. As stated earlier, citizenship is learned 'all over'. Bits and pieces of information as well as solid knowledge are constantly available and pieces of advice or directives or orders are plentiful along anyone's learning path.

Teaching, Learning and Democracy

We will now seek to combine many of the aspects mentioned so far in order to present a view on democracy. First, however, a few remarks on democracy. 'Democracy' can be defined in many ways. Some political scientists have found more than 40 definitions of democracy, and more than 100 countries claim to be democratic. In order not to enter discussion of, for example, the number of representatives, houses or secret balloting, let me suggest a definition which has a strong bearing on civic education and, besides, has proven itself to be useful in many contexts.

9. *Democracy builds on the participants' agreement on how to handle conflicts.* This definition, democracy as agreement on how to handle conflicts, starts to summarise some of the insights so far. The way to start is with the individual *learning* that takes place through active *participation*. It is through participation that we train and develop our

democratic skills. These, in turn, are further developed in the *handling of conflicts.* This handling takes place on a negotiated basis, within a frame. Basically, democracy is characterised by rules and procedures for conflict resolution. The learning comes to some degree from teaching but in particular from the *micro-social environment.* In addition, *freedom of expression* and *independent media* are basic building blocks in a democratic society.

The learning of democratic skills is more likely to take place where the content of the educational system and forms used correspond to that of the family and other micro-social systems.

10. *Democracy has two sides, a* structural *one dealing with distribution of power and access to decision-making, and a* procedural *one dealing with communication in the power structure.* Living together in a democratic way is not to stand still. Democracy develops according to its own logic. I sincerely think of regulated conflicts as being productive. Conflicts can be equally as stimulating to innovation and creativity as – sadly enough – the 'real' wars have been. Democracy is a dynamic concept.

11. *Civic education is influencing and influenced by the degree of openness and transparency in community and society.* It is evident (I hope) that the portrait of civic education given here is to be seen on the background of an open society. In that case, civic education can be an efficient tool in fighting corruption and bribery.

12. *Democratic pluralism denotes the coexistence of several power centres.* In countries in transition, it may be hard to locate the power centres, from the monolithic state to civil society. It is not unfair to claim that quite a few of the former Soviet-dominated countries have had severe difficulties in establishing a new public bureaucracy with the tasks of controlling the 'wild' market forces.

Implementation of Civic Education

13. *The implementation of civic education must take into consideration the time lag between centre and periphery. Even in the so-called homogeneous societies, the time lag varies up to two generations.* We do not share the same time, in much the same way as we do not share the same place. When considering ways of installing, implementing or renewing civic education, we have to take these time differences and their implications seriously. If the gap is one generation, i.e. 30 years, from the centre to the locality in question, the point of departure for the learners will be the normative background of the parent generation. The

governmental bureaucrat making rules and regulations for everybody to follow easily overlooks this.

Civic Education and Citizenship: some concluding remarks

14. *Civic education must encompass the spheres of the market (the consumer), the politics (the voter) and the bureaucracy/administration (the citizen).* The conception of society underlying the pointers and recommendations is that of a political democracy based on a free market and supported and regulated by a perfect bureaucracy. These subsystems operate in a dynamic balance.

> At the 'bottom' or at the centre of each we find the *voter*, the *consumer* and the *citizen*. Each of these roles has to be learned. Each has a constitutional basis, consisting of rights and freedoms.
> Strong forces urge producers to fight for monopoly in the market. After all, the concept of 'the market' is now being used as we 30 years ago used the term 'capitalist'. The logic of money has not changed.
> The political struggle for power sometimes gives one of the political parties a temporary dominance. How is this majority used? And do the parties reflect the electorate or are they self-contained?
> Are the bureaucrats public servants? Or do bureaucracies have their own agenda in conflict with their political owners and the public at large?

By way of a conclusion: we have only just started to realise that the complexity of being a citizen has been dramatically increased.

PART THREE

Democratic Ways
of Working and Researching

The five chapters in this section consider the nature of democratic partnerships in five very different settings. What unites the chapters is that by deconstructing existing power relationships, or by advocating a different approach, they call into question traditional hierarchical, non-participative ways of working which have dominated so many fora in education, from the classroom to the international policy arena.

The chapter by Caroline Dyer et al reports on a research project in India on the professional development of primary school teachers. It shows how teachers' voices reveal the gaps between training inputs and their needs, and, at another level, the constraints that decentralised authorities experience in trying to act with autonomy in addressing those needs. The research is based on collaboration between Northern and Southern participants.

The next two chapters explicitly examine relationships between researchers from the North, and their colleagues in the South, and how an egalitarian and democratic approach can be developed to inform findings and action. Keith Holmes's chapter analyses the dynamics of relationships in his research in St Lucia, and Rob McBride uses his research on HIV/AIDS in Malawi to illustrate how reflexive interactions between researchers, and between researchers and subjects, can lead to illuminating insights.

In the fourth chapter, Ikuko Suzuki examines how parents participate in schools in Uganda, including some of the less obvious, but equally important, ways in which they support their children's schools, and how accountability is a factor in the relationship. Finally, Kenneth King & Simon McGrath consider new, supposedly democratic, patterns in development cooperation, taking a critical approach to the assumptions embedded in the current discourse about partnerships and power.

Research and the Participatory Professional Development of Primary Teacher Educators in India

CAROLINE DYER, ARCHANA CHOKSI, RENU MOYADE & NEETU PUROHIT

Introduction

In this chapter, we discuss experiences of participatory teacher educator development in two Indian States (Madhya Pradesh and Rajasthan), gathered in a 2-year, three State collaborative project involving a North-South research team from the University of Manchester, and Southern teacher educators and teachers. Two of us had already carried out a short project on teacher education [1] (Dyer & Choksi, 1997) in a research 'on' mode but found little scope for development and practical application of the useful findings it generated. In this larger project, we adopted a participatory paradigm – research 'with' – to explore whether processes of supportive collaboration with teacher educators could help them move towards the more proactive, locally embedded style of functioning envisaged in the 1986/92 National Policy on Education.

Improving Teacher Education: the role of District Institutes of Education and Training

Over the last decade, efforts have been made to refocus primary teachers away from the 'chalk and talk' mode, institutionalised by the British, and towards a teaching-learning process that is characterised by a child-centred, joyful, activity-based approach, structured around a competency-based curriculum. Reform efforts must engage with elementary school teachers [2] who are characterised as having low levels of professional competence and commitment (e.g. Kumar, 1991; UNICEF, 1991; Programme of Action on the National Policy of Education

[PoA], 1992; World Bank, 1996; *Public Report on Basic Education in India* [PROBE], 1999); and for many of whom:

> *teaching activity has been reduced to a minimum, in terms of both time and effort. And this pattern is not confined to a minority of irresponsible teachers – it has become a way of life in the profession. (PROBE, 1999, p. 63)*

Official commentators hold the inadequate professional pre- and in-service preparation of teachers responsible for this state of affairs:

> *The system still prepares teachers who do not necessarily become professionally competent and committed at the completion of initial teacher preparation programmes. (National Council for Teacher Education [NCTE], 1998a, p. 5)*

> *A considerable investment is made in further training and development of teachers but the benefits flowing from it in terms of improvement in pupils' learning outcomes are not visible ... It is generally observed that the training provided to teachers is often irrelevant, excessively theoretical, outdated and far removed from the work situation. (Arora, 1998, pp. 1-2)*

Pervasive in these commentaries is the notion of teachers as 'technicians' (McNiff, 1991). Teachers are the 'implementer of ideas' generated elsewhere by 'experts' who are responsible for curriculum development, textbook writing and materials production. Instead of encouraging teachers to 'build up the wisdom to judge their own practice in terms of its educational competence' (McNiff, 1991, p. xiv), teachers learn to look to others to provide the 'solutions'. This not only curtails individual creativity, but also nurtures dependency and the oft-noted passivity: it is essentially undemocratic.

Until the late 1980s, in-service education was undertaken sporadically across the States, but it was not unusual to find primary teachers who had served for 30 years without a single day of refreshment training (Dyer, 2000). Developing systemic capacity to provide all teachers with regular in-service education and training (INSET) was thus one of the reasons for setting up the District Institutes of Education and Training (DIETs) advocated in the National Policy on Education (NPE) 1986. DIETs were expected to match teacher education to local needs and pursue three key functions:

> *1. Training and orientation of the following target groups (elementary school teachers; Head Masters, officers of Education Department up to Block level; NFE [Non-formal Education] and adult education instructors and supervisors; members of District Boards of Education and Village*

Education Committees, other community volunteers; resource persons who will conduct suitable programmes ... at the centres other than the DIET).

2. Academic and resource support to the elementary and adult education systems in the district in other ways ...

3. Action research and experimentation to deal with specific problems of the district in achieving the objectives in the areas of elementary and adult education. (Ministry of Human Resource Development [MHRD], 1989, p. 8)

It is widely felt, both within and beyond the DIETs themselves, that DIETs are not staffed by persons with the necessary professional confidence and capacity to manage these three functions. Staff are expected to have a master's degree in both a subject area and in education, and 7 years of primary sector experience. These qualifications are anyway in themselves virtually mutually exclusive, since (with one exception) primary teacher education does not take place within universities. During the initial recruitment drives, certificated qualifications took precedence over the requirement of practical experience, although the Government of Rajasthan has recently recognised the inappropriateness of the MEd qualification:

It has to be acknowledged that MEd provides only theoretical background and orientation in some research techniques. It does not prepare teacher educators for educating teachers. It does not train trainers. (NCTE, 1998b, p. 53)

DIET staff in Madhya Pradesh and Rajasthan are mostly ex-upper secondary school teachers with no experience of working in primary schools – and little or no professional reorientation since this was not consistently offered in either State by the nodal agency for the DIET, the SCERT (State Council of Educational Research and Training or equivalent). In a focus group discussion early in our project, DIET staff in Madhya Pradesh said:

TT1: They have made branches for the DIETs but the SCERT is not giving the training that is required for that. Work is not going to happen just by making branches ... they tell us these are the functions but to make it function we require training programmes, which we are not getting. We are trying to work from our experiences but we need training from SCERT or other branches from above.

TT2: We have suggested and demanded many times that we need training.

In three out of four of our case study DIETs in these States, we found that most staff were unfamiliar with the DIET guidelines or the expected workings of their own or the other branches of the DIET. Only a handful of them had read or were familiar with the policy document which provided the overarching conceptual framework for the educational reforms. The lack of support for DIET staff from their parent institute was worrying; but so was the lack of initiative at the DIET level to understand their own role. Our observations and interactions with teachers, officials and DIET staff in the early months of the project indicated various avenues for exploration: DIETs were treated as sites for the onward transmission of training programmes designed from above; feedback loops or evaluations of the impact of training were not in evidence; and teachers consistently indicated a lack of confidence about applying what they were supposed to have learned during training.

Collaborative Research with DIETs

Our starting point for collaboration was action research: DIETs are expected to include action research in their portfolio of activities and, acknowledging this area is weak, they welcomed our offer of support to develop it. It quickly emerged that we understood very different things by this term. The project team were familiar with action research as a mode of enquiry that had arisen in a Western context, partly via the 'teacher as researcher' movement. Action research thus depends crucially on the notion of a teacher being a reflexive and expert practitioner, ready to engage in critical reflection on his/her own practices, and committed to making changes by taking action (e.g. Elliott, 1991; McNiff, 1991). Underlying such commitment, however, must be a sense of agency, and 'democratic intent' (Elliott, 1991).

The prevalent view of action research among DIET staff was of small projects which involved action, i.e. fieldwork, but had no reflective component. Indeed, the term seems to have been hijacked to serve centralising tendencies: the State Councils ask DIETs, in the name of action research, to undertake surveys on topics specified by the Councils, which may not directly concern DIETs. The few members of DIET staff with research experience then do the project and send SCERT the results: this perpetuates the notion of 'expert doing research on' and contributes to elitism within the DIET, but not necessarily to use of the findings at source. Since the positivist research paradigm dominates, all this research is quantitative.

Despite these initial differences in understandings of action research, it was an umbrella term we all used to generate small research projects with elements of seeking out teachers' reactions to recent changes, their perceptions of how training has equipped them to accept and implement those changes, and the role of DIETs in mediating training messages. Action research projects could thus serve as a means of generating feedback which was not being undertaken at present by DIETs in their 'throughput' mode, and later – in a gradual process of democratising the teacher education process – towards evaluating and reflecting on those findings with a view to taking action on them.

We were reminded of the extent to which the latter would mark a significant departure for DIET staff in the early stages when we were jointly working out 'initial ideas' on which research projects might build. The concerns which the DIET staff listed were consistently seen as created by, and the responsibility of, others. Many DIET staff in both States shared the conviction that teachers were not implementing their training in the field because they were not interested or properly motivated. This made the DIET staff feel that if teachers' attitudes were like that, there was not much they could do. (Day's [1997] comments on 'beyond comfortable collaboration' reflect some of our feelings when encountering this ideology.) Action research, derived from contexts where practitioners tend to have a well-developed sense of personal agency, looked quite problematic in this respect. Considerable prompting from the project team was required to consider the possibility that the quality or relevance of the in-service training might be related to both interest and motivation. We also suggested that teachers might not have fully understood the training messages, or could have found it difficult to see how to implement a training idea in school. The teacher as technician model tends to construct non-implementation by the technician as a wilful choice, and so these workshops offered for DIET staff a new perspective on matters.

This was the first time these DIETs had generated their own research agenda. Action research thus took on significance as a medium by which DIETs might begin to define their own role in relation to the *impact* of their training programmes on teachers and their practices, rather than completing a training programme and viewing teacher attendance as the criterion of success. The project team had consciously tried to demystify doing research and in so doing, change the DIETs' perception of research to create a more positive sense of it. We jointly designed tools, such as open-ended questionnaires, which would be administered in forthcoming training programmes, and later the project team trained DIET staff in thematic analyses of data that were subsequently generated.

For all of us there was a professional development component, lying in the way we respectively approached the challenges of identifying issues in our own practices that might be changed, designed and implemented the changes, and evaluated the results. We were all, whether explicitly or not, engaging with the democratisation of teacher education, by trying to give teachers' voices a more prominent place in shaping the agenda for their own development.

The Action Research Projects

Three of the four DIETs generated at least one small and complete project which could be written up.

DIET D (Madhya Pradesh/DPEP)

DIET D has 11 staff members, one of whom has elementary experience. Twelve of the 13 blocks of this District are designated 'tribal' and it is part of the District Primary Education Programme (DPEP). The DIET, however, has largely been bypassed by the DPEP, which deliberately set up its own 'parallel DIET' (personal communication, District Project Officer, 1999) consisting of selected elementary teachers. Only three members of DIET staff are drawn into DPEP activities. Although its large new building has been on the verge of completion for at least 2 years, by early 2001 the DIET was still housed in three rooms of a school, whose halls it uses for training; it has no toilets for women staff. Morale is low and staff required considerable orientation from the project team to the work of the DIET and their roles within it.

The DIET's action research project on teachers' attitudes to change revealed that while high proportions of teachers (some 80%) endorse the 'play-way' method, and use of teaching-learning aids, far fewer of them felt that these things were appropriate in their own classrooms. A low proportion (17%) mentioned the competency-based approach which underpins these 'methods'. Teachers object to the schemes which appear to come and go without evaluation, and stress the importance of regular monitoring visits to schools by DIET staff. Despite the DPEP 'parallel', there was from teachers a clear call for staff of the official DIET to visit them and make suggestions. Few of the DIET staff were, however, willing to engage with this call or respond to the teachers' demand: they completed the action research project but did not take on board the implications of their findings.

DIET I (Madhya Pradesh)

DIET I (MP) is fully staffed. Although this status had since lapsed, it was established as a model DIET, and still enjoys the services of a small enthusiastic group who were hand picked by a former principal. This DIET's first project concerned transmission loss in the cascade model. After the initial workshops, DIET staff requested an interim workshop with us, for which Cluster Centre Coordinators [3] were called to ensure field officers were drawn into the action. This was a completely new initiative. The staff attempted an initial analysis on their own, identified numerous possible future action steps, and asked us for another workshop on analysis. Their data revealed that while teachers see the

DIET as helpful, they are less positive about Master Trainers (who carry out the next tier of training in the cascade); they called for the DIET to improve the quality of the Master Trainers, and the DIET responded by developing more training inputs for the Master Trainers.

Although the initial project began with a few committed staff members, the momentum spread across the DIET in a fascinating process by which, after the enthusiasts (forming one of the DIET's three 'lobbies') had set the ball rolling, the other 'lobbies' took up a project so they were not left behind. Within a year, four new projects on various aspects of teacher motivation had been added and a large proportion of staff were involved in some aspect of ongoing research. Gradually, as their research topics overlapped, the lobbies converged a little, and began to consider how to evaluate training programmes at the school level; attitudes towards teachers became more positive.

DIET U (Rajasthan)

In DIET U (Rajasthan), an overstaffed urban DIET, orientations to the role and functions of the DIET preceded any further project activities, as had been the case for DIETs I and D too. Processes that had led quickly to research projects in all the other DIETs did not evoke much response here, and we could only identify two people who regularly and enthusiastically visited schools. This DIET is also failing to attract teachers to its INSET programmes, and although programmes are carried out, staff showed little interest in investigating or improving the quality of the programmes, constantly referring to a lack of interest or will on the part of teachers, or problems elsewhere in the system. For all DIETs, politics surround postings to more coveted locations: the city in which DIET U is located is very desirable and as a high proportion of staff had engineered their presence there as a place of convenient employment, this personal agenda often conflicted with one of the project's inbuilt assumptions – that staff wished to improve their practices.

DIET M (Rajasthan/Lok Jumbish)

DIET M (Rajasthan) was adopted by Lok Jumbish, and staff who met the specially-designed criteria for posting to the DIET were deputed by government or on contract to Lok Jumbish. The Government was not cooperative about deputing staff (personal communication, LJ Chairman, 1998) and the DIET was severely short-staffed. The DIET was open to the project team and quickly confided that with so few people, disputes about workloads were common. We agreed this was a research topic: the DIET staff initiated a time management action research project, seeking inputs from the project team on key principles, and documenting their activities to feed back to each other. Analysis of how individuals sought temporal opportunities to seek each other out to exchange information indicated that the absence of a regular full-staff planning meeting was a key source of problems. Their action step was to implement regular staff meetings to increase transparency about allocation of workloads, with a revolving chair and previously agreed agenda. One such meeting was held and staff found it useful and wanted to carry on. However, at the same time, they were in a state of debilitating anxiety about their futures as the overseas funding agency had withdrawn its financial support for Lok Jumbish in protest at the Pokhran nuclear tests. More members of staff left as their contracts expired, and while those remaining tried to continue their own development for as long as possible in highly unconducive circumstances, by August 2000 – and still, as we write – there was a staff of only five who are expected to maintain a full pre- and in-service training schedule.

Research Findings: indications for future DIET actions

As pieces of research in their own right, these projects have had important outcomes. We all worked together to develop projects that were immediately relevant and useful without being methodologically complex, which has encouraged the DIETs in this sphere of activity.

Secondly, teachers' opinions and views both explicitly and implicitly point out for the DIET staff a variety of possible directions for improvements to training inputs. Teachers' responses reflect confusions about new policy programmes – both in terms of what they are supposed to do, and why they should be doing it. Specifically, they raise doubts about managing multigrade situations; a range of queries about competencies, from why they are necessary to how to evaluate them; insecurities about how and why to use teaching-learning aids; and so on. The action research project findings, which have drawn written responses from over 500 teachers, show that teachers believe current training arrangements are providing them with neither the practical expertise nor the conceptual understandings to match training messages with processes in their own classrooms. Importantly, teachers' voices underline the inadequacies of the ways in which training programmes are conceived and delivered at present: implicitly, they reflect the need for a DIET which functions with local sensitivity, just as the policy idea envisaged.

Democratising Teacher Education:
structural and professional constraints

The collaborative projects described implied some movement towards a democratisation of the teacher education process by inviting teachers to comment on the quality of their training programmes, with the intention that DIETs would act on those comments. Our account of the action research projects indicates difficulties in linking teachers' voices with a commitment to act on the part of teacher educators, although, as we noted earlier, a commitment to action is pivotal to action research, and action research implicitly has 'democratic intent'. Theoretically, DIETs are part of a national drive towards decentralisation aimed at encouraging greater public participation in educational processes, reflecting democratic intent at other levels of the education system. It is important, therefore, to locate our investigation of practice in the wider contexts in which the practice occurs, in order to reveal tensions surrounding the possibilities of developments in the directions indicated by the action research findings. Specifically, we consider here training programme design; budgets and financial dependence; and linkages with other administrative entities at the District and sub-District levels. All of these provide examples of a context in which a DIET wishing to take action on its own research findings will experience considerable obstacles; and these examples also help explain some of the attitudes shaping DIET staff's responses to what teachers had to say.

Training programmes of each DIET are planned according to an annual calendar of activities, which is first developed by the State-level agency. This is sent to DIETs, who are supposed to amend it in the light of the District's training needs, progress and so on. State-level actors expect DIETs to tune it according to the District requirements:

> *You see, this is just suggestive. It's a guideline. This is guidance for you. This is one way in which you can work. Like ... if a stone gets underfoot on your way, you can move it. It can be changed. It is flexible. Based on the necessities of their own areas, you take programmes and get them approved in these meetings. (personal communication, teacher education section, RAJ/SC 2000)*

In practice, this 'flexible guideline' is taken as a blueprint from which DIETs tend not to deviate and no fine-tuning is done. DIET staff *believe* they are regulated by the constant need to seek permission, although this need is disputed by the state level. The definition of training needs is encapsulated in the module which comes from the state, rather than the local knowledge of the DIET staff:

> *I told you, here everything comes from the top ... Normally the types of training programme are decided at the State level, and modules are developed by SCERT. The training module is for all and it's the same for all. If I want to add something of mine in the module, I am not free to do that. The module they have prepared and given us, we have to work on that only. (personal communication, DIET D, 1999)*

The pervasive lack of belief in the existence of the autonomy to make even minor changes in module content reflects a much wider agenda of power and control which dominates many aspects of DIET functioning. The DIET's nodal agency in both States easily retain its role of 'idea generator' because of centralised financial arrangements, which deprive DIETs of any possibility of running a locally designed programme.[4] Budgets, largely to cover teachers' daily and travel allowances, are tied to training programmes whose content and length is decided either at the state or national level. The widespread teacher discontent about training programmes which the action research reflected is fuelled by teachers' dissatisfaction with travel and daily allowances which, they claim, do not cover costs, and are often reimbursed late.

Teacher attendance at training programmes depends heavily on the support of the District Education Officer, as the DIET does not have the administrative mandate to issue teachers with an order to attend training. Without an order, they cannot be released from school; and not every DIET enjoys cooperation in this respect. Non-attendance of teachers is a major problem in Rajasthan, and in the two case study DIETs there, sometimes as many as half the training places would be unoccupied because teachers were not deputed, leaving DIET staff further demoralised. But DIETs themselves have created poor will towards training because their internal planning is weak: systematic records of teacher career development have so far been kept neither by the DIET nor the District Education Officer, and so sometimes one teacher is sent several times for the same training or called to attend a training programme in an area s/he does not teach. In the absence of any cover arrangements, District Education Officers may also object to teachers going for training and leaving children unattended.

Acute lacks of links between the various bodies constituted to work for elementary education have left the DIET in a situation of dependency, handicapped by its lack of administrative authority in a system dominated by written orders:

> *Power is very important. If we want any information we face problems. Now here we don't have any power so we can write a letter to a school. If a school is good they will send it otherwise it doesn't come. The most we can do is write to the DEO office, or we have to go personally to the DEO office and request there. They will send a letter from there. After that – out of fear – the information will come. If we had power, we won't face problems in our work. (personal communication, I DIET staff member, 1999)*

In the absence of mandated administrative powers, the functioning of the DIET becomes largely dependent on the institute's ability to generate good will. Its own credibility thus becomes a major factor. The inappropriate staffing of DIETs has considerably undermined, or prevented from developing, such credibility, since it is an open secret that people who cannot contribute effectively to the DIET's portfolio of activities continue to work there:

> *Actually, DIET should guide and carry out all the educational and academic activities of the district. But what has happened is that people who were in the Basic Training Institute already have remained. Or people who wanted to come to the city and were not needed anywhere else have got their transfer here. Do they have this type of thinking or are they suitable for it or not? They were all appointed without that. This has had a big effect on the DIET. The basic feelings for the DIET is destroyed if you are imposing on it people who are not capable. What work do they have except they want to stay in ... a city. They are not required anywhere else so they were brought here. What will one gain from that? You tell me. Can something happen from that? Nothing will materialise from that. They have come from higher secondary and they don't know what happens in a DIET. They only understand that classes should be held. (personal communication, I DIET staff member, 1999)*

The constant emphasis by DIET staff on the need for power (i.e. the capacity to invoke administrative sanctions) suggests that the decentralisation initiatives of the state have not opened up spaces for more democratic ways of working.

Commitment to Change – the link gone missing?

The first part of this chapter illustrated the possibilities of introducing professional teacher educator development via collaborative action research projects. The project attempted to model a more democratic way of working, and to strengthen DIETs through building both responsivity to their constituency, and a sense of agency. The resulting action research projects illustrated successes and constraints in these directions, but reminded us that our attempts to develop a more democratic model of practice were shaped by the much larger socio-political forces in which DIETs are embedded. This wider context shapes the extent to which action on the research findings might be conceived as possible, or undertaken, since the possibilities of sustaining this momentum are interlinked with a much larger set of processes which are unsupportive of developing a sense of agency, and lacking in democratic intent.

In our case study sites, the relationship between the state and the DIET remains centralised, while relationships between agencies at the District and sub-District levels have either broken down, or not been

Caroline Dyer et al

created. The resulting fragmentation and compartmentalism had combined to create a disempowering context for the DIET as an institution and for the individuals within it, although a small number of teacher educators responded positively to the opportunity for professional growth predicated on a democratic and self-reflective approach.

Despite the rhetoric of decentralisation, the explicit dissatisfaction with the quality of teacher education at the national level, and the establishment of what were apparently intended to be decentralised institutes of teacher education, conditions supportive to democratisation of teacher education processes have not yet been created. We would argue that if the promises at the policy level are to take shape in practice, the 'teacher as technician' model which prevails must be challenged. Action research shows some promise as a challenge, but it may end up as more of a frustration than a democratising strategy unless comprehensive structural changes become a reality and are accompanied by wide-ranging commitments to heeding what action research has to say. The rapid movement towards comprehensive restructuring in Madhya Pradesh, however, offers some optimism that teacher education may emerge as a site where links can be made between the potentially potent forces of individual and collective agency, and creative, democratic educational processes.

Notes

[1] We are grateful to the United Kingdom's Department for International Development for funding the project 'District Institutes of Education and Training: a comprehensive study in three Indian States'.

[2] We refer in this chapter only to elementary (lower and upper primary) teachers within government sector schools.

[3] 10-12 schools are grouped into a Cluster, each of which has a coordinator.

[4] In 2000, Madhya Pradesh embarked on a major process of institutional reform which intends to achieve convergence between various agencies that are all charged with assisting in providing education for all, but have been operating independently and sometimes at cross purposes with one another (cf. Sharma & Gopalkrishnan, 1999). Processes of decentralisation have made the District the centre of all development activities, and all local government bodies report to the head of the District, the Collector. DIETs are now required to work very closely with the reformed educational administration agency at the District level; DIETs themselves had yet to reform but sweeping changes are expected during 2001 (personal communication, Amita Sharma, Secretary, Elementary Education, GoMP, March 2001). Our observations here refer to the situation prevailing in the field during 1999-2000.

References

Arora, G.L. (1998) *Needs Assessment: a conceptual framework, in Assessing Primary Teachers' Training Needs: self-learning package for trainers and data collection tools* (DPEP Activity no. 2, 1997-98). New Delhi: National Council of Educational Research and Training.

Day, Christopher (1997) Working with the Different Selves of Teachers: beyond comfortable collaboration, pp. 190-203 in S. Hollingsworth (Ed.) *International Action Research: a casebook for educational reform.* Lewes: Falmer Press.

Dyer, Caroline (2000) *Operation Blackboard: policy implementation in Indian elementary education.* Wallingford: Symposium Books.

Dyer, Caroline & Choksi, Archana (1997) *District Institutes of Education and Training: a case study of Baroda DIET*, mimeo, University of Manchester.

Elliott, John (1991) *Action Research for Educational Change.* Milton Keynes: Open University Press.

Kumar, Krishna (1991) *The Political Agenda of Education.* New Delhi: Sage.

McNiff, Jean (1991) *Action Research: principles and practice.* London: Routledge.

Ministry of Human Resource Development (1989) *District Institutes of Education and Training: guidelines.* New Delhi: Ministry of Human Resource Development, Government of India.

National Council for Teacher Education (1998a) *Curriculum Framework for Quality Teacher Education.* New Delhi: National Council for Teacher Education.

National Council for Teacher Education (1998b) *Teacher Education in Rajasthan.* New Delhi: National Council for Teacher Education.

National Policy on Education 1986 (with modifications undertaken in 1992). New Delhi: Ministry of Human Resource Development, Government of India.

Programme of Action on the National Policy of Education 1986/1992 (1992). New Delhi: Ministry of Human Resource Development

Public Report On Basic Education in India (1999). New Delhi: Oxford University Press.

Sharma, Amita & Gopalkrishnan, R. (1999) *Universal Primary Education and Total Literacy in Madhya Pradesh: a proposal for institutional reform*, Rajiv Gandhi Mission Occasional Paper (not numbered). Bhopal: Rajiv Gandhi Mission.

UNICEF (1991) *Basic Education and National Development: the Indian scene.* New Delhi: UNICEF.

World Bank (1996) *India: primary education achievements and challenges.* Washington, DC: World Bank.

Whose Knowledge for Educational Development? Reflections on Collaborative Fieldwork in the Small State of Saint Lucia

KEITH HOLMES

Introduction

There is a strong rationale for strengthening research capabilities in post-colonial societies to reduce the dangers of the inappropriate cross-cultural transfer of research findings. Small states (taken here as countries with populations of less than 1.5 million) are especially vulnerable to international educational development agendas that are ill suited to local realities (Bacchus & Brock, 1987, p. 6). The transfer of existing research methodologies and research paradigms is also problematic, since small states have 'an ecology of their own' (Commonwealth Secretariat, 1986, pp. 5-6).

My doctoral dissertation used a case study of Saint Lucia in the Eastern Caribbean to explore some of the main issues, challenges and priorities for the development of educational research in a small post-colonial society. As an English researcher, I sought to develop, and test, the potential of a collaborative methodology to avoid some of the above pitfalls. A collaborative approach was conceived as a way of working 'with', rather than 'on', 'in' or even 'for' a postcolonial society.

After conducting educational research in Jamaica several years ago, I felt that I had short-changed some of the most disadvantaged young people I had ever met. They had given freely of their time, knowledge and enthusiasm without getting anything in return. This experience, which is by no means unique, posed serious ethical questions about the research process and especially the role of 'Northern' researchers in the

'South'. Although a collaborative approach inevitably raises other ethical issues, the process of identifying common research goals and establishing more equitable and democratic relationships potentially avoids some of the exploitative aspects of social research.

There are additional philosophical and pragmatic arguments in favour of collaborative research. It 'confronts traditional assumptions about the nature of knowledge, ideas about scientific privilege and the process of mystification underpinning academic culture' and, 'treats participants as competent knowers and co-researchers' (Shuttleworth et al, 1994, p. 94). Collaborative research should therefore be of particular interest to educationalists and sociocultural theorists who recognise the value of participatory activities for shared, reciprocal learning (Bruner, 1966) and developing research skills. A collaborative approach also fits with what Gibbons et al (1994) describe as a 'new mode of knowledge production', whereby knowledge is increasingly produced by teams and judged on its contribution to the solution of transdisciplinary problems (Gibbons et al, 1994, p. 33).

In Saint Lucia and other small states, some development consultants have a poor reputation as overpaid, interfering 'outsiders' who are blinkered by their previous experiences. Their so-called 'findings' are often common knowledge and their recommendations often ignore crucial contextual factors. This reputation presents immediate challenges to 'outsiders' proposing to conduct research in a small state. A collaborative research design that begins with locally identified priorities and seeks to generate useful knowledge *with* the research participants is a realistic and appropriate alternative. One of the challenges is to achieve both process and outcome benefits for everyone involved.

Why Were My Efforts to Collaborate with Saint Lucian Researchers Successful?

Whether Saint Lucians would agree that my efforts to collaborate were successful depends on the extent to which their own objectives were met. From this experience, I would concur with Griffiths (1998, p. 113) that 'collaboration is fun, satisfying, motivating, mind-stretching and a way of working to one's strengths. At the same time, it is very difficult to do well'. Having worked with personnel from the Ministry of Education, the Folk Research Centre, the National Research and Development Foundation, the Sir Arthur Lewis Community College and other organisations and individuals in Saint Lucia, I have been reflecting on why this 15-week field visit went as well as it did. In particular, what led to such good collaboration with the Research Officer at the Ministry of Education? In this brief chapter, several instrumental factors are identified and some of the major dilemmas arising from a collaborative approach are explored. Many of these are relevant to broader issues concerning North-South collaborative research partnerships.

Interpersonal Factors

The University of Bristol has strong links with Saint Lucia. The Governor General, herself a former doctoral student in Bristol, was supportive of the study. This was my third visit to Saint Lucia in two years, and on each visit I had prioritised building relationships of trust and mutual respect. In the complex, plural societies of the Caribbean, skin colour, language, educational background and age are prominent signifiers of social status. Somehow, the combination of these factors helped to create a balanced, non-threatening relationship between the Research Officer and myself. The low status ascribed to my relatively young age and my lack of teaching experience compensated for the high status ascribed by many Saint Lucians to my skin colour and language. Our educational backgrounds were broadly similar so we could relate well at an intellectual level. The Research Officer might easily have felt threatened if I had been an older, more senior academic. Importantly, we shared similar views on education and the potential benefits of educational research, especially qualitative research. Being from an 'outside' university was an advantage for developing trust, as I had no established allegiances to personal networks, political parties, or development agencies in Saint Lucia.

Common Objectives

The research design, and to some extent the topic itself, built upon previous work by Saint Lucian graduate students in Bristol. Research development was already known to be high on the agenda of the Ministry of Education and other organisations. From the outset, the Research Officer recognised how involvement in this study was relevant to her ongoing work and career development. One of her work objectives was to find out what educational research was currently going on and to explore the potential for closer collaboration between organisations in order to reduce duplication and to share costs. I was able to build these objectives into the research design. Until May 2000, the Research Officer had not had much opportunity for networking. By collaborating with me, she could obtain information about who is involved in educational research and what research they are engaged in. The Research Officer was also enthusiastic about the fact that this study would stimulate awareness about the potential value of educational research across the country.

Communication

Communication was crucially important for the success of the fieldwork. The Research Officer and I spent time sharing findings and information of joint interest and closely negotiated over our weekly schedules. Several long telephone conversations and social meetings away from the office helped to strengthen trust, mutual respect and cross-cultural understanding. Use of a mobile phone and email enabled me to stay in touch even while I was away from my home base.

Flexibility

Before arriving in Saint Lucia, I had not known for sure who my main collaborators would be. Even when it became clear that I would be working closely with the Research Officer, we were both prepared to be flexible about the project and how our work should develop. Commitment to an emergent research design was especially important for the benefits of collaboration to be realised (Tom, 1996, p. 347). On several occasions, the Research Officer asked me to attend meetings that I would not otherwise have attended but which turned out to provide valuable data and contacts for the study. In return, I helped the Research Officer to identify Saint Lucians who had recently conducted educational research for higher degrees.

★★★★★

As mentioned earlier, a collaborative methodology raises a number of practical challenges and ethical dilemmas. Some of these are discussed below.

Multiple Loyalties

Working collaboratively with different organisations inevitably generated multiple loyalties. At times, this meant an awkward process of juggling meetings and priorities. Although each of the organisations knew that I was working with the other organisations, the extent of these relationships was not known. I needed to maintain an appearance of impartiality that was difficult to achieve in practice. For example, at a National Consultation on Adult and Continuing Education, I had to be careful which participants I was seen to be sitting with or talking to.

Appropriate Distance

Maintaining appropriate distance was also difficult at times. It was not always clear which conversations with the Research Officer were confidential, which activities were part of our collaborative research, or which activities were necessary for strengthening the research relationship. For example, the Research Officer asked me to comment on a draft report and to help her prepare a PowerPoint presentation. While I agreed to these activities, I declined the offer of using a desk and a telephone in the Ministry, as this would have positioned me too close to the Ministry relative to the other collaborating organisations.

Independence

A collaborative approach necessarily compromises the independence of the researcher. Since my research role within the Ministry depended on an interest in the development of educational research in Saint Lucia, it was not possible to take a neutral, detached perspective. Indeed, my legitimacy and credibility depended on sharing my views on several occasions. Furthermore, research relationships were built on the implicit understanding that any publicly available reports or articles would not portray the individuals or their organisations in a bad light. At times, I felt that I was being trusted with too much sensitive information. Researchers with less integrity might have exploited this situation to the detriment of those involved.

What, if Any, Role is there for 'Outside' Researchers in a Small, Postcolonial Society?

A collaborative methodology raises many dilemmas, because it challenges conventional wisdom about research relationships, and even the nature of knowledge itself. Some social scientists still claim that it is their job to analyse and interpret data, and that it is up to others to implement research findings. However, this posture looks increasingly untenable in small, crisis-prone societies like Saint Lucia. If, on the other hand, researchers do take a more proactive role in national development, how can they maintain enough impartiality to work effectively with a wide range of organisations and individuals?

Another dilemma for the 'outside' researcher is the tendency to collaborate primarily with established institutions run by members of the educated elite. Working with, for example, illiterate French Creole speaking farmers as 'co-researchers' would have been more democratic, though less feasible. As BrockUtne (1996) has argued, in North-South research partnerships, the missing link is often between the elites in the country and the ordinary people. Surely, due to their closer understanding of French Creole language and culture, most Saint Lucians are better placed than 'outsiders' to work with ordinary folk.

One well-established role for 'outside' researchers in the field of comparative education is to illuminate what 'insiders' cannot see. In

Saint Lucia, it was observed that some Saint Lucians would prefer to assist 'outside' researchers than 'inside' researchers with their enquiries. This was explained to me by way of an analogy with a goldfish bowl. Goldfish apparently like to be looked at from the outside, swimming round in their bowl, but they get uncomfortable if they are being watched by other fish inside. It might have been more difficult for an 'inside' researcher to negotiate such good access to the Ministry of Education. Interestingly, one of the main reasons given why the Government of Saint Lucia engages external consultants is because they do not have prior personal, business or political interests within the country. However, there may also be a role for 'outside' academics as advocates. For example, Saint Lucia would benefit from advocates within respected universities who understand both the local and the global contexts, and who may able to influence multinational corporations, and international institutions, including the World Trade Organisation.

To What Extent Are Current Models of Research Partnerships Appropriate for Conducting Collaborative Research in a Small State?

Whereas many of the above factors and dilemmas would exist for 'outside' researchers working collaboratively in large post-colonial societies, there are distinctive issues for researchers in small states. Although useful in broad terms, current models for 'North-South' collaborative research partnerships (e.g. KFPE, 1998) have not taken population size into consideration. For successful collaboration, the importance of allowing time to build relationships and to understand the local micro-politics may be greater in a parochial context where there is more suspicion of the 'outsider'. In Saint Lucia, politics pervades every area of life, as does the use of social networks to achieve personal and career objectives. Personal contacts and individual personalities can be more influential than qualifications, job titles or official roles on what actually happens in research and practice.

To collaborate successfully in a small state, 'outside' researchers need to get a feel for the 'social ecology'. For example, in Saint Lucia, I became aware of unfamiliar perceptions of social and physical space. On several occasions I was surprised that a Saint Lucian had not visited a certain place or spoken to a certain person, even though it seemed to me as if they were only a small physical or social distance apart. This is an example of the kind of social regulation in small states that Lowenthal (1987, p. 39) describes as 'managed intimacy'. In such a context, an 'outsider' can unwittingly trample on established social spaces and boundaries, because the wiring of interpersonal, economic and political relations is invisible at first. Trust may take longer to generate precisely because small state 'insiders' know that 'outsiders' are not familiar with the complex rules and social mechanisms that guide their everyday lives.

Conclusion

I began by introducing the rationale for a collaborative approach. Several factors that contributed to the success of the main field visit to Saint Lucia were then identified, and I noted some of the key challenges and ethical dilemmas arising. Current models of North-South collaborative research partnerships do not necessarily fit the social ecology of small states. Although the relationship between 'inside' and 'outside' researchers is invariably problematic, a collaborative approach can nevertheless enable a two-way process of illumination. Indeed, the knowledge generated by bringing together 'inside' and 'outside' research perspectives can potentially contribute to education policies that are well suited to local contexts and cultures, within this rapidly globalising world.

Acknowledgements

I am grateful to Catherine Albert and Michael Crossley for their professional support and advice, and for financial assistance provided by the Economic and Social Research Council.

References

Bacchus, K. & Brock, C. (1987) *The Challenge of Scale: educational development in the small states of the Commonwealth.* London: Commonwealth Secretariat.

BrockUtne, B. (1996) Globalisation of Learning – the role of the universities in the South with a special look at sub-Saharan Africa, *International Journal of Educational Development,* 16, pp. 335-346.

Bruner, J.S. (1966) *Towards a Theory of Instruction.* Cambridge, MA: Belknap Press.

Commonwealth Secretariat (1986) Educational Development: the small states of the Commonwealth. Report of a Pan-Commonwealth Meeting of Experts, Mauritius, 1985. London: Commonwealth Secretariat.

Gibbons, M., Limoges, C., Nowotny, H., Schwartzman, S., Scott, P. & Trow, M. (1994) *The New Production of Knowledge: the dynamics of science and research in contemporary societies.* London: Sage.

Griffiths, M. (1998) *Educational Research for Social Justice: getting off the fence.* Buckingham: Open University Press.

KFPE [Kommission für ForschungsPartnerschaften mit Entwicklungsländern] (1998) *Guidelines for Research in Partnership with Developing Countries: 11 principles.* Bern: Swiss Commission for Research Partnerships with Developing Countries.

Lowenthal, D. (1987) Social Features, in C. Clarke & T. Payne (Eds) *Politics, Security and Development in Small States*, pp. 26-49. London: Allen & Unwin.

Shuttleworth, S., Somerton, M. & Vulliamy, D. (1994) *Collaborative Research for Social Change: shared learning between workers and academics*. Hull: University of Hull Centre for Continuing Education Development and Training.

Tom, A. (1996) Building Collaborative Research: living the commitment to emergent design, *Qualitative Studies in Education*, 9, pp. 347-359.

Playing down Presence: the importance of in-depth research for education for development

ROB McBRIDE

Introduction

The main thrust of this chapter is not to directly criticise any form of research or to suggest that all or the majority of research in education for development should be in-depth research. Rather, the argument is in favour of a 'broader church', which includes *more* in-depth research. In addition, there are no direct criticisms of any individual or journal, or practitioners in 'the field'. The intention is to present an argument that may benefit all who work in, and may be helped by, education for development.

A Brief Portrayal of In-depth Research

During September 1999, two researchers, myself and a Malawian academic, initiated a small research project which considered HIV/AIDS education in primary and secondary schools in the Zomba area of Malawi. We visited eight schools, interviewing the headteachers, and teachers responsible for HIV/AIDS education. At the end of the interviews, we invited the eight teachers to a meeting to discuss our perceptions of their views and to help us understand further the work they were engaged in and the issues they faced (the research is ongoing).

During visits to schools and at the group meeting we heard:

When we meet, drama is used and children are encouraged to write poems and sing songs. Yet it is sometimes difficult to talk about AIDS as some of the words we need are embarrassing to say in our local language.

> We advise our girls not to indulge themselves in immoral behaviour such as chatting with boys, that can lead to the killer disease.

> I associate the term AIDS with a punishment from God because of our bad behaviour.

> There seems to be a contradiction. We aim to stop the disease but we are promoting condoms which encourage children to be loose. Abstinence should be the message – one line.

Some headteachers told us that their schools were unaffected by HIV/AIDS, while another (a secondary head) told us:

> The biggest issue that affects us is the loss of parents. Pupils have no one to support them so I have to contact organisations who are able to help them. Almost every term this happens. This term two boys have lost both parents.

Other comments were:

> For the children, just losing a parent is emotionally bad enough but the children suffer from guilt and fear. [Showing us a letter] Here is a letter from a child who does not admit his parents died from AIDS but indicates this and adds, 'I think I will suffer in the same way as my parents'.

> Remember, we are a mission school and the Bishop lives nearby. The mission view is that you must abstain. But what if they cannot, what should they do? The mission view is that if they cannot abstain they are sinners. I am the buffer and we have two sets of regulations – those of the mission and the ones we use.

> Around 45% of our children's families have been affected by AIDS. We notice that the attainment of some children who have been affected is very low and they often drop out. AIDS affected children are unhappy, they do not mix and they absent themselves. Some children insult them. As a headteacher, I feel overwhelmed by this cloud over the school.

> We have lost three teachers in the last two years. It has not been disclosed but we believe they died as a result of AIDS.

> AIDS brings more administration work, frequent illnesses and possible loss of life. It corrupts our way of working and we do not reach our objectives. This year we have lost two teachers.

From this and other evidence, we drew the following tentative conclusions:

the term 'AIDS' has a set of meanings that are not just about the disease;

cultural expectations and Chichewa (the spoken language) meant that matters associated with AIDS were 'unspoken';

teachers needed help and advice to develop their understanding of the teaching of controversial issues;

teachers in schools seem to have received less help than they would have liked. No evidence of advice, guidance or support from government could be found (this has since begun to change);

it seems there are orphans in schools whose parents have died from AIDS. There was a lack of understanding about the sorts of lives experienced by orphans, their educational needs and school responses.

It might be argued that the early parts of this chapter include too much raw data – it is deliberate. Some of these teachers' comments might be interpreted in a number of ways and the reader has the opportunity to question the writer and the writer's interpretations. They are intended, in part, to encourage an 'active' reader and to reduce the influence of the writer.

Equally significantly, we can also ask which of these issues might have remained unseen had the researchers not talked to teachers and met them more than once to discuss these matters. Let us consider one issue – the support for teachers in teaching controversial issues. We have since spoken to ministry officials and inspectors, local politicians, non-governmental organisations (NGOs) and organisations engaged in HIV/AIDS support. This matter has never been raised.

Other methods, however useful in different ways, might not have seen this issue emerge. For example, had we entered schools with a hypothesis or an agenda in order to find out something about teaching materials used, numbers of orphans and so on, we may not have come across this matter. Another method, such as observation, with its hit and miss element ('there are no AIDS education lessons today') may not have helped. Certainly, we were surprised when we drew our conclusions about teaching controversial issues.

It is also significant to realise that there were variations in perceptions and interpretations in the responses received. The writing of this chapter and our reports intentionally sought to demonstrate that responses we received were different in each school we encountered. Some were running anti-AIDS clubs successfully, had some teaching materials, had fewer orphans, had staff with a range of ideas and so on; others had different experiences and were taking alternative approaches. This is not to say that we can say nothing general about them. For example, some headteachers wanted to stress one message, that of complete abstention outside of marriage. Some of these felt that the teaching materials available to them were effective and others did not – indeed, we could go on and consider other variables and paint a more complex picture. This has ramifications for policy and teacher development and, as we shall see, it will be argued that perceptions of the nature and effectiveness of policy often go hand in hand with other views about research and teachers' roles.

Prior to turning to these issues, let us consider what is called in this chapter 'in-depth research'.

What is In-depth Research?

In-depth research takes place in natural settings; it is naturalistic, as exemplified by some of the research described above. Like much qualitative research, it is interpretive in that it deals with the perceptions of ordinary people in their daily lives, including both routine and problematic activities. Much in-depth research is small scale, dealing with a single case. It recognises the reality of power in the research situation, between the researcher and the researched (whom it endeavours to put on as level a footing as possible), between researchers (see the example above) and between those researched.

The power that researchers can exercise has been the subject of considerable debate (see MacDonald, 1974; Rorty, 1980; Geertz, 1983; Van Maanen, 1988; Denzin & Lincoln, 1994, to name a few), and of particular interest here is the researcher's interpretation, especially as expressed in his/her writing (see Clifford & Marcus, 1986; Geertz, 1988; and more on this topic in a later section). Objectivity is not possible for the social researcher who changes the natural situation through studying it and, as Manning has written: 'self-construction is as much a part of sociological method as theory construction' (Manning, 1982/1991, quoted in Vidich & Lyman, 1994, p. 58). The lack of objectivity means that the outcomes of such research comprise soft knowledge that acknowledges its weakness in the areas of certainty and prediction. This, in turn, implies that a simplistic notion of research providing straightforward guidance to practitioners or policy-makers is not an option, but this does not imply that soft knowledge is of no use.

Rather, let us briefly consider how we learn and how we might lose our knowledge. Plainly, there are forms of research that give us what are considered firm and hard outcomes, knowledge that is considered certain. This may be used by policy-makers to directly inform their decisions. This makes up the bulk of research in the field of education for development and this will probably continue. The central argument of this chapter is that alongside these approaches there should be space for in-depth research. In this sort of research, knowledge consists of a compote of cases rather than generalisations. In the words of MacIntyre:

Objective rationality is therefore to be found not in rule-
following, but in rule-transcending, in knowing how and when
to put rules and principles to work and when not to. Consider
how practical reasoning of this kind is taught, whether it is the
practical reasoning of generals ... of surgeons or of natural
scientists. Because there is no set of rules specifying necessary
and sufficient conditions for large areas of such practices, the
skills of practical reasoning are communicated only partly by
precepts but much more by case-histories and precedents.
Moreover the precepts cannot be understood except in
terms of the history of both precepts and case-histories.
(MacIntyre, 1977)

Notions of generalisation will be discussed later. At this stage, we need to say something more about policy and the subject of MacIntyre's statement, practical knowledge, for practice is often associated with in-depth research.

Samoff (1999a), in a paper delivered at the Oxford International Conference in September 1999, sheds some light on the matter of policy (see also Samoff, 1999b). He argues that: 'Assumptions about *what is policy* and *how policies are made* influence both research and political action' (Samoff, 1999a, p. 8). He continues:

The aid business distinctly prefers a rational-technical
orientation to policy making, with unambiguous policy
directions, systematic planning and orderly implementation,
all supported by applied research. Education itself, however,
is more process than product. A rational-technical orientation
to education policy disdains interactive and participatory
policy making that is necessarily clumsier, muddier and
slower. Characterizing itself as neutral and apolitical and
seeking to avoid an explicitly political approach to setting
education policy, a rational-technical orientation is ill-
equipped to address learning as popular mobilisation.
(Samoff, 1999a, p. 9)

Samoff confirms the detached and mechanistic nature of policy-making in much of the field of Education for Development. Local people are too often removed from the central decision-making process and there are few serious means of including their views – the role that in-depth research could take. Moreover, aside from his comment about applied research, which is not used as in this chapter, these comments are reminiscent of those of Schön (1971), Havelock (1971), House (1974) and Sarason (1990), who all argued that educational change and improvement does not take place as planned without some kind of local involvement. Policy could be, in other words, a process which involves people rather than an event in the form of legislation, commands or instructions. A dynamic and ongoing understanding of complex and changing situations can be a major factor in *sustainable* educational development.

From the involvement of people in this way, it is a small step to discuss practical knowledge. Aristotle distinguished practical reasoning (phronesis) and knowledge from scientific knowledge (episteme) and technical knowledge (techne). In the words of philosopher Richard Bernstein:

> *phronesis is a form of reasoning that is concerned with choice*
> *and involves deliberation. It deals with what is variable and*
> *about which there can be differing opinions (doxai). It is a type*
> *of reasoning in which there is a mediation between general*
> *principles and a concrete particular situation that requires*
> *choice and decision. In forming such a judgment there are*
> *no determinate technical rules by which a particular can*
> *simply be subsumed under that which is general or universal.*
> *What is required is an interpretation and specification of*
> *universals that are appropriate to the particular situation.*
> *(Bernstein, 1983)*

Moreover, phronesis is fostered by a community; practical knowledge is often socially constructed, especially by practitioners such as professionals or small groups of ordinary people who live together. It is this knowledge, similar to what Geertz (1983) called local knowledge, and which for Dewey (1916/1966) was the form of reasoning that guided action in a democratic society, that is often brought to the surface by in-depth research.

Action research is one form of research that is often in-depth, and could be used to gather and process practical knowledge (see Elliott, 1991). It is also ongoing, that is to say, it is not a form of research which is usually about someone coming up with hard and fast conclusions that then require implementation. Rather, action researchers spiral between gathering data, making reasoned decisions, monitoring and evaluating – often to find that new issues arise from previous activities which then require further deliberation and action.

Sometimes the movement into connected issues is called *progressive focusing*. This involves trying to establish one set of issues and then going on to ask respondents to try and deconstruct further to see if there are unspoken or unthought matters that emerge from further reflection. Terms and ideas used by respondents are treated as complex and requiring further investigation. Progressive focusing is often used in action research to provide insights and a basis for change and improvement (see O'Hanlon, 1996).

In the Department for International Development's practical guide for research (DfID, 1999), action research is included as an approach that might be commissioned, yet other statements in the Education Section (Section 2), e.g. 'fills a gap in international knowledge' (p. 13) and 'has the potential to make a significant contribution to international understanding' (p. 13), suggest a rather limited understanding of this approach. These statements appear to reveal a view of action research as producing propositional or theoretical knowledge when it is better conceived as an approach that informs action, i.e. practical knowledge. To reinforce this perception when I recently suggested to the DfID that I would like to submit a proposal which used storytelling as a form of data collection, the reply included the (however well-intentioned) statement: 'and it would do no harm if you concentrated upon the macro, rather than the micro, and orientated towards informing policy on the issue' (email, 18 July 2000). What can DfID mean by action research? Generalisation as a basis for policy development is plainly a significant concept for the DfID, if this reply is anything to go by.

Small-scale educational evaluation is another form of research which can be in-depth and which has common roots with action research (see Adelman, 1993). Parlett & Hamilton's (1972/1987) seminal paper describes how evaluation, to be effective, needed to take into account the views of ordinary people who have a stake in the programme being evaluated. MacDonald (1974/1987), in an equally seminal paper, argued for similar reasons that evaluation has to be careful of the control and power that emerges from bureaucracies and from autocratic evaluators. He argued in favour of democratic evaluation in which *all* stakeholders had opportunities to influence, and be influenced by, the debate that surrounded educational programmes. MacDonald's 'key justificatory concept' was 'the right to know' (MacDonald, 1987, p. 45). It is suggested here that both papers see forms of in-depth research as being associated with evaluation.

If this is in-depth research, let us see if we can find evidence of it in the field of education for development.

Where is it Scarce?

If in-depth research is used in the field, we ought to find evidence of it in the journals that can be considered to reflect the work of a good number of practitioners. To this end, all editions of the *International Journal of Educational Development* (*IJED*) and *Compare* from 1998 to the time of writing (August 2000), that is, volumes 18-20 of *IJED* and 28-30 of *Compare*, have been considered. This is not a Tooley type survey which judges papers according to their perceived quality (Tooley et al, 1998). Rather, it has been a search for papers that demonstrate that they have conducted in-depth research. Indicators of in-depth research have been taken as the presence of independent research rather than bureaucratically dominated (this is not just a matter of funding); that the 'voices' of stakeholders are present, not just representations of them; that writers have been cautious about generalising to 'big' theory and/or policy, especially 'big' policy; that there is evidence of some kind of practical involvement; that writers show an awareness of their relationship with their writing (see below); and that there is some kind of small-scale element (in-depth tends to restrict time for large-scale survey).

Plainly, these indicators have been subject to interpretation and there has been no effort to look for all in a single paper. Yet, even after a fairly positively disposed perusal, it can be argued that we would all benefit if we, i.e. those engaged in education for development, endeavoured to do, and publish, more in-depth research. In the *IJED* volumes, less than one in five papers can be described as having a significant in-depth element, though with each volume this is increasing to not far from one in three, in volume 20. In *Compare*, there is a slight tendency to decrease from one in 10 to one in 12 of the papers in the volumes considered.

It should be added that a sizeable number of writers claimed that they have conducted fieldwork, yet provided no evidence. In-depth research has a tendency to yield large amounts of quotable discourse and if this is not present it is possible that the views of people on the ground were considered insignificant for policy development or could be better written in the words of the writer, i.e. stakeholders could be represented better by the writer than by their own words. The first substantiates the need for more in-depth research; researcher representation will be the subject of comment below.

This analysis and these sorts of conclusions have appeared before. For example, in his Presidential Address to the United Kingdom branch of the Comparative Education Society in Europe in 1978, Lawrence Stenhouse commented:

> *Experience is made public to invite judgement in dialogue,*
> *and such judgement rests upon the possibility of an appeal to*
> *evidence. This evidence, the fundamental data source for*
> *comparative education, must be description: and I am going to*
> *argue that, since it became a self-conscious and academic*
> *study, comparative education has paid too little attention to*
> *observation and description, preferring to emphasise such*
> *abstractions as statistics and measurements on the one hand*
> *and school 'systems' on the other. (Stenhouse, 1979, p. 6)*

He goes on to suggest that many comparativists use largely documents as source data and do not 'provide the student with some protection against misreading his [sic] documents' (1979, p. 6) He concludes by 'asking that we develop in our field a better grounded representation of day-to-day educational reality' (p. 10), and casts doubt on the worth of so much 'research conducted without the polluting intimacy of fieldwork' (p. 9). Detached research reports (perhaps rather than papers) do not encourage the reader to question; indeed they endeavour to present a singular, certain and authoritative view that in-depth research would, of its experience, undermine.

A recent paper by Ninnes & Mehta (2000, p. 206) comments similarly and refers to others who have done so, particularly in *Comparative Education Review*. If all of this sounds unduly negative, there are plainly some cases of excellent in-depth research to be found in these journals and elsewhere, in particular, the papers by Dyer & Choksi (1998) and by Stephens (2000). If we look more broadly, there are some good in-depth papers in the collection edited by Crossley & Vulliamy (1997), though it has to be said that from a book with this title the reader might have expected more evidence of in-depth research and greater recognition of the issues previously raised by, for example, Clifford & Marcus (1986) or Denzin & Lincoln (1994) in their widely available publications.

It is as if education for development deals largely with policy and that policy has no dynamic or contentious features and is implemented without problems. Research, in general, is separated from practice and, if this is the case, it is likely that in-depth research is seen as unimportant, irrelevant and probably a little quirky. Perhaps as significantly for education for development, its means of regeneration are being constrained, for around the ideas of in-depth research, a number of virulent debates are taking place in nearly all of the social sciences. Some of these are the subject of the next section.

The Accompanying Debate

In those areas where in-depth research is mostly found – ethnography, for example – virulent debates have been waging for a number of years. These had been preceded by more fundamental concerns raised in numerous disciplines and areas of study ranging from art and architecture to philosophy (see Jameson [1991] for a very full account). We reached a point some time ago where the terms 'new ethnography' and 'postmodernism' were widely used and there are numerous publications (it is not possible to completely dissect what is postmodern and what might have a different 'source' – see Marcus, 1994).

We will now consider a small number of the debates that have arisen from these literatures and others that are concerned with the sorts of issues that arise from in-depth research. The central argument is that education for development, with its paucity of concern with in-depth research, is missing out on these debates and that its *academic development and practical effectiveness are undermined.* Of fundamental concern are the issues that hover around the use of the term *presence*, though this term will be left until last.

Let us return to the HIV/AIDS research in Malawi that was referred to earlier. Our interest was to understand how teachers and pupils make sense of AIDS, how they respond to the messages they receive and which of the messages change their perceptions. In addition, we sought means of supporting teachers and schools. Let us now consider the matters that we, as researchers, have had to be mindful of.

We deliberately started 'on the ground', i.e. in schools, with just a little scepticism towards the multilevel analysis approach of Bray & Thomas (1995). It was our view that while such an approach is worthy of consideration, it will provide background only. We are concerned that an analysis at a range of levels, prior to immersion in schools, may create hypotheses and perceptions that could reinforce researcher bias in data collection and early analysis. We prefer the major foci and hypotheses to emerge from the respondents and to be evidentially based (see Weinstein & Weinstein, 1991, p. 161).

There has been the relationship between we two researchers. To what extent do I, the most experienced researcher, lead in selecting schools, interviewees, asking questions and so on – indeed, how do we treat my whiteness and my European research background.(see Wright, 1988; and Vidich & Lyman, 1994). We find some teachers prefer to speak to him, others to me. Some break into Chichewa, others prefer English (we see why later). We have some problem, we think, discussing sexual matters with female teachers. Indeed, we are both male researchers and there is a set of major gender issues in any AIDS research. There is a little religious tension in that I have no religious affiliation while my colleague is a Methodist but not a member of the church that has influenced the most widely used teaching materials (they are strongly religious in my view) and which is the largest church in the country. Most of the teachers see the whole matter of AIDS in religious terms. Once we begin to analyse our data, we begin to find differences between us (see Stronach & MacLure, 1997, ch. 2 for a similar story). We need to explain these differences and also to decide whether there is need for reconciliation. We go further and begin writing. Do we write our own versions of the whole, stick to our favourite parts or agree a division? What style or genre do we adopt?

Van Maanen (1988) helped us come to terms with the messiness of the fieldwork we were undertaking. In particular, there were issues of reflexivity, some of which have been referred to earlier. Marcus argues that, in postmodern anthropology (multidisciplinarity – see earlier), at least: 'The crucial turn, it seems to me, has been the position taken toward self-critical reflexivity in ethnographic writing' (Marcus, 1994, p. 568), and in particular, the 'radical or surplus difference' (see Marcus, 1994, p. 566 and Welch, 1998) that cannot be accounted for. I was aware of being from the 'North', white, male and so on, and that this affected the data I was collecting and my use of it. I was always cautious. Indeed, writing is problematical. Geertz (1988) has eloquently pointed out that while there are historically great concerns about the relationship of researchers to what they know, there should also be questions asked of the relationships of the researcher to his/her writing. What writing genre should be used? Should the writer seek to reveal personal biases? Is a detached 'scientific' style appropriate or does such an approach discourage, rather than encourage, reader participation and questioning?

General caution, in turn, prompted a sense of a lack of certainty, what Denzin & Lincoln (1994, pp. 10-11) call a 'crisis of representation' in representing the people who were subjects of the research and also caution about the legitimacy of the outcomes. No matter how much data were gathered, we tried to keep conclusions open to further question. Caution about the outcomes (called by Denzin & Lincoln [1994, pp. 10-11] the crisis of legitimacy) is connected to issues such as validity, generalisability and reliability.

Generalisability is one form of what the eminent American psychologist, Lee Cronbach (1983), called external validity. He suggested that the external validity of evaluation rests in the human domain, that is, rather than make a claim that some knowledge is true in all situations, the transfer of that true knowledge should rest with people in different situations. If somebody finds an outcome from some research that they consider to be useful in their situation, they should attempt to use it. By testing that knowledge in their practice, they will conclude whether it can 'travel' or not. The range of possibilities is so great, the perceptions so vastly different that we must be cautious, as we were in Malawi about generalising – it must remain in the human domain.

Cronbach argued that: 'When we give proper weight to local conditions, any generalization is a working hypothesis, not a conclusion' Cronbach (1975, p. 125). This does not stop us softly generalising or making naturalistic generalisations (see Stake, 1980). This can be achieved by what is sometimes called theoretical sampling, i.e. considering whether our conclusions from a small in-depth study have application in some way in similar (but not the same) situations. The close understanding that emerges from much in-depth research leads neatly to an increased valuing of human beings (especially those without power), an appreciation of the differences between people and a reticence to generalise in hard or absolute terms.

Validity refers to whether we are clear that we have measured what we set out to measure. In the complex and fluid situations where in-depth research occurs, such certainty is not possible. Janesick offers the following:

Validity in the quantitative area has a set of technical microdefinitions ... Validity ... has to do with description and

151

> explanation, and whether or not a given explanation fits a
> given description. In other words is the explanation credible?
> (Janesick, 1994, p. 216)

Crossley and Vulliamy (1997, p. 20) observe a similar set of reasonings and suggest that the concept of 'trustworthiness' replaces both reliability and validity as long as it is supported by, for example, an audit trail – this is further support for Stenhouse's ideas reported earlier.

We found our constant questioning of simple dichotomies, used by our interviewees and by us in our own analysis, useful. We sought complexity rather than simplicity. For example, the more we asked about the term AIDS, the more it became clear that this term brought forward a host of complex feelings among our respondents – fear of the disease; uncertainty about how it was contracted or identified; a veritable snake's nest of feeling about ungodly and unworthy behaviour; often a denial of the nightmare that AIDS orphans existed in large numbers; a desire to return to 'traditional behaviour' (according to which sex took place only in marriage) and to reject the undermining behaviour usually found in more technologically advanced countries. I add that this form of semiotic discourse analysis, inspired by the 'linguistic turn' of postmodernism, enabled us to open up numerous new lines of investigation and of helping the teachers we were working with to come to new understandings of their own perceptions, thoughts and feelings.

So, even in this necessarily limited case, what might be called postmodernist ideas supported our in-depth study and aided our analytical vision. Indeed, such considerations encouraged us to reflect continuously on our research activities. Yet, it is the uncertainty and caution, the necessary softness of the conclusions that sometimes causes concern and a rejection of the influence of postmodernism. This leads us conveniently to the notion of *Presence*.

To Conclude

'Presence' is a term used by Derrida to allude, in part, to the transcendental thinking that, in his view, has dominated the history of the West.[1] Metaphysical ideas associated with, for example, religion, the natural sciences, philosophy and others tend to provide a 'centred structure' that enables their adherents to return to 'an origin or to a "priority" held to be simple, intact, normal, pure, standard' (Derrida, 1988, p. 93). From such centres (phallogocentrism is another), other ideas and people who hold them are marginalised and excluded. Moreover, from the Archimedean point which stands as a foundation for certain knowledge, other terms are presented with clarity – essence, God, man, objective and so on. Simple, ordered hierarchies become mantras – normal/abnormal, positive/negative, ideal/non-ideal and others.

We can argue, too, that there is a 'living presence', the assured researcher who produces authoritative texts without detailed reference to his/her research subjects; who has a prior personal or bureaucratic agenda; who has few problems with his/her knowledge or text; and who produces valid and reliable generalisations for policy-makers.

There is a strong case for carrying out, using the results of, and publishing more in-depth research. By providing a dynamic commentary, more flexible policy programme directors can keep in touch with the views of ordinary people and support more sustainable action. The study of education for development could be seen as an aspect of practice. At the Oxford International Conference in 1999, 'partnership' was a central issue. Partnership, as the term is often used, is not going to emerge from sector development programmes or similar processes alone. They may help, but more genuine (or symmetrical) partnerships will depend upon human interaction and mutual understanding. In-depth research, by playing down presence, can foster such developments.

Note

[1] This term is not used lightly here but to help illuminate the argument presented here – it is not an example of detached theorising.

References

Adelman, C. (1993) Kurt Lewin and the Origins of Action Research, *Educational Action Research*, 1, pp. 7-24.

Bernstein, R.J. (1983) *Beyond Objectivism and Relativism: science, hermeneutics, and praxis*. Oxford: Blackwell.

Bray, M. & Thomas, R.M. (1995) Levels of Comparison in Educational Studies: different insights from different literatures and the value of multilevel analyses, *Harvard Educational Review*, 65, pp. 472-490.

Clifford, J. & Marcus, G. (1986) *Writing Culture: the poetics and politics of ethnography*. Berkeley: University of California Press.

Cronbach, L. (1975) Beyond the Two Disciplines of Scientific Psychology, *American Psychologist*, 30, pp. 116-126.

Cronbach, L. (with the assistance of K. Shapiro) (1983) *Designing Evaluations of Educational and Social Programs*. London: Jossey-Bass.

Crossley, M. & Vulliamy, G. (Eds) (1997) *Qualitative Educational Research in Developing Countries: current perspectives*. New York: Garland.

Denzin, N.K. & Lincoln, Y.S. (1994) *Handbook of Qualitative Research*. London: Sage.

Department for International Development (DfID) (1999) *Re:search Guide. A Practical Guide for Those Wishing to Obtain Research Funding from DfID*. London: DfID.

Derrida, J. (1988) *Limited Inc.* Translated by Samuel Weber. Evanson, Ill: Northwestern University Press.

Dewey, J. (1916) *Democracy and Education: an introduction to the philosophy of education.* New York: The Free Press; reprinted in 1966, New York, Free Press/Collier Macmillan.

Dyer, C. & Choksi, A. (1998) Education is Like Wearing Glasses: nomads' views of literacy and empowerment, *International Journal of Educational Development*, 18, pp. 405-414.

Elliott, J. (1991) *Action Research for Educational Change.* Milton Keynes: Open University Press.

Geertz, C. (1983) *Local Knowledge.* New York: Basic Books.

Geertz, C. (1988) *Works and Lives: the anthropologist as author.* Cambridge: Polity Press.

Havelock, R.G. (1971) *Planning for Innovation through the Dissemination and Utilisation of Knowledge.* Ann Arbor: Centre for Research and Utilisation of Knowledge.

House, E. (1974) *The Politics of Educational Innovation.* Berkeley: McCutchan.

Jameson, F. (1991) *Postmodernism: or, the cultural logic of late capitalism.* London: Verso.

Janesick, V.L. (1994) The Dance of Qualitative Research Design: metaphor, methodolatry, and meaning, in N.K. Denzin & Y.S. Lincoln (Eds) *Handbook of Qualitative Research.* London: Sage.

MacDonald, B. (1974) Evaluation and the Control of Education. Reprinted in R. Murphy & H. Torrance (1987) *Evaluating Education: issues and methods.* London: Harper.

MacIntyre, A. (1977) Epistemological Crises, Dramatic Narrative and the Philosophy of Science, *Monist*, 60, pp. 453-472.

Manning, P.K. (1987) *Semiotics and Fieldwork.* Newbury Park: Sage.

Manning, P.K. (1991) Analytic Induction, in K. Plummer (Ed.) *Symbolic Interactionism, Vol. 2: Contemporary Issues.* Brookfield, UT: Edward Elgar. [Reprinted from R. Smith & P.K. Manning (Eds) (1982) *Qualitative Methods.* Cambridge, MA: Ballinger.]

Marcus, G.E. (1994) What Comes (Just) After 'Post'? The Case of Ethnography, in N.K. Denzin & Y.S. Lincoln (Eds) *Handbook of Qualitative Research.* London: Sage.

Ninnes, P. & Mehta, S. (2000) Postpositivist Theorizing and Research: challenges and opportunities for comparative education, *Comparative Education Review*, 44, pp. 205-212.

O'Hanlon, C. (1996) Why is Action Research a Valid Basis for Teacher Development, in R. McBride (Ed.) *Teacher Education Policy: some issues arising from research and practice.* London: Falmer Press.

Parlett, M. & Hamilton, D. (1972) Evaluation as Illumination: a new approach to the study of innovatory programmes. Reprinted in R. Murphy & H. Torrance (1987) *Evaluating Education: issues and methods.* London: Harper.

Rorty, R. (1980) *Philosophy and the Mirror of Nature.* Oxford, Basil Blackwell.

Samoff, J. (1999a) When Research Becomes Consulting, paper delivered at the 1999 Oxford International Conference, 'Education and Development: poverty, power and partnership', UK Forum for International Education and Training (UKFIET).

Samoff, J. (1999b) No Teacher Guide, No Textbooks, No Chairs: contending with crisis in African education, in R.F. Arnove & C.A. Torres (Eds) *Comparative Education. The Dialectic of the Global and the Local*. Oxford: Rowman & Littlefield.

Sarason, S. (1990) *The Predictable Failure of Educational Reform*. San Francisco: Jossey-Bass.

Schön, D. (1971) *Beyond the Stable State: public and private learning in a changing society*. Harmondsworth: Penguin.

Stake, R.E. (1980) The Case Study Method in Social Enquiry, in H. Simons (Ed.) *A Science of the Singular*. Norwich: Centre for Applied Research in Education [CARE], University of East Anglia.

Stenhouse, L. (1979) Case Study in Comparative Education: particularity and generalisation, *Comparative Education*, 15, pp. 5-10.

Stephens, D. (2000) Girls and Basic Education in Ghana: a cultural enquiry, *International Journal of Educational Development*, 20, pp. 29-44.

Stronach, I. & MacLure, M. (1997) *Educational Research Undone. The Postmodern Embrace*. Buckingham: Open University Press.

Tooley, J. with Darby, D. (1998) *Educational Research: a critique*. London, Office for Standards in Education.

Van Maanen, J. (1988) *Tales of the Field: on writing ethnography*. Chicago: University of Chicago Press.

Vidich, A.J. & Lyman, S.M. (1994) Qualitative Methods: their history in sociology and anthropology, in N. Denzin & Y. Lincoln (Eds) *Handbook of Qualitative Research*. London: Sage.

Weinstein, D. & Weinstein, M.A. (1991) Georg Simmel: sociological flaneur bricoleur, *Theory, Culture and Society*, 8, pp. 151-168.

Welch, A. (1998) The End of Certainty? The Academic Profession and the Challenge of Change. Guest Editorial Essay, *Comparative Education Review*, 42, pp. 1-15.

Wright, C. (1988) Internationalising Educational Research Paradigms: a West African perspective, *Compare*, 18, pp. 39-51.

The Notion of Participation in Primary Education in Uganda: democracy in school governance?

IKUKO SUZUKI

Introduction

'Participation' in education has been much debated both in the Western and developing worlds, though with different purposes and implications. The focus of the recent debate in the United Kingdom and USA is placed on parental participation in terms of choice of schools and school governance (see, for instance, Vincent, 1996; Dimmock et al, 1996), while in developing countries, the debate centres on community participation in school construction, financing and management (see, for instance, Bray, 1996; Gershberg, 1999). The tendency in the latter debate to treat parents as a collectivity and as equivalent to community suggests implicit assumptions regarding schools and communities: firstly, that 'a distinct community exists' (Leach et al, 1997, p. 4); secondly, that communities can work collectively, based on consensus; thirdly, that parents are a subunit of a community where they share the same concerns with other members of the community; and, fourthly, parents do not have or do not need choice when priority is given to access to education. The first two assumptions about homogeneous and consensual communities are contested elsewhere (for example, Leach et al, 1997; Lee, 1994; Cleaver, 1999).[1] The latter two, however, have not been given as much attention as they deserve.[2] Likewise, the word 'participation' itself has been subject to diverse interpretations and is thus controversial (see the following section). Moreover, the historical and sociocultural background of each country influences the way people understand 'participation'. Thus, it is deemed necessary to analyse the forms of participation and understand their implications in a specific context, and to reconstruct the notion of participation in education in a broader conceptual framework. This is the starting point of this study.

Uganda is chosen as the setting for the research because of its decentralised and participatory political and administrative structure called the Local Council (LC) system (see the following section). It is one of the poorest countries in East Africa whose history after independence in 1962 was turbulent until Museveni took power in 1986. During the early years of independence, the country had a reputation for its high standard of education, which, however, later declined due to the decades of political turmoil and civil strife (Ssekamwa, 1997). Currently, several reforms are being undertaken by the Government. The most notable development is the introduction of a policy of free primary schooling (the UPE policy) in 1997, by which each school receives a capitation grant (the UPE grant) in replacement for the school fees previously collected from the parents. In this process, the role of the school governing bodies is given emphasis, as articulated in the government policy that 'the successful implementation of UPE ... greatly depends on them' (Ministry of Education and Sports, 1998, p. 17). Although the programme has been successful in terms of increased enrolment [3], it is facing several quality problems at the school level.

Having set the research in a context informed by decentralisation and democratisation, this research aims to explore the notion of participation in education, starting from investigating who participates in what, how and for what purpose. Particular reference is made to the perception of teachers and parents. This is because of a relative lack of research on participation described from parents' and teachers' perspectives in the developing countries. The unit of analysis is the school governing body, which comprises representatives of different stakeholders and is thus seen as a potential avenue for exercising representative democracy (Martin & Vincent, 1999). As we shall see, however, the findings from the field do not support this anticipation. In this chapter, based on the findings of my field research in Uganda, the notion of participation is analysed with regard to the issue of accountability in decentralised and 'democratic' school governance structure.

Participation, Decentralisation and Accountability

'Participation' is currently one of the key words in the analysis of social development (see, for example, Chambers, 1995), yet its purposes, meanings and implications are subject to diverse interpretations and are thus controversial. Some researchers associate the notion of participation with *influence* (see Davis, 1981; Chell, 1985; Munn, 1998), while others contend that participation means *empowerment* (Mayo & Craig, 1995; Nelson & Wright, 1995) or consider it as *democracy* (da Cunha & Peña,

1997). Despite these divergences, there seems to be an assumption that participation is 'a good thing' (Cleaver, 1999).

It is pointless to discuss the meanings and implications of participation without considering the actual forms of participation. Several attempts have been made to categorise the different forms of participation and the levels of involvement, such as a ladder-style linear scale of participation starting from mere consultation to a stage of self-control (Arnstein, 1969; Shaeffer, 1994), and a list of dimensions of participation (Malen & Ogawa, 1988; Colletta & Perkins, 1995; Manikutty, 1998) to name but a few. These categorisations, however, tend to overlook, if not ignore, the distinctions between individual (private) and collective as well as direct and indirect (representative) forms of participation. This is particularly pertinent to education, because of the value conflict inherent in mass education between private interest and public good (Golby, 1993; Ward, 1997). For instance, the World Bank (1995) advocates community participation in school governance and the provision of parental choice of schooling places as a means of increasing the accountability of educational institutions. This is contradictory because in the former (school governance), parents are expected to act collectively while in the latter (choice), they are encouraged to pursue their private interest, which may conflict with collective interest.

Participation of parents in school governance is often debated in relation to decentralisation. Decentralisation, again, takes several forms and levels, reflecting different rationales underpinning it (Rondinelli, 1981; McLean & Lauglo, 1985; Lauglo, 1995).[4] In general, decentralisation means redistribution of power and responsibilities from central to local levels of the government structure. By shifting the point of decision-making close to local levels, greater participation by local people is envisaged (Rondinelli, 1981; Crook & Manor, 1998).

As far as schools (primary and secondary levels) are concerned, there is a tendency in many countries to decentralise financing and administrative functions to the provincial or district levels, and further to the school level (Fiske, 1996). In countries such as the United Kingdom and USA, school governing bodies are given power and authority as decentralised institutions. Generally, school governing bodies comprise representatives of parents, teachers, communities and the government. They therefore have the potential as fora for citizen participation in a form of representative democracy, as well as to form a part of an administrative unit in a decentralised governance structure (Kogan, 1984). Research on the participation of parents in school governing bodies in the United Kingdom shows, however, that decentralisation does not necessarily lead to greater participation (Golby, 1993; Deem et al, 1995; Vincent, 1997; Ball et al, 1997). The reasons are adduced as the power imbalance between professionals and lay citizens, and the uneven representation of the different groups, attributed to social structures such as class, gender and race. In the developing countries, not much research has been done on representation and participation of parents in school governance. As the myth of 'homogeneous communities' has been falsified, there is a need to disaggregate 'parents' in the analysis of parental participation. With regard to school governance, attention has to be paid to who participates, who does not, and why.

Although decentralisation does not automatically enhance participation, decentralisation and participation are two sides of a coin. It is often argued that when there is citizen participation, decentralised institutions will become more responsive and accountable (Crook & Manor, 1998; Blair, 2000). However, in this relation, the mechanism of participation affects the degree of accountability (Blair, 2000). In the case of the school governing bodies in Uganda, some of the representatives are elected from among the parents, whilst some are appointed by the local government. This makes the locus of accountability of the governing bodies elusive; the existence of the parents' representatives makes school governing bodies accountable to the parents (citizens), whilst appointees create accountability of the governing bodies to the local governments (bureaucrats). To this extent, it is appropriate to examine the meaning of accountability.

There are two strands of definitions of 'accountability'. One is the narrower sense found in Kogan (1986, p. 25) and Fearon (1999, p. 55), which can be summarised as: A is accountable to B when (1) A is obliged to act on behalf of B, and (2) A is subject to application of sanction or reward by B for his/her action. In this definition, if B cannot pose an effective sanction against A, A is not accountable to B, but can be responsible to B. Fearon calls it 'moral responsibility' and distinguishes it from 'accountability'. The other definition takes the concept of accountability more broadly so that it subsumes 'responsibility' or 'responsiveness' (see, for instance, Eraut et al, 1980; Bovens, 1998).

Logically, the participation of the wider population enhances information sharing and thus increases 'accountability' of the governing towards the governed (Paul, 1991; Crook & Manor, 1998). However, as Jenkins & Goetz (1999) point out, such arguments tend to ignore the power inequality between the two parties, thus assuming automatic information sharing, which often does not take place in reality. Therefore, it is deemed important to unravel the power relations between the parties concerned when analysing accountability relations. Since the narrower definition of Kogan mentioned earlier involves such notions of power, reflected in the application of sanctions, it has proved useful in framing this study. Thus, it becomes possible to highlight the power relations that exist in a school and analyse their impact on the participation of the parents in school governance.

Field Study

The field data collection was conducted between January and April 2000. One District (Mukono) was selected, considering that it has both rural and urban areas and is predominantly inhabited by the largest ethnic group (Baganda) in the country. Within the District, four schools (all government-aided) were chosen, based on the following criteria: locality, size, physical condition of the school, and type of foundation body.

Each school was visited for 2-3 weeks, during which the headteacher, School Management Committee (SMC) members, teachers, parents and the LC I chairperson were interviewed. All the interviews were semi-structured, conducted in English or Luganda (the interviewee's choice) with the help of an interpreter, tape-recorded, and then transcribed into English. In addition, various school activities, including staff meetings, SMC meetings and PTA meetings, were observed, along with observation of classroom teaching and casual contact between teachers and parents.

Findings

School Governance Structure in Uganda

The present Government of Uganda has been committed to the democratisation and decentralisation of the political and administrative structure, which is manifested as the Local Council (LC) system. It is meant to be a popular participation mechanism, starting from LC I at the village level, in which all the villagers directly participate, to LC V at the District level. LC III and V are recognised as local governments entrusted with decision-making power, and authority over wide-ranging local matters, while LC II and IV are administrative units. These LCs are expected to play an important role in the implementation of the UPE policy.

Levels – responsibilities with reference to primary education
District (LC V) – develop, approve and implement educational policy, development plan, and budget
County (LC IV) (administrative level)
Sub-County (LC III) – identify needs of the community, disburse grants to primary schools
Parish (LC II) (administrative level)
Village (LC I) (administrative level)

Table I. The LC system and its responsibility in primary education. Sources: compiled from Tukahebwa (1998) and Ministry of Education and Sports (1998).

Table I shows the LC system and its responsibility in primary education.

According to government policy, LC III is expected to play the major role in monitoring primary education (Ministry of Education and Sports, 1998). At the four schools studied, however, the LC I was more notable. It is likely that LC I officers make more frequent visits to the school and meet the parents over educational matters, because they are physically closer to the school compared with LC III and are considered to have legitimacy in contacting the parents in the village.

Technically, educational administration is done by the District Education Officers (DEOs), who are appointed by the District Council (LC V), while the management of primary schools is the responsibility of the school governing bodies called the School Management Committees (SMC). All the government-aided primary schools are, by law, required to have an SMC, which according to the law of 1969, comprises:

> *4 members appointed by the education committee of the area [refers to the Education Committee of LC V] and one of whom shall be appointed as a chairman;*
>
> *2 members elected by the parents; and*
>
> *3 members appointed by the chief education officer [refers to the Commissioner for Education of the central government]. (Uganda, 1969)*

In addition, the 'Headmaster' (*sic*) is supposed to sit on the SMC as 'a secretary'. The two parent members are usually the PTA chairperson and the treasurer, who are directly elected from among the parents. Before the introduction of the UPE policy, school financing heavily depended on the PTA, which consolidated fees from the parents and even supplemented teachers' salaries. This gave the PTA substantial power in school governance. Under the UPE policy, however, the role of the SMC has been revitalised. It is now the SMC that manages the UPE grant and the entire school affairs. Given the importance of the role of the SMC in the implementation of the UPE policy, the Ministry is now considering amendments to the law, in order to give the SMC more power and wider representation of the stakeholders.

In theory, all the parents and teachers are represented in the SMC through the PTA executives, and thus are subsumed in it. In reality, however, the PTA executives, parents and teachers do not recognise themselves as part of the SMC but rather consider themselves as external groups. For ordinary parents, both the SMC and the PTA are distant organisations. Most of the parents interviewed did not know the functions of the PTA and the SMC, the differences between them and even who the members were. The relations between the headteacher and other actors within school vary from school to school. At one school

(Omutwe), the power of the SMC seemed to be comparable to that of the headteacher, whereas at another school (Mukasa), the former headteacher monopolised the SMC but was criticised by the PTA. However, at all the four schools, the headteacher obviously dominated the ordinary teachers, thus hardly representing *all* the teachers in the SMC.

'Bringing Children to the School'
as a Form of Participation of Parents

[In order to support the school] [a]s parents, we bring our
children here. Instead of taking the money elsewhere, we keep
it here in this school. (Young male parent of Miyembe,
translated from Luganda)

Many parental activities were described by the interviewees, most of which are judged to be forms of participation, such as contributing to school development, and attending school events. Amongst others, 'bringing children to the school' was found to have significant implications for the issue of accountability. In the following part, I delineate the background of this action in an attempt to reconstruct its contextual meaning.

It is plausible that 'bringing children to the school' is implicitly understood by parents, teachers and the local leaders as a fundamental form of parents' participation in education. By bringing their children, parents participate in the development of a particular school. It is different from 'sending children to [any] school'. The distinction is made because the latter, 'sending children to [any] school', means to support the government policy on UPE, while 'bringing children to *the* school' can be seen as a manifestation of parents' support for the particular school.

The mechanism is as follows: under the UPE programme, schools receive the UPE grant in accordance with the total enrolment; thus, an increase in the number of pupils leads to a bigger grant allocation to the school. In addition, most schools still rely on contributions from the parents for the maintenance and development of school facilities, despite the ban on fee collection under the UPE policy. In consequence, more pupils means more funding, both from the Government and from parents. Conversely, withdrawal of children results in a decrease in school funds. Most parents and teachers seem to be aware of the consequences of transfer of children for school development. Some parents were critical of other parents and local leaders who sent their children to schools in other areas. The reasons for the transfers of children given by parents were (a) disagreement with the administration (headteacher), and (b) dissatisfaction with the academic standard of the school.

At two schools studied (Mukasa and Miyembe Primary School), the former headteachers committed malpractice where they allegedly embezzled school money, including the UPE grant, teachers' salaries and parental contributions. Because the schools lacked basic records of past years, it was not possible to establish if the incidents led to a decrease in enrolment. However, some parents mentioned withdrawing their children as a response to embezzlement by the headteacher. This year, since the 'administration has changed', parents are said to be 'coming back'.

On the other hand, many parents are concerned about the academic standard of the school. Anxious parents have sometimes transferred their children, if another school has performed better in the previous year's examination. One parent at Miyembe said that she had transferred one of her children because the academic standard of other pupils was found to be very low. Also, at Miyembe, some parents expressed their discontent with the working attitude of the teachers. As the deputy headteacher of Mukasa pointed out, the quality of education seems to be an important factor influencing parents in their decision as to whether to bring their children to *the* school.

Discussion – accountability and participation

Accountability in the Ugandan Context

In illustrating malpractice by the headteacher, interviewees often used the term 'accountability'. In Uganda, 'accountability' is often used in a specific monetary sense, such as 'the accountability report on the UPE grant', which accounts for the money received. The interviewees used the term in the same narrower sense, although there seemed to be a broader concept implicit in its verbal use, but reflected in the actions of the parents. The following example illustrates how parents perceive 'accountability'.

At a PTA General meeting held at Miyembe, the PTA and SMC chairmen proposed that the parents pay a further contribution on top of the money collected last year, but were met with objections from the parents on the grounds of 'accountability'.

LC I chair [5]: It seems there is no feedback towards the parents to know what the money they have paid has done. If they don't know then they won't pay, but if they do then they will surely start paying.

Headteacher: I was suggesting that we forget the past and start anew. Let us begin accountability as the chairman [LC I] has said. This money was set by the Gombolola [sub-county: LC III Government]. So what is your question?

Male Parent: I appreciate the interest to build the office. But the problem was that parents did not know what the 5000 shillings was for and that the Gombolola set it. There has never been a meeting to inform the parents about it.

PTA chair: Those who don't know about it are those who send their children and never follow up!

[Several parents protest.] (translated from Luganda)

In this example, the headteacher understood 'accountability' in terms of an accounting report, which is the *outcome* of the spending activities. In contrast, both the LC I chairperson and the male parent requested explanation on the decision-making *process*, and contested that the parents' actions (non-payment) were a result of the lack of that explanation. Although not explicit, their accounts capture the concept of accountability, and the parents' action of non-payment can be seen as a measure of sanction.

Parents' Perception of Accountability

Before embarking on a discussion about whether these actions, the non-payment and withdrawal of the children analysed earlier, can be effective sanctions or not, I delineate factors affecting the perception of parents. From the comparison among the four schools, the following are deemed significant in determining the perceived (lack of) accountability: (a) lack of transparency, (b) power imbalance between the (head)teacher and the parents, and (c) weak representation of ordinary parents in the SMC.

First, in both embezzlement cases at Miyembe and Mukasa, the parents were not informed of the incidents until a late stage. They were not involved in budgeting and planning school development and had no access to the information, such as the income and expenditure. At both schools, the financial records were not available to the researcher either. However, at two other schools (Town and Omutwe) the accounting reports of the UPE grant were displayed, though not in a public place as stipulated in the government policy, but in the headteacher's office.[6] Judging from the contrast among the four schools, the lack of information, in other words, lack of transparency, in Miyembe and Mukasa may have created speculation among parents about the credibility of the financial management by the headteacher.

Second, there is an apparent power imbalance between the parents and the headteacher, which hinders parents from accessing the information they need. Some teachers and local leaders noted that the parents are not interested in school governance. Many parents are, however, concerned about the school but feel intimidated when asking questions of the headteacher or teachers in general. When asked if they came to school and observed classes, one parent lamented, 'We can't do it because the teachers may take it badly and say that you have a big head' (male parent, Miyembe, translated from Luganda).

The same feeling of intimidation applies even to a member of the SMC. One female SMC member at Mukasa commented on her work as SMC, 'It isn't easy because it is to supervise the people who know better than we are [do]. The teachers, because for we find it that they know better than I am [do]' (female SMC member, Mukasa and LC II councillor, interviewed in English). In this situation, parents are unable to force the headteacher to disclose information, even when they perceive that there is a lack of transparency. The result is the informational asymmetries between parents and headteacher, which, as Paul (1991) argues, can be a serious obstacle for parents considering taking any further action.

Third, according to the government policy, a school is governed by the SMC, which has legitimacy in requesting information from the headteacher on financing and any school matters. The PTA chairperson and the treasurer sit on the SMC, purportedly representing the parents. In reality, however, the representation of parents in the SMC is ambiguous because of the perceived gap between the leaders and ordinary parents. For the majority of the parents, the PTA and SMC chairpersons are both 'big people' who are in close relations with the headteacher. Often, these chairpersons hold other posts in the villages, such as LC councillors and church leaders. This problem of a local elite dominating every aspect of local governance and thus hindering the democratic participation of the wider population is evinced elsewhere (for instance, Golby, 1993; Deem et al, 1995; Mehta, 1997; Wilkes, 2000). At the four schools studied, formal meetings were well attended. Yet, most of the parents seemed to be reluctant to express any opinions which challenged the leaders. It is tenable that because participation does not take place in a vacuum but in a prefabricated social structure, it can result in replicating and reinforcing the existing social relations (da Cunha & Peña, 1997; Plank, 1997). In this sense, participation does not necessarily mean democracy.

Another problem with parents' representation on the SMC is the lack of an accountability mechanism between parents and the SMC chairperson. While the PTA chairperson is directly elected from among the parents, the SMC chairperson is appointed by the District Education Officer, over which ordinary parents have no power. This means that there is no mechanism for parents to pose sanctions on the SMC chairperson, which, according to the definition of Kogan (1986), makes the SMC chairperson only *responsible* to the parents but not *accountable*.

To sum up, ordinary parents do not have information on school finance and management and structurally cannot perceive whether they are given an avenue to participate in school governance. These conditions could have affected parents' perceptions regarding the lack of accountability of the school.

Effectiveness of the Sanctions Posed by the Parents

Now I come back to the question posed earlier: whether the actions taken by parents, namely, 'non-payment of contribution', and 'withdrawal of the children', are effective sanctions on the school. The analysis primarily focuses on the headteacher and not the SMC. The reasons are twofold: First, as discussed in the previous section, the SMC chairperson is not accountable to the parents; Second, it is the headteacher who is questioned about accountability due to the fact that the school financing and administration is often solely managed by the headteacher.[7]

The non-payment of contributions directly affects the school fund. However, since the headteacher is not the owner of the school, decreases in revenue are not a direct blow to him/her, at least in theory. This is particularly true if one considers the introduction of the UPE policy, and that teachers' salaries are no longer supplemented by the parents' contribution, and thus the headteacher's salary will not be reduced. The withdrawal of children from the school also means decreased revenue from both the Government and parents, as explained earlier. In this sense, withdrawal of children seems to be an expression of dissatisfaction with the service, which Hirschman (1970) calls 'exit'. Paul (1991) asserts the effectiveness of exit as a mechanism for improving accountability (in the broader definition in this case) of the service provider. However, in this case, as in the case of non-payment, it does not affect the headteacher. If there is massive exodus of children from the school, the headteacher may be questioned by the District Education Office. Nevertheless, the former headteachers at Mukasa and Miyembe had eventually been transferred to larger schools where they could receive higher salaries than before. Thus, the two actions taken by the parents cannot be effective means of sanction towards the headteacher. While parents seek accountability in their relationship with the headteacher, the headteacher is not held *accountable* to the parents but can be *responsible*. What is lacking here is a mechanism to transform parents' warning signals to a 'hierarchical control function of the agency' (Paul, 1991, p. 4), such as formal incentives/sanctions by the District Education Office.

Thus far, I have assessed the effectiveness of the means of sanction available for the parents. They are all ineffective, mostly due to the structure and process of school governance. Despite the insignificant impact on the headteacher, parents do opt to stop paying contributions or withdraw their children when they perceive the school lacks accountability. If these actions cannot hold the headteacher accountable, a question arises about the meanings of such actions taken by parents.

As mentioned earlier, 'bringing the children to the school' and 'contributing to school developments' are proved to be forms of participation. Conversely, 'withdrawing the children from the school' and 'not paying requested contribution' can be seen as forms of 'non-participation'. This implies that the perceived accountability affects the decision of parents to participate in education or not. Often, such non-participation is regarded as a rational 'choice' made by the parents derived from the comparison between the cost and benefit accruing from educating their children. However, in reality, the parents' decision-making, such as in this case of Uganda, does not always neatly fit into the explanation in economic terms. Those parents who have no other schools nearby (and in rural Africa it is often the case), hence no exit options, will simply 'drop out' of educational services. If they remain in the service but refuse to pay the requested contributions, the result will be services of less quality and quantity, which their own children have to depend on. Furthermore, such an action runs a risk of negative repercussions from the teachers. One parent illustrated how they felt about the way the teachers treated their children:

> There is this mentality some teachers in this school have, that a child may bring a[n exercise] book to a teacher [for marking] to whom the teacher says, 'You go away! After all you are studying for free'. This thing hurts us parents. Maybe lack of parents bringing those things [contribution for schools and teachers] is what causes this teacher's attitude. (female parent at Mukasa, translated from Luganda)

A point made by Cleaver (1999, p. 607) may well explain this decision-making by parents in a situation where non-participation may bring a backlash. He suggests that such 'non-participation and non-compliance' may be not a simple, rational decision but a complex mixture of a rational strategy and 'an unconscious practice embedded in routine, social norms and the acceptance of the status quo'. This point, the motivation and implications of non-participation of parents, needs further empirical investigation.

Conclusion

The discussion reveals a negative cycle, as follows. The level of participation of parents in the forms of 'bringing children to the school' and 'contributing to the school development' is affected by the perceived accountability of the school management. The perception is influenced by the access (or lack of access) to information, which reflects the level of participation of parents in planning and monitoring school development. The summary of the discussion thus far can be, rather paradoxically, that participation affects accountability, which then determines the level of participation.

The Government of Uganda stresses the importance of the participation of parents and communities for the successful implementation of the UPE programme. It seems that accountability is one of the keys to enhancing the involvement of parents in education, bringing children to the school and participating in school development. To achieve this, the negative cycle needs to shift to a positive cycle, which includes financial and academic accountability . For this, several changes are necessary, including: (a) increasing transparency by disclosing information; (b) involving parents in the planning and monitoring process; and (c) strengthening the representation of parents in the school governance structure. Achieving an increase in transparency may require 'direct confrontation' between the parents and the headteacher and the SMC, which may be an inevitable and crucial process (Jenkins & Goetz, 1999, p. 612) when there is significant power disparity between the two parties. In this regard, Wilkes (2000) suggests the role of external actors in enabling the powerless to have a 'voice'. In the case of Ugandan primary schools, this is where the LCs (LC I and LC III), which are directly elected from among the parents and communities, are expected to play the role of external monitors. Because of the present situation, where many of the SMC members are LC councillors, this mechanism does not function. Following the direction from the central ministry, the District started to advise schools not to nominate LC councillors as SMC members. This is an important step towards improved accountability, and greater democratic participation by parents.

Involving parents in the planning and monitoring process and strengthening the representation of parents in the school governance structure mean structural and procedural changes in the school organisation, which require 'internal' as well as 'external' 'negotiat[ion] and manage[ment]' among the people concerned in school governance (Cornwall et al, 2000, p. 7). These measures are not easy options. However, they are crucial to the democratisation of school governance, which could be one of the keys to the successful implementation of the UPE programme.

Notes

[1] For a review of the debates on the nature of 'community', see, for example, Awortwi (1999).

Ikuko Suzuki

[2] In their analysis of educational governance in South Africa, Sayed & Carrim (1998) question 'stakeholder-based' participation, for it runs the risk of excluding the non-stakeholders in the community.

[3] The enrolment in primary school jumped from 2.9 million in 1996 to 5.7 million in 1997. According to the Headcount exercise, the enrolment in 2000 has increased to 6.6 million (Ministry of Education and Sports, 2000).

[4] McGinn (1997) built up a counter-argument on the rationales for decentralisation.

[5] This LC I chairperson (male) does not have children at Miyembe primary school. He was invited at the discretion of the headteacher to the PTA General Meeting 'because schools must be in a close relation with LC' (Headteacher).

[6] Although the headteacher's office is not recognised as a public space (see International Development Consultants, 2000), it is often relatively open to the parents. In many schools, it is used as a de facto accounting and administration office, and parents frequently go into the office for various purposes such as registration, payment and consultation.

[7] At the four schools studied, the dominance of the headteacher in school management was obvious. The same trend is reported by International Development Consultants (2000).

References

Arnstain, S.R. (1969) A Ladder of Citizen Participation, *Journal of the American Institute of Planners*, 35, pp. 216-224.

Awortwi, N. (1999) *The Riddle of Community Development: factors influencing organisation, participation and self-management in 29 African and Latin American communities*, Working Paper Series No. 287. The Hague, Institute of Social Studies.

Ball, S., Vincent, C. & Radnor, H. (1997) Into Confusion: LEAs, accountability and democracy, *Journal of Education Policy*, 12, pp. 147-163.

Blair, H. (2000) Participation and Accountability at the Periphery: democratic local governance in six countries, *World Development*, 28, pp. 21-39.

Bovens, M. (1998) *The Quest for Responsibility: accountability and citizenship in complex organisations*. Cambridge: Cambridge University Press.

Bray, M. (1996) *Decentralization of Education: community financing*. Washington, DC: World Bank.

Chambers, R. (1995) Paradigm Shifts and the Practice of Participatory Research and Development, in N. Nelson, & S. Wright (Eds) *Power and Participatory Development: theory and practice*. London: IT Publications.

Chell, E. (1985) *Participation and Organization: a social psychological approach*. London: Macmillan.

Cleaver, F. (1999) Paradoxes of Participation: questioning participatory approaches to development, *Journal of International Development*, 11, pp. 597-612.

Colletta, N.J. & Perkins, G. (1995) *Participation in Education*. Washington, DC: World Bank.

Cornwall, A., Lucas, H. & Pasteur, K. (2000) Accountability through Participation: developing workable partnership models in the health sector, *IDS Bulletin*, 31, pp. 1-13.

Crook, R. & Manor, J. (1998) *Democracy and Decentralisation in South Asia and West Africa: participation, accountability and performance*. Cambridge: Cambridge University Press.

da Cunha, P.V. & Peña, M.V.J. (1997) *The Limits and Merits of Participation*, policy research working paper 1838. Washington, DC: World Bank.

Davis, D. (1981) Citizen Participation in Decision Making in the Schools, in D. Davis (Ed.) *Communities and Their Schools*. New York: McGraw-Hill.

Deem, R., Brehony, K. & Heath, S. (1995) *Active Citizenship and the Governing of Schools*. Buckingham: Open University Press.

Dimmock, C., O'Donoghue, T.A. & Robb, A.S. (1996) Parental Involvement in Schooling: an emerging research agenda, *Compare*, 16, pp. 5-21.

Eraut, M., Barton, J. & Canning, T. (1980) *Accountability in the Middle Years of Schooling, Working Paper 3. Some Teachers' Perspectives on Accountability*. Falmer: University of Sussex.

Fearon, J.D. (1999) Electoral Accountability and the Control of Politicians: selecting good types versus sanctioning poor performance, in A. Przeworske, S.C. Stokes & B. Manin (Eds) *Democracy, Accountability and Representation*. Cambridge: Cambridge University Press.

Fiske, E. (1996) *Decentralization of Education: gaining consensus*. Washington, DC: World Bank.

Gershberg, A.I. (1999) Fostering Effective Parental Participation in Education: lessons from a comparison of reform process in Nicaragua and Mexico, *World Development*, 27, pp. 753-771.

Golby, M. (1993) Parents as School Governors, in P. Munn (Ed.) *Parents and Schools: customers, managers or partners?* (London, Routledge).

Hirschman, A.O. (1970) *Exit, Voice, and Loyalty: responses to decline in firms, organizations, and states*. Cambridge: Harvard University Press.

International Development Consultants (2000) *Tracking the Flow of and Accountability for UPE Funds*. Kampala: Ministry of Education and Sports.

Jenkins, R. & Goetz, A.M. (1999) Accounts and Accountability: theoretical implications of the right-to-information movement in India, *Third World Quarterly*, 20, pp. 603-622.

Kogan, M. (1984) Relevant Concepts in Understanding Governing Bodies, in M. Kogan (Ed.) *School Governing Bodies*. London: Heinemann.

Kogan, M. (1986) *Education Accountability: an analytic overview*. London: Hutchinson.

Lauglo, J. (1995) Forms of Decentralisation and Their Implications for Education, *Comparative Education*, 31, pp. 5-29.

Leach, M., Mearn, R. & Scoones, I. (1997) Challenges to Community-based Sustainable Development: dynamics, entitlements, institutions, *IDS Bulletin*, 28, pp. 4-14.

Lee, Y.S.F. (1994) Community-based Urban Environmental Management: local NGOs as catalysts, *Regional Development Dialogue*, 15, pp. 158-176.

Malen, B. & Ogawa, R.T. (1988) Professional-patron Influence on Site-based Governance Councils: a confounding case study, *Educational Evaluation and Policy Analysis*, 10, pp. 251-270.

Manikutty, S. (1998) Community Participation: lessons from experience in five water and sanitation projects in India, *Development Policy Review*, 16, pp. 373-404.

Martin, J. & Vincent, C. (1999) Parental Voice: an exploration, *International Studies in Sociology of Education*, 9, pp. 231-252.

Mayo, M. & Craig, G. (1995) Community Participation and Empowerment: the human face of structural adjustment or tools for democratic transformation? in G. Craig & M. Mayo (Eds) *Community Empowerment: a reader in participation and development*. London: Zed Books.

McLean, M. & Lauglo, J. (1985) Rationales for Decentralization and a Perspective from Organization Theory, in J. Lauglo & M. McLean (Eds) *The Control of Education: international perspectives on the centralization-decentralization debate*. London, Heinemann.

Mehta, L. (1997) Social Difference and Water Resource Management: insights from Kutch, India, *IDS Bulletin*, 28(4), pp. 79-89.

Ministry of Education and Sports (1998) *The Way Forward; guidelines on policy, roles and responsibilities of stakeholders in the implementation of Universal Primary Education (UPE)*. Kampala: Ministry of Education and Sports.

Ministry of Education and Sports (2000) *The Major Achievements of the NRM Government in the Ministry of Education and Sports*; <http://www.educationsectoruganda.com/nrm/achievements.php3>

Munn, P. (1998) Parental Influence on School Policy: some evidence from research, *Journal of Education Policy*, 13, pp. 379-394.

Nelson, N. & Wright, S. (1995) Participation and Power, in N. Nelson & S. Wright (Eds) *Power and Participatory Development: theory and practice*. London: IT Publications.

Paul, S. (1991) *Strengthening Public Service Accountability: a conceptual framework*. World Bank Discussion Papers No. 136. Washington, DC: World Bank.

Plank, D.N. (1997) Dreams of Community, *Politics of Education Association Yearbook, 1996*, pp. 13-20. London: Falmer Press.

Rondinelli, D.A. (1981) Government Decentralization in Comparative Perspective: theory and practice in developing countries, *International Review of Administrative Sciences*, 47, pp. 133-145.

Sayed, Y. & Carrim, N. (1998) Inclusiveness and Participation in Discourses of Educational Governance in South Africa, *International Journal of Inclusive Education*, 2, pp. 29-43.

Shaeffer, S. (1994) *Participation for Educational Change; a synthesis of experience*. Paris: IIEP.

Ssekamwa, J.C. (1997) *History and Development of Education in Uganda*. Kampala: Fountain.

Tukahebwa, G.B. (1998) The Role of District Councils in Decentralisation, in A. Nsibambi (Ed.) *Decentralisation and Civil Society in Uganda: the quest for good governance*. Kampala: Fountain.

Uganda, the Republic of (1969) *1969 No. 224 The Education (Management Committee) (Amendment) Rules 1969*.

Vincent, C. (1996) *Parents and Teachers: power and participation*. London: Falmer Press.

Vincent, C. (1997) Community and Collectivism: the role of parents' organisation in the education system, *British Journal of Sociology of Education*, 18, pp. 271-183.

Ward, J.G. (1997) Theories of Politics and the Legitimacy of Public Schools in a Democratic State, *Politics of Education Association Yearbook, 1996*, pp. 21-28. London: Falmer Press.

Wilkes, A. (2000) The Functions of Participation in a Village-based Health Pre-payment Scheme: what can participation actually do? *IDS Bulletin*, 31, pp. 31-36.

World Bank (1995) *Priorities and Strategies for Education*. Washington, DC: World Bank.

Who is in the Driving Seat? Development Cooperation and Democracy

KENNETH KING & SIMON McGRATH

Democracy and a 'New Way of Working' in Development Cooperation

Development cooperation is experiencing a dramatic range of new understandings and approaches that appear to amount to a 'new way of working', both in how development cooperation takes place and in how it includes the knowledge and wishes of its assumed recipients in the South. New possibilities of information and communications technologies (ICTs), new understandings of the role of knowledge in development, and a new rhetoric of North-South partnership form the core of the new discourse.

The emphasis on the importance of knowledge includes a strand that stresses the centrality of local knowledge for development. The concern with partnership highlights the key role of more equitable partnership in development and talks even of the 'country being in the driving seat' of development. Importantly, the country is taken to encompass civil society rather than just the government in an apparently radical shift from previous formulations. Thus, development appears to be becoming more democratic.

However, arguments about the empowerment of the South through the new approach to knowledge can be contrasted with concerns about a 'digital divide' through which ICTs serve to magnify rather than eliminate exclusion from knowledge, from power and from wealth. Equally, notions of partnership seem to ignore issues of power and assume consensus. Moreover, the greater collaboration amongst development cooperation agencies, and the strong convergence of official Northern views on the merits of themes such as globalisation and liberalisation, appear to limit severely the possibilities for alternative models of development to be pursued by Southern countries. Nothing exemplifies this narrowing of possibilities for debate and policy more than the set of International Development Targets (IDTs) that are now set at the core of development cooperation thinking for a number of agencies. Thus, as this chapter will explore, there appear to be serious questions that need asking about the extent to which trends in development cooperation facilitate greater democracy in the policy arena. We will not focus exclusively on the education sector but it is clear that our explorations have strong implications for debates on both democratic control over education policy and about an education for democracy and citizenship.

Studying the New Way of Working

This chapter reflects on fieldwork on the Department for International Development (DfID – UK), the Swedish International Development Cooperation Agency (SIDA) and the World Bank. We shall focus on the two principal themes that have emerged from this fieldwork: knowledge and partnership. These will be examined in turn for each agency and their overall implications for democratic ownership of development will be considered. However, before we can turn to case studies, a sketching out of the context in which the agencies are operating is necessary.

The New Knowledge Theory

Since the late 1990s, a series of overlapping models of knowledge have emerged that have permeated academia, politics and development cooperation policy and practice. The notion of a 'knowledge economy' has appeared that situates knowledge at the centre of economic success, North and South. Emanating from the corporate sector, but now in the development field, is a notion of 'knowledge management' that stresses the importance of systems and approaches within organisations to capture and use knowledge (both their own and others') as the central competitive tool for success in the knowledge economy. Moreover, the World Bank has served to popularise amongst development actors the notion of knowledge for development (World Bank, 1998a). As well as incorporating the two concerns above, this stresses the promotion of multidirectional knowledge flows on development and claims that this will be more important in future than disbursement of official development assistance. Such a view seeks to move beyond knowledge management within an agency for purposes of internal efficiency, to knowledge sharing between an agency and its partners, in order to make development more effective. All three strands, in differing ways, also link into a more theoretical literature about the nature of knowledge that raises questions about the relationship between knowledge and context, thus questioning the applicability of universal accounts and prescriptions.

Partnership in Development

There is an apparent donor consensus on the need for partnership and that such partnership should be Southern-driven. However, there does not appear to be any balancing Southern consensus on either the desirability or detail of partnership.

In the donor discourse of partnership, there is a series of positive elements. Partnership is seen as privileging local ownership and as inclusive of civil society (Wolfensohn, 1999). It is seen as contributing to the development of local capacity and better adjustment of donors to local procedures (Chang et al, 1999). It is seen as promoting openness, transparency and humility (Gustafsson, 1999). However, as we shall note below in the case of the World Bank, it is also linked to pragmatic views of better aid efficiency.

Partnership appears antithetical to conditionality. However, whilst there is a growing sense about the ineffectiveness of conditionality, there is still a strong agency view of what are good policies. In particular, a number of agency policies are closely linked to the IDTs.

In spite of its apparent merits, there are critical voices about the nature of partnership. It is necessary to reinfuse partnership debates with power. How can we talk of partnership in the context of falling development expenditure by the North or asymmetrical and exploitative economic relations? How does partnership face up to a history of past exploitation?

The International Development Targets

In 1996, the Development Assistance Committee (DAC) of the Organisation for Economic Cooperation and Development (OECD) produced a document entitled *Shaping the Twenty-First Century* (DAC, 1996). This sought to synthesise the recommendations of the series of world conferences of the first half of the 1990s into a shortlist of IDTs against which developmental practice could be measured.

The simple account presented by DAC of the IDTs being derived from the world conferences is problematic. First, it obscures the issue of the extent to which the world conferences had a mandate from civil society or were essentially gatherings of states' representatives. Would the processes by which these conferences were organised and their decisions made really satisfy the criteria that many donors increasingly wish to use for governance and transparency? Second, transition from world conference to IDT is also obscured. It is open for debate whether the six IDTs can be seen as an accurate and exhaustive distillation of the key commitments of the world conferences, or of global civil society opinion about development priorities. Nor does it seem reasonable to argue that the world conferences amount to a systematic programme of meetings to discuss all the world's outstanding issues. Equally, the IDTs do not concern themselves directly with a whole range of issues. To take just a few of those mentioned in the final report of the Copenhagen Social Summit, key absences include debt, unemployment, the arms trade, AIDS and trade (United Nations, 1995). Moreover, the right of DAC, a representative organisation of the North, to establish these IDTs is also questionable. Thus, the democratic credentials of these central elements of development policy are dubious.

The World Bank

Under the Presidency of James Wolfensohn, the World Bank appears to be going through a period of considerable change. There is a perceptible shift from the neo-liberal certainty that seemed to characterise much of the organisation's work in the 1980s and early 1990s. Under Wolfensohn, the World Bank has become the major agency proponent of new knowledge thinking and has also placed considerable emphasis on partnerships that 'put the country in the driving seat' (Wolfensohn, 1997).

In 1995, Wolfensohn committed himself to turning the World Bank into a 'knowledge bank' by 2000 (World Bank, 1998a). This has resulted in a wide range of knowledge-related activities within the World Bank that have propelled it far on the way to this aspiration, but which have also resulted in a considerable spread of positions and practices regarding knowledge and its use in development.

In some of the more theoretically rich accounts (e.g. Ellerman, 1998; Stiglitz, 1999), associated with the central knowledge sharing team, and with Joseph Stiglitz in his time as Chief Economist, new understandings of knowledge have been developed with powerful implications for the way in which the World Bank thinks, and these understandings are intended to transform its practices. The most detailed expression of this position is the *World Development Report 1998/99* (World Bank, 1998a). In the Report, knowledge is seen as the key to development and the importance of developing national capacities for knowledge generation and acquisition are emphasised. Moreover, the Report argues that knowledge exists and must be applied within contexts. This is crucial for the World Bank's way of working as it suggests that universal accounts of best theory and practice, so central to the World Bank's previous neo-liberal approach, are downplayed in favour of learning from comparative experiences and adaptation to local circumstances.

The World Bank's policy centrepiece, the Comprehensive Development Framework (CDF), also sees knowledge as central. Included in its vision for comprehensive national development strategies is a component to develop national knowledge strategies. Two other major projects, the Global Development Network (GDN) and the Global Development Gateway (GDG), are also very concerned with the development of knowledge strategies. Moreover, the development forum part of the World Bank's external website (http://www.worldbank.org/devforum) is one of the best sources of online sharing of development knowledge.

Across these initiatives, it is possible to discern a strong awareness of the possibilities that new ICTs provide for multidirectional knowledge flows. There is also a stated commitment in the CDF, GDN and GDG programmes to capacity building in the South in the area of knowledge.

However, there remain concerns within and outside the World Bank about the extent to which the new knowledge vision has been enacted or, indeed, whether there is a variety of visions that are sometimes in conflict with each other. As the GDG continues to develop, these concerns remain to be voiced but with little apparent impact on the project's operation.

As the GDN develops, concerns have also been raised about the extent to which it privileges economics over other disciplines and, therefore, skews development thinking. The GDN Secretariat sought to respond to this by entitling the December 2000 GDN conference, 'Beyond Economics', but concerns remain about the ability of the GDN to develop a truly holistic view of development.

The World Bank has sought to further its own learning through the development of thematic groups bringing together staff to discuss key thematic areas. Some of these groups do have excellent links to external groups and individuals but a perusal of the external websites of the education-related thematic groups gives an overwhelming sense of them being about synthesising existing World Bank knowledge first, with external Northern knowledge sources a distant second and Southern knowledge sources hard to find at all. From the available lists of partner institutions in mid-2000, there appeared to be few in the South.

There are also question marks regarding the World Bank's willingness to listen to critical voices. The resignation of Ravi Kanbur, lead author of the *World Development Report 2000/01* (World Bank, 2000a), has widely been seen as due to pressure from within the World Bank to ignore the critical comments that had been generated during what was an extensive consultation phase.

It is clear that the new account of knowledge and its stressing of the importance of context and learning from the South have been influential within the World Bank (e.g. Stiglitz, 1999). However, it appears that these influences exist alongside the continuation of older practices and the emergence of less radical practices related to knowledge sharing. In particular, new attitudes towards dialogue and authority are often absent in World Bank documents and statements. Given its size and influence, the World Bank has the potential to transform the relationship between knowledge and development in a progressive manner. However, divergences in its vision and the effect of organisational culture and external suspicions of the World Bank's motives suggest that such a transformation cannot simply be assumed.

Country ownership of and broader participation in development decision-making have also formed a central theme of the Wolfensohn presidency, as reflected in a number of his speeches (Wolfensohn, 1997, 1998, 1999). This notion of partnership and ownership seeks to move beyond state-to-state relations. The World Bank has emphasised the need for partnership to be driven by the Southern partner and to include civil society. It is also very clear about the undesirability of donor domination of development (World Bank, 1998b). The Bank is concerned in the CDF to develop Southern capacity to lead the partnership and to construct clear rules and mechanisms for evaluating partnerships and ending them if necessary.

However, the argument for partnership is primarily pragmatic rather ethical:

> *It must be remembered that the goal is not partnership* per se.
> *Partnership is* a means to an end. *The real goal is the shared*
> *objective. Partnership is a tool to reach this goal more*
> *effectively, and more efficiently, for the benefit of all involved.*
> *(World Bank, 1998b, p. 5)*

Whilst the CDF documentation talks of partnership and ownership as key principles, it also talks of a stronger focus on outcomes (World Bank, 2000b). This points to a potential tension that cuts across the three case study agencies' attitudes to development partnership. Is partnership to be primarily about the South signing up to a set of non-negotiable policies or is it primarily about a process designed to strengthen cooperation in order to promote development, without seeking to define this too closely, e.g. in terms of the IDTs? Given the past record of the World Bank on conditionalities, this will be a very sensitive issue for the World Bank to deal with in its development partnerships.

There are signs of the World Bank becoming more of a 'listening bank' with regard to its attitudes about partnership. Nonetheless, there continues to be considerable scepticism, in both the North and the South, of the extent to which it has cemented this change (as can be seen from the range of hostile comments across the various online discussions of World Bank policies and programmes over the last 2 years). For instance, the way that the GDG project has interacted with civil society is widely seen as showing that the World Bank can still be insensitive about the need to grow partnerships.

The World Bank's account of partnership implicitly assumes that there will be little or no conflict over vision among donors, between donors and Southern states, and between government and civil society. Consensus is seen as easy to achieve. However, this account appears very naive about the policy process and the impact upon it of power, conflict and ideology.

There are continuing external concerns that conditionalities are still important to the World Bank's way of working. Most recently, there have been external criticisms of the way the Heavily Indebted Poor Country (HIPC) initiative and the Poverty Reduction Strategy Papers (PRSPs) contain heavy sets of conditionalities (Martin, 2000; Wood, 2000). The Bank is far from monolithic and new practices and commitments to more democratic ways of working appear to exist alongside a continued certainty about what good development is and a belief in the efficacy of using the Bank's power to ensure that its views are adopted into policy.

The Department for International Development

Since its renaming in 1997, the DfID has embarked on a major policy development phase. As well as two White Papers, the core of this effort has been a series of nine Target Strategy Papers (TSPs) organised around the six IDTs. Given the importance of these documents, we shall focus largely on the TSPs in what follows, although also referring to other sources.

The Nine Target Strategy Papers
1   Halving world poverty by 2015 (DfID, 2000a)
2   Better health for poor people (DfID, 2000b)
3   Education for all: the challenge of universal primary education (draft) (DfID, 2000c)
4   Poverty elimination and the empowerment of women (DfID, 2000d)
5   Realising human rights for poor people (DfID, 2000e)
6   Addressing the water crisis (draft) (DfID, 2000f)
7   Achieving sustainability (DfID, 2000g)
8   Making government work for poor people (draft) (DfID, 2000h)
9   Urbanisation (draft) (DfID, 2000i)

The TSPs process has taken place whilst DfID is still trying to codify its knowledge strategy (see below) and this probably accounts for some of their lack of explicit engagement with the themes of knowledge theory, of the kind expressed in the World Bank's *Knowledge for Development* report. Instead, the TSPs often mention knowledge in ways that suggest its interchangeability with concepts such as information and research.

In our earlier discussion of the World Bank, we noted the difficulty in moving from highlighting the importance of Southern knowledge to building such knowledge into agency learning and policy. The TSPs are another example of the distance that still needs to be travelled in this regard. A calculation of citations in footnotes or bibliographies suggests that only 4% of sources cited were from the South, whilst more than 84% could be identified readily as either published or commissioned by agencies or international non-governmental organisations (NGOs). Moreover, much of this agency literature is global or regional in its focus. Thus, at this level of analysis, it would appear that the TSPs are quite far from encompassing Southern knowledge. Moreover, their tendency towards reliance on broad generalisations rather than country-level data is at variance with the argument that knowledge is highly contextualised. It is intended that future Country Strategy Papers (CSPs) will provide an important local contextualisation of the global arguments of the TSPs, but it will be important to ensure that the global arguments of the TSPs do not prevent acceptance of local arguments that disagree with them.

Knowledge theory stresses the importance of allowing multiple accounts to be learnt from. However, the writing of policy documents conventionally stresses the importance of strong storylines. Thus, it is not surprising to find that the TSPs tend not to reflect the complexity of debates about issues such as privatisation of health care or the East Asian Miracle and Crisis. However, from the references provided it is not possible to see whether alternative points of view were considered prior to the TSPs being written.

Knowledge, as conceived of and used by the TSPs, is tightly linked to the IDTs. This has the effect of ensuring major absences. For instance, the draft Education TSP (DfID, 2000c) is noticeably narrower in terms of subject matter and references than the education sector paper of the previous year (DfID, 1999). The TSP focuses on universal primary education and girls' education, in line with the IDTs, whereas the paper, 'Learning Opportunities for All', considers education far more holistically and includes concerns with skills and knowledge development, and further and higher education.

However, there are signs in the TSPs that DfID is concerned about the need to build more Southern knowledge into its future research, and, by implication, policy. Thus, a number of draft or final TSPs (Education, Health, Human Rights, Water) speak of the need to develop Southern research capacity. The increased concern with Southern involvement in knowledge generation may also be seen in practical terms by research competitions held during 2000 by the Education Department and the Economic and Social Committee for Overseas Research, which required significant Southern involvement in all research bids. Nonetheless, there arguably is too little emphasis across the TSPs about the need to support South-South and South-North knowledge flows more generally and to make these critical to policy-making in ways that would open up DfID policy-making to more critical Southern commentary.

As we noted earlier, DfID has not used the term 'knowledge' in documents such as the TSPs or the first White Paper in a way that reflects the current knowledge debate. However, it is the case that DfID has embarked on attempts to understand and respond to these debates through less high-profile actions. The Knowledge Policy Unit has been established to coordinate and innovate regarding DfID's use of knowledge for achieving its policy goals. In August 2000, a draft document was produced that sought to examine how DfID's practices measured up to knowledge management practice in the corporate sector, the donor cooperation community and Whitehall (DfID, 2000j). This paper argues that whilst DfID does a lot of management of knowledge, it has not yet done much in the way of deliberate knowledge management. One part of a knowledge management strategy that the paper does recommend is a focus on deliberately learning from partners, including in the South:

> *We are also recognising that we need to* learn more *from our partners and from the countries and organisations with whom we work, and allow them to influence and inform more what we do. There is a need to incorporate their wisdom and learning more effectively in our working and to link with centres of knowledge in the South as much as in the North. (DfID, 2000j, p. 10)*

The second White Paper (DfID, 2000k) does contain a stronger sense of knowledge for development but it can be argued that there is still insufficient evidence, both in its arguments and in its own sources of knowledge, that it has fully explored the democratic implications of the new knowledge debates.

DfID has also made partnership a key theme of its activities since 1997. The first White Paper (DfID, 1997) made frequent use of the term. DfID sees partnership as encompassing its relationships to Northern partners (other agencies, the private sector, universities and NGOs) as well as to Southern collaborators. Nonetheless, it appears that much of the criticism of the notion of partnership that has been made generally can also be applied to the case of DfID.

There is some reference to the partnership notion in some of the TSPs. The Health TSP, for instance, mentions the importance of partnership with civil society and NGOs, both North and South. However, it promises DfID support for 'international leadership with the authority to hold countries to account for the achievement of the international development targets' (DfID, 2000, p. 28), regardless of the questionable legitimacy of the IDTs. Such a commitment could be construed as partnership with a prior agenda.

Yet, at the same time, DfID is increasingly supportive of the new Sector Wide Approach (SWAP), which sees greater donor coordination around a national policy strategy. As we shall see when we turn to SIDA, there are strong ethical arguments in favour of SWAPs. In the education sector, it is evident that SWAPs are seen by DfID staff as a way to be both more effective and more partnership-oriented. However, there are also concerns about the extent to which SWAPs can lead to greater donor control over policy as they increasingly speak with a single voice. With its strong emphasis on the IDTs, DfID may face a particular challenge in listening to its Southern partners. Moreover, given that not all Northern agencies are so supportive of the IDTs as is DfID, it is possible to see in the TSPs an attempt to gain Northern agency support for DfID's strategy. It is clearly legitimate for agencies to seek to lobby for support for their positions, but DfID will need to guard against appearing to be more concerned with telling than listening.

There is little sense in the TSPs about the responsibilities of development cooperation agencies. Most crucially here, there is no acknowledgement of Britain's continued failure to match the target agreed at both the United Nations (UN) and the OECD of 0.7% of gross national product (GNP) to be committed to official development assistance (ODA). The Economics TSP boasts an increase from 0.27% in 1997 to 0.33% in 2004 (DfID, 2000a, p. 42) but is silent on how long it will take to reach the 0.7% obligation. Partnership appears hollow if donors are not living up to their own commitments to this basic international development target.

Whilst still engaged in a range of project delivery, often on a considerable scale, DfID has begun to stress its role as a policy advocacy agency in the past 3 years. One challenge in adopting such a role is the need to base that advocacy on a careful listening to Southern knowledge on development and a powerful commitment to forging genuine partnerships with the South. If these challenges can be met, then it is possible that DfID will make real its commitment to 'making government work for poor people'. However, much still needs to be done.

The Swedish International Development Cooperation Agency

SIDA underwent a reorganisation in the late 1990s that has seen an amalgamation of previously independent elements of the Swedish development cooperation effort. Whilst the new SIDA has not developed anything like the number of policy documents as DfID, it has spent considerable time and effort in articulating an approach to partnership and process in development cooperation and, under the lead of the Ministry for Foreign Affairs, has participated in major reviews of

Sweden's policies for Asia and Africa (Ministry for Foreign Affairs, 1997, 1998, 1999).

> *Knowledge is our most important resource. During the next five years we shall implement an investment programme for the long-term renewal of knowledge and skills in our partner countries, of our Swedish partners and at SIDA. (SIDA, 1997a)*

> *In all operational programmes the development of knowledge, in the widest sense of the term, is the most important working method. (SIDA, 1997b)*

> *The central issue of all development cooperation is to contribute to developing knowledge – in the partner country, in Sweden, and internationally. (SIDA, 1997c)*

These extracts from the SIDA website are indicative of a concern with knowledge. In August 2000, SIDA also began to sketch out in more detail an approach in which it sees knowledge as being created in partnership with others, particularly in the South (SIDA, 2000). Moreover, a concern with knowledge sharing can be seen as embedded in SIDA's more developed concerns with learning. In this formulation, learning is not simply important for better policy and programme development, but is also closely intertwined with partnership concerns.

This learning-partnership focus is clear in SIDA's continued focus on research in partnership with the South. Research is seen in SIDA as being important for capacity building both North and South and as a catalyst for more cooperative relationships. The desire to learn from others is also evident in the processes that accompanied the development of SIDA's new Africa policy, in which there was a very serious attempt to listen to the voices of the South, both in the region under focus and within Sweden. However, as with other agencies, SIDA will have to work hard to overcome past failures in listening to and learning from the South, as papers in a recent Swedish produced volume on development learning indicate (Carlsson & Wohlgemuth, 2000; Wieslander, 2000).

Sweden's recent development of an Africa policy is an exemplar of concerns with partnership both in the process of developing policy and in the content of the policy itself. The development of the *Partnership with Africa* was built in large part on consultations in Africa and with Africans living in Sweden. Throughout the policy document and the accompanying statement, *Africa on the Move* (Ministry for Foreign Affairs, 1998), there is a powerful emphasis on partnership as a core concept of Sweden's new approach. The need for long-term relationships is affirmed and the wide range of non-governmental linkages between Africa and Sweden applauded and encouraged.

These documents and our fieldwork highlight Swedish concerns about the asymmetrical nature of the development cooperation relationship. There is a strongly expressed desire to tackle this issue. For instance, it has been suggested that a move away from placing the financial element of being a donor or recipient at the core of the development cooperation process would be advantageous as a way of downplaying a key area of asymmetry. Nonetheless, given that SIDA has just as strong a disbursement culture as other agencies, such sentiments will be difficult to put into practice. The concern to move beyond monetary relationships is evident in a desire to stress cooperation over aid.

This desire for cooperation seems linked to SIDA's focus on twinning programmes and long-term sustainability of relationships, particularly through the period when SIDA support is being reduced and finally withdrawn. This desire for cooperation also emerged during fieldwork in terms of partner country leadership of development cooperation. There appears to be a sense that SIDA is more concerned with processes and values than with outcomes and products, although it would be impossible for the former to be pursued exclusively. In his foreword to the volume *A New Partnership for African Development* (Kifle et al, 1997), Karlsson presented a vision of partnership built on seven principles:

1. *a subject-subject attitude;*
2. *explicitness regarding values;*
3. *transparency regarding interests;*
4. *clear standards;*
5. *sticking to agreements;*
6. *equality of capacity;*
7. *code of conduct. (Karlsson, 1997, pp. 7-8)*

The importance of processes and values is most clearly seen in SIDA's leading role in the development of the SWAP. This approach is justified as an ethical as well as an effective way of pursuing development cooperation. The language used is very striking. SWAPs are seen as forming the basis of a new code of conduct in development cooperation based in part on donor attitudes of openness, humility and transparency (Gustafsson, 1999).

Whilst SIDA will continue to come to dialogue with partners with its own values and priorities, Karlsson makes it clear that it must also come ready to listen and learn. This commitment is not entirely unproblematic, however. There is a rather unconvincing argument put forward that conditionalities are no longer problematic as there is shared agreement on major policy issues (e.g. Ministry of Foreign Affairs, 1998, p. 85). The line between Sweden coming to discussions with legitimate policy views and concerns and coming with preconditions for partnership seems to be a fine one (Caddell, 1998; King, 1998).

Moreover, SWAPs are not universally admired and questions continue to be raised about their desirability and feasibility. Nonetheless, the SIDA vision of SWAPs does point, in comparison to existing cooperation models, to a longer time period in which to build better relationships, a greater stress on civil society involvement in policy-making, and a sense that development decisions are political rather than technical in nature. Thus, of the three agencies explored in this chapter, it is SIDA that, in theory at least, appears to have the most sophisticated understanding of the challenges of democratic development cooperation.

How Does the New Development Discourse Affect Democracy?

The three case studies suggest that there is considerable complexity and tension surrounding these two key themes of the new development cooperation discourse. In their most rigorous and radical forms, the new accounts of knowledge and partnership offer the possibility of a more democratic model of development. The knowledge account provides an opportunity to step back from universal theories and to explore good practices and real contexts, and empowers countries to develop their own approaches through adaptive learning. Moreover, it raises the possibility of a strengthening of Southern knowledge generation capacity and a more equitable process of multidirectional knowledge flows that include South to North and South to South flows. Such a reduction in the dominance of Northern knowledge for policy-making purposes brings with it the possibility of national policies that are better grounded in local practical concerns, cultural approaches and epistemological systems.

The partnership account explicitly seeks to move away from the excessive conditionalities and donor direction of development in the 1980s and early 1990s. It promises national leadership of development strategies and goes beyond the state to incorporate a vision of active citizenship for development planning. It highlights the need for long-term relationships and planning and the need for a focus on processes and values.

However, in practice, partnership can be very closely linked to conditionalities. Agencies often argue that 'real' partnerships can only be between like-minded partners. Thus, Southern partners are expected to share a whole range of values, targets and policies with donors, if they want to be supported. As far as democracy is concerned, three issues quickly arise. First, what do partnerships mean for democracy if they lead to policies being designed in the North rather than in the country whose policies they allegedly are? Second, good governance is often one of the most explicit of the conditionalities that are required for partnership. Is a requirement for good governance, as defined in the North, actually good for democracy in the South? Third, recent agency efforts at SWAPs and PRSPs have sought to use 'civil society' in the South as a means of strengthening democratic ownership of development policies. However, these civil societies appear often to be imagined, and the agency analyses of national political processes are often inadequate. Does the current focus on civil society participation in partnerships serve to obscure the power dynamics of policy-making rather than ensure widespread ownership of development policies?

There are existing imbalances in knowledge and power that mean that new knowledge and partnership relationships cannot simply be willed into being. Inevitably, overall agency practices lag considerably behind the visionary edge of the most progressive agency documents. Moreover, organisational cultures and opposing mindsets mean that the new ways of thinking and doing are not dominant. Asymmetries of current knowledge production will be hard to overcome and political imperatives in the policy arena inevitably will cut across any attempts to build policy on good and diverse knowledge foundations. Development partnerships too are necessarily asymmetrical at the current juncture, given the huge disparity in resources and the often pressing need to receive aid. Moreover, the need by Northern agencies for quick disbursement will continue to undermine a focus on long-term processes and the careful development of partnerships and alliances for development. Whilst better practices regarding knowledge and partnership have democratic potential, they are by no means guarantors of democracy.

Although this chapter is not about the education sector per se, it is clear that all of these arguments do have major implications for education systems as a core area of focus for aid. Moreover, education systems are heavily influenced by donor views on education, not least because a large proportion of non-recurrent (i.e. non-salary) education budgets are externally financed. Donor certainties about the appropriate nature of education also combine with the current orthodoxies and trends associated with globalisation to impact upon the democratic control of education. Globalisation and the views of many agencies encourage the growth of private schooling, with major implications for national education systems and the notion of education for citizenship. Decentralisation can be seen as increasing democratic control over education, but can alternatively be seen as another way of increasing the power of the market and reducing that of the state and democratic structures. The globalisation of other educational ideas, about school management and efficiency, about pedagogy, about curriculum, etc., also serves to reduce the possibility of local ownership of educational policies. Thus, the close relationship between globalisation and development, so clearly admitted in the 2000 British White Paper, has profound implications for the education sector.

In conclusion, our case studies point to much that is positive in the statements and actions of these three agencies. In particular, they point to new understandings and new attitudes that seek to move away from donor dominance of cooperation towards local leadership. However, they also point to a continued tendency within agencies to push their own agendas more strongly than they listen to the needs and aspirations of others, and to come to a supposed dialogue with their minds already made up about what they will fund. It is important that agencies have visions and priorities but, as Karlsson (1997) and Gustafsson (1999) have written, trust and humility are also vital. Given the existing imbalance in power in development cooperation, such values from the Northern side are essential if democracy in development is to be a possibility, in the often harsh light of globalisation.

References

Caddell, M. (1998) Beyond the White Papers: an overview of the debate, in K. King & M. Caddell (Eds) *Partnership and Poverty in Britain and Sweden's New Aid Policies*. CAS Occasional Paper No. 75. Edinburgh: University of Edinburgh.

Carlsson, J. & Wohlgemuth, L. (2000) Learning in the Development Debate, in J. Carlsson & L. Wohlgemuth (Eds) *Learning in Development Cooperation*. Expert Group in Development Initiatives (EGDI), Studies in Brief, 2/00. Stockholm.

Chang, H-S., Fell, A. & Laird, M. with Seif, J. (1999) A Comparison of Management Systems for Development Co-operation in OECD/DAC Members. Development Cooperation Directorate, DCD(99)6. Paris: Organisation for Economic Cooperation and Development.

Department for International Development (DfID) (1997) *Eliminating World Poverty*. London: HMSO.

Department for International Development (DfID) (1999) *Learning Opportunities for All*. London: DfID.

Department for International Development (DfID) (2000a) *Halving World Poverty by 2015*. London: DfID.

Department for International Development (DfID) (2000b) *Better Health for Poor People*. London: DfID.

Department for International Development (DfID) (2000c) *Education for All: the challenge of universal primary education*. London: DfID.

Department for International Development (DfID) (2000d) *Poverty Elimination and the Empowerment of Women*. London: DfID.

Department for International Development (DfID) (2000e) *Realising Human Rights for Poor People*. London: DfID.

Department for International Development (DfID) (2000f) *Addressing the Water Crisis.* London: DfID.

Department for International Development (DfID) (2000g) *Achieving Sustainability.* London: DfID.

Department for International Development (DfID) (2000h) *Making Government Work for Poor People.* London: DfID.

Department for International Development (DfID) (2000i) *Urbanisation.* London: DfID.

Department for International Development (DfID) (2000j) *'Doing the Knowledge'. How DfID Compares with Best Practice in Knowledge Management.* Final Draft, August. London: DfID.

Department for International Development (DfID) (2000k) *Making Globalisation Work for Poor People.* London: HMSO.

Development Assistance Committee – Organisation for Economic Cooperation and Development (1996) *Shaping the Twenty-First Century: the contribution of development cooperation.* Paris: Development Assistance Committee – Organisation for Economic Cooperation and Development.

Ellerman, D. (1998) *Knowledge-based Development Institutions.* Washington, DC: World Bank.

Gustafsson, I. (1999) New partnership possibilities, *Norrag News,* 25, pp. 4-6.

Karlsson, M. (1997) Foreword, in H. Kifle, A. Olukoshi & L. Wohlgemuth (Eds) *A New Partnership for African Development.* Uppsala: Nordic Africa Institute.

Kifle, H., Olukoshi, A. & Wohlgemuth, L. (Eds) (1997) *A New Partnership for African Development.* Uppsala: Nordic Africa Institute.

King, K. (1998) New Challenges to International Development Cooperation in Education, in K. King & M. Caddell (Eds) *Partnership and Poverty in Britain and Sweden's New Aid Policies.* CAS Occasional Paper No. 75. Edinburgh: University of Edinburgh.

Martin, B. (2000) *New Leaf or Fig Leaf? The Challenge of the New Washington Consensus.* London: Bretton Woods Project/Public Services International.

Ministry for Foreign Affairs, Sweden (1997) *Partnership with Africa.* Stockholm: Ministry for Foreign Affairs.

Ministry for Foreign Affairs, Sweden (1998) *Africa on the Move.* Stockholm: Ministry for Foreign Affairs.

Ministry for Foreign Affairs, Sweden (1999) *Our Future with Asia.* Stockholm: Ministry for Foreign Affairs.

Swedish International Development Cooperation Agency (SIDA) (1997a) A World in Imbalance; downloaded on 22 October 1999 from: http://www.sida.se/SIDA/articles/600-699/645/global3.html

Swedish International Development Cooperation Agency (SIDA) (1997b) The Task is to Create the Right Conditions; downloaded on 22 October 1999 from: http://www.sida.se/SIDA/articles/600-699/649/global7.html

Swedish International Development Cooperation Agency (SIDA) (1997c) Knowledge is the Key to Development; downloaded on 22 October 1999 from: http://www.sida.se/SIDA/articles/600-699/653/global11.html

Swedish International Development Cooperation Agency (SIDA) (2000) Capacity Development as a Strategic Question in Development Cooperation: policy and guidelines for SIDA. Final Draft. SIDA Working Paper No. 8, Policy Secretariat for the Sector Departments. Stockholm: SIDA.

Stiglitz, J. (1999) Scan Globally, Reinvent Locally: knowledge infrastructures and the localisation of knowledge. Keynote address to the First Global Development Network Conference, Bonn, December.

United Nations (1995) Report of the World Summit for Social Development; downloaded on 27 March 2000 from: http://www.un.org/esc/socdeve/geneva2000/docs/summit.pdf

Wieslander, A. (2000) When Do We Ever Learn? in J. Carlsson & L. Wohlgemuth (Eds) *Learning in Development Cooperation*. Expert Group in Development Initiatives (EGDI) Studies in Brief, 2/00. Stockholm.

Wolfensohn, J. (1997) The Challenge of Inclusion; downloaded on 21 October 1999 from: http://www.worldbank.org/html/exdir/am97/jdw_sp/jwsp97e.htm

Wolfensohn, J. (1998) The Other Crisis; downloaded on 21 October 1999 from: http://www.worldbank.org/html/exdir/am98/jdw_sp/am98-en.pdf

Wolfensohn, J. (1999) A Proposal for a Comprehensive Development Framework (A discussion draft); downloaded on 9 June 1999 from: http://www.worldbank.org/cdf/cdf.pdf

Wood, A. (2000) *The ABC of the PRSP*. London: Bretton Woods Project/Public Services International.

World Bank (1998a) *World Development Report 1998/99. Knowledge for Development*. Oxford: Oxford University Press.

World Bank (1998b) Partnership for Development: proposed actions for the World Bank. A discussion paper; downloaded on 21 October 1999 from: http://www.worldbank.org/html/exdir/pfd-discpaper.pdf

World Bank (2000a) *World Development Report 2000/01. Attacking Poverty*. Oxford: Oxford University Press.

World Bank (2000b) Comprehensive Development Framework: mid-term progress report; downloaded on 7 July 2000 from: http://www.worldbank.org/cdf/cdfinfo.doc

PART FOUR

Curriculum and Learning for National Identity

In this section, four authors examine in different ways how the official and unofficial curriculum is used to try to forge citizenship and nationalism. Wai Chung Ho's is a unique study which relates culture, political socialisation and music in Hong Kong and Taiwan. Both countries transmit national identity and solidarity through the music curriculum, in particular national and nationalistic songs, but also through songs stressing Confucian values of family, the role of the mother and filial piety. However, the motives are different: in Hong Kong, the hidden curriculum of music, or 'non-musical learning' relates to promoting a greater understanding of China, whereas in Taiwan, it is to intensify an emotional and ethical nationalism.

Joseph & Rea Zadja's chapter on textbooks in Russia focuses, in contrast, on the history curriculum, but the theme of the creation of a national identity is similar. Textbooks are being rewritten, but with complications over funding from Western donors. Confusion arises over the loss of the Soviet grand narrative, and now books are emphasising pluralism, tolerance, patience and a 'romantic quasi-humanistic perception of historical event'. Interestingly, Zadja & Zadja also examine how history is integrated into music lessons, where students are asked to analyse music dedicated to the struggle against fascism.

Clive Harber's chapter, on the other hand, takes a more futuristic look at the overt promotion of citizenship in the introduction of the new citizenship curriculum in England. He recognises that this may not fall on fertile ground, as it is being inserted into an education system which is currently undemocratic. The context and contradictions of the introduction – the overall National Curriculum, assessment, league tables of school achievement – is shown to be crucial in determining the fate of what could be a radical innovation.

In his chapter on values and citizenship in the Asian Pacific Rim, Elwyn Thomas also analyses the revival of citizenship education, but uses cross-cultural dimensions of individualism-collectivism and universalism-relativism to compare countries and assess future trends. The challenges are to incorporate global values and to deliver a form of civics education which promotes participation in decision-making as well as questioning the role of authority. While the first two chapters of this section relate to indirect political socialisation and the last two to direct civic education, all four chapters point to contradictions and challenges for curriculum design in an increasingly globalised world with shifting boundaries and loyalties.

Democracy, Citizenship and Extra-musical Learning in Two Chinese Communities: Hong Kong and Taiwan

WAI-CHUNG HO

Introduction

When the British Association of International and Comparative Education designated 'Learning Democracy and Citizenship' as the theme of its conference in 2000, it underlined concerns that have been at the heart of recent worldwide discussions of educational reforms. Questions of citizenship and problems of promoting democracy through education are the key challenges of contemporary global education. My purpose here is not to review the philosophical issues underpinning these challenges, but to describe the practices of educating for citizenship and democracy in two contemporary Chinese societies. This chapter explores the extra-musical functions of music education for overall national cultural developments.

Toward the end of the twentieth century, debates over political development and democracy in Asia increasingly came to focus upon the states of Hong Kong and Taiwan (officially named as the Republic of China). Both have histories of colonialism, predominantly Chinese populations, and extraordinarily successful records of economic growth. Hong Kong is situated off the south-east coast of China, incorporating a small portion of the mainland east of the Pearl River, adjoining the Guangdong Province of the People's Republic of China (PRC). Almost 95% of the 7.2 million-population are ethnic, Cantonese-speaking Chinese, whilst the remaining 5% comprises various nationalities. Since the 1984 Sino-British Joint Declaration, Hong Kong has become a closely watched laboratory in which the conflict between Asian values and Western democratic ideals is played out on the world stage. When Hong

Kong was returned to China on 1 July 1997, its inhabitants were guaranteed a high degree of individual freedom within the framework of the policy of 'One Country, Two Systems' laid down in the constitutional document, *Basic Law*. This guarantees a 50-year right for Hong Kong to run its own capitalist system and way of life according to principles which are very different from the socialist system and way of life in Mainland China.

Taiwan is bounded by the Pacific Ocean to the east and by the Formosa Strait to the west, which separates it from Mainland China by over 100 km of sea. Taiwan was colonised by Japan from 1895 to 1945 as a result of the Sino-Japanese War. In 1945, Civil War broke out in China between the Kuomingtang (KMT) led by Chiang Kai-shek and the Chinese Communist Party (CCP) led by Mao Zedong. In 1949, the KMT was defeated and Chiang with 2 million Nationalists fled to Taiwan and founded the Republic of China (ROC), with a capital in Taipei. The ROC advocates the capitalist teachings of Sun Yat-sen in opposition to Chinese socialism. Both the Beijing and Taipei authorities have attempted to rebuild cross-strait interactions, but because the Chinese Government insists on Taiwanese unity with 'the mainland', there has been no consensus over the issue 'one country, two systems'. In 1971, when Taiwan was expelled from the United Nations, it started to adopt the policy of Taiwanisation to promote the ideology of Taiwan as a homeland of, for and by Taiwan's people. In July 1998, 84% of the population of 21,908,135 were native Taiwanese (descendants of Chinese who migrated from Fujian and Guangdong Provinces on the mainland, primarily in the eighteenth and nineteenth centuries), 14% were original Mainland Chinese (who came from all parts of Mainland China after 1945), and 2% were aborigines.

The purpose of this study is to analyse to what extent the return of Hong Kong's sovereignty to Mainland China after 1997, and the indigenisation of Taiwan after 1945, have shaped the extra-musical components of music lessons, by examining a selection of music education publications that are used in the primary and secondary schools of the two countries. A 9-year public educational system has been in effect since 1978 and 1979 in Hong Kong and Taiwan respectively. Six years of elementary school and three years of junior high are compulsory for all children. Most schools have music lessons up to junior high. Sources of data include school music textbooks, government documents concerning educational policies and curricula, school music syllabuses, and other relevant studies. I shall argue that education for citizenship in Hong Kong and Taiwan music classes is carried out by means of Confucian nationalistic educational principles that serve to bind people together from different social backgrounds. This chapter examines some theories of cultural transmission through the school curriculum that have influenced both societies, and then explores dimensions of nationalistic, Confucian and democratic education.

The Theoretical Problem:
cultural transmission and educational values

Karl Marx argued that each significant period of history is built around a particular 'mode of production', or way in which a society is organised to produce, which determines the political, social and cultural shape of that society and its possible future development (see Marx, 1976, p. 3 & Storey, 1997, pp. 101-102). However, confusions arise about understandings of the word 'culture'. With reference to the cultural development of western Europe, Raymond Williams (1983, p. 87) calls culture 'one of the two or three most complicated words in the English language', and suggests three broad definitions: (1) 'a general process of intellectual, spiritual and aesthetic development'; (2) 'a particular way of life, whether of a people, a period or a group'; and (3) 'the works and practices of intellectual and especially artistic activity'. The term 'culture' also has several different meanings and connotations within the theories and practices of curriculum planning and development (see Kelly, 1981, 1986). Questions about the transmission of culture through the school curriculum may be considered functionally in terms of socialisation, and/or neo-Platonically in terms of universal forms of knowledge, irrespective of particular national or class cultures (see Eliot, 1948; Bantock, 1968, 1971).

No matter which approach is adopted, cultural development through music education is generally linked to the country's sociocultural context. This has been illustrated by Lawton's cultural analysis model (1973, 1975), which argues that all forms of curriculum development select and promote those aspects of our lives, knowledge, attitudes and values that are thought essential to the culture of a society, and which can contribute to nation-building in accordance with state ideals. In his *Education, Culture and the National Curriculum*, Lawton (1989) quotes the definition of the curriculum as being a selection from the culture, using the term 'culture' to refer to every thing that was 'man-made' in society, including language and literature, music and art, and attitudes and values (see also Lawton, 1983). Music education in any country tends to include traditional types inherited from the past in order to cultivate a sense of national identity among students.

There are always arguments about the process of transforming cultural forms, values, and practices into political symbols in school education. In practice, the use of the word 'culture' creates more difficulties than it resolves in the music curriculum. In the Western world, music education in school generally appreciates the value of classical music as artistic knowledge (see Green, 1988). Nevertheless, the rationale for Chinese music education adheres to the discipline of moral education as a way of encouraging people to conform to more virtuous living and to promote understanding of the Chinese heritage. That is the reason why Confucianism, one of China's major philosophical systems, considered that music should have its proper roles to educate people and the use of ritual to embellish harmony with the universe so as to build ethical character among people. And classical music has been treated as a national, high-cultural treasure and source of pride in the non-Western world.

Every curriculum has a particular educational function which upholds the values of the educational developers and the society at large. The pedagogical discourse of educating for citizenship and democracy in schools uses a variety of key terms: citizenship education, political socialisation, nationalistic education, patriotic education, democratic education, civic education, multiculturalism, etc. Citizenship education or political education usually takes the form of ethnic nationalism in most Asian countries.

Although the study of culture is nothing new in various disciplines of the humanities and social sciences, relating culture to music education in Chinese communities is still rare. We may consider how the Hong Kong and Taiwanese music education systems transmit their cultures' demands for an education for citizenship and democracy along three axes.

To what extent has the political context influenced the transmission of nationalism and Chinese culture through music education in the two Chinese communities?

How is Confucian education integrated into the learning of citizenship in music education?

Does school music education reflect democratic principles in its curriculum?

The Transmission of Nationalism and Chinese Culture through Music Education

Music education in Hong Kong and Taiwan promotes national identity and/or national solidarity through the use of traditional Chinese and Taiwanese music respectively. The definition of 'nationhood' in this chapter is narrowed to the sense of belonging to Mainland China or Taiwan. The preservation of community culture, including common language and unity of music traditions, are important means to sustain a sense of national identity. Smith (1991), for example, recognised the importance of intellectuals, artists and folklorists to the promotion of nationalism. Guibernau (1996) suggested that the relationship between national identity and culture depends on individuals' emotional investment in their culture, which provides the basis for the formation of national consciousness. But dilemmas arise over the nature of national sentiment and national consciousness as expressed through various musical styles and types of nationalistic songs. Within this patriotic education, national sentiment refers to emotional attachment, whilst national consciousness is derived from shared values, traditions and memories of the past. By thinking about both these contrasting 'discourses of identity', we can compare the meaning of the two countries' inclusion of Chinese music and nationalistic or patriotic songs in their school curricula.

Being inhabitants of a British colony ceded by China in 1842, the predominantly Chinese population of Hong Kong has no independent national identity to speak of. Hong Kong students were alienated from China and the sense of being Chinese was extremely weak. Education for national identity was absent from Hong Kong schools, since students were discouraged from identifying either with Chinese or local society (Tse, 1998). Since the late transitional period of Hong Kong (i.e. during the time that Chris Patten was Governor of Hong Kong, leading up to the return of Hong Kong to China), more nationalistic education has been called for both in society and the education sector. In September 1995, the Civic Education Team of the Board of Education began publishing a series of teaching materials titled 'Affection for Hong Kong, Heart for China' for primary and secondary school students (Yuen, 1997). This concern to preserve political and national identities is also illustrated in official educational documents from before and after the changeover of Hong Kong (see Curriculum Development Council, 1996, 1998; Curriculum Development Institute, 1999a, 1999b).

The promotion of Chinese music and the singing of the PRC's anthem are two signs of how nationalisation is emerging to various degrees in Hong Kong music education. The preservation of national culture, including the presentation of projects on Chinese music delivered by the Education Department and other educational institutes, represents an attempt to enhance students' feelings of national pride. Other audio and visual teaching materials, such as CD-ROMs on Chinese music, were also produced by the Hong Kong Institute of Education and the Education Department. The national anthem of the PRC ('March of the Volunteers') is promoted to cultivate a sense of belonging amongst students. Nevertheless, unlike Mainland Chinese music education materials, no revolutionary or patriotic songs are found in primary music textbooks. There are a few patriotic songs in music textbooks for secondary schools, such as 'Protection of the Yellow River' (see Editorial Board, Hong Kong Music Publisher, 1997a, pp. 36-37; Wu, 1998, pp. 92-93), 'Song of the Great Wall' (Wu, 1998, p. 108) and 'A War Song for Defending the Daioyutai Islands' (Lam & Ip, 1997, pp. 158-160). However, most students neither commit their sense of belonging to their motherland nor feel the importance of understanding Chinese culture and history. In a civic education survey conducted in a crowded industrial district of Sham Shui Po in Hong Kong in 1997, it was found that love of one country was rated lowest in priority, especially among students. Only 46% of the students interviewed felt that understanding Chinese culture and history is important (source: <http://www.mailing-list.net/cditt/chinahk/sub-hk9698.htm>). Most music teachers also feel as little enthusiasm as their students toward the teaching/learning of Chinese music or the singing of the anthem (see Ho, 1999a, 1999b; Ho & Fung, 1999).

A rather different process of musical nationalisation through education has been occurring in Taiwan. Though traditional Chinese musical instruments and folk songs are used in both primary and secondary schools, the promotion of 'China culture' idealises Chinese music within a larger utopian vision of a nationalist state grounded in shared myths, values, beliefs, ethnicity and history. The inclusion of traditional Chinese music is in celebration of Taiwan's own sense of its cultural past, and has nothing to do with the cultivation of national sentiment toward the mainland. Music composed in Communist China is never mentioned in the school curriculum. Rather, a 'Taiwanisation' of the political system and culture has solidified feelings of national identity towards the Taiwan state itself. The construction of a new 'multiethnic' nation has been an attempt 'to solve the old "provincial" conflict between mainlanders and Taiwanese, to integrate the aborigines and to achieve a broad consensus on Taiwan's national identity' (Schubert, 1999, p. 62). Taiwanisation in music education and the Taiwanese independence movement are closely related to each other. Article 158, one of the most important articles of the Constitution of the ROC, stipulates that national autonomy, national citizenship, national morality, healthy physicality, and social responsibility are to be regarded as key aims for the development of education and culture (Ministry of Education, 1997). Thus, Taiwanese music and the history of Taiwanese music have emerged as key learning areas as more emphasis on Taiwan as 'homeland' was introduced (see Ministry of Education, 1995; Lau, 1998).

Nationalism in school music education is designed to encourage love of the country of Taiwan, and pride in citizenship of the ROC (see various volumes of primary music textbooks published by the National Institute for Compilation and Translation; Kuo, 1987; Ministry of Education, 1995; <http://content.edu.tw/primary/music/tn-dg/content/standard/standard.htm>). Taiwanese students who are proud of their country far exceed those who are not proud of their country, and junior and senior high school students tend to identify themselves as 'Taiwanese' (see Chen, 1999). Primary school students are required to learn more about Taiwanese folk songs and children's songs (Liu, 1994). The music syllabus also outlines the proportion of national songs and foreign songs that should be taught/learnt in music lessons: for primary 1-2, 70% for national songs and 30% for foreign songs; for primary 3, 65% and 35% respectively; and primary 4-6, 60% and 40% respectively. According to data obtained from the Taiwan Ministry of Education, 238 schools were sponsored to promote traditional and native music, and these programmes were welcomed by both teachers and students (source: <http://www.cdn.tw/live/1999/09/06/text/880906e2.htm>).

Three common nationalistic songs are included in most music textbooks for primary schools: the national anthem of the ROC, 'The Three Principles' (San-min Zhu-yi) (i.e. nationalism, democracy, and social well-being), composed by Cheng Mao-yun; 'Song for the National Flag' (Guo-qi Ge), which takes pride in being Chinese as one of the major ancient civilisations in the world, and stressing the value of hard work for the Republic, composed by Wang Zi; and 'Song of the National Father' (Guo-fu Ji-nian Ge), composed by Li Jia-hui. Other new nationalistic songs are used, such as 'My Country' (Guo-jia) and 'Praise the Republic of China' (Zhong-hua Min-guo Song), written by the Taiwanese composer Li Jin-hui (see Liu, 1999, pp. 34-39). Some people have ideological or emotional conflicts when they sing the ROC's anthem, because it was originally that of the KMT (source: <http://www.taipei.com/news/20000/05/28/story/0000037814>; Li, 1998), and some people have even criticised its compulsory use in schools (Li, 1998).

To conclude, traditional Chinese and local Taiwanese music in Hong Kong and Taiwan education is used to develop their respective Chinese collective identities and their differing ideals for a national consciousness. Chinese music and the PRC anthem in schools are supposed to provide the basis for a greater understanding of China in Hong Kong, whilst native music and nationalistic songs in Taiwan music education are designed to intensify an emotional and ethical nationalism.

Citizenship Education and Confucian Education

To some extent, one may recognise that being a good citizen of the ROC or Hong Kong can be considered vastly different from being a good citizen of the United Kingdom, the USA or Canada. Fei Hsiao-tung, a leading sociologist in China during the 1940s, made a crucial distinction between Chinese hierarchical social organisation and Western associative organisations (Cheng, 1997). For thousands of years, Confucianism's 'language of moral and political organization' (Bergen & Mi, 1995, p. 41) permeated Chinese culture, stressing the achievement of social harmony through the practice of individual moral conduct in a hierarchical society (Lau et al, 1991; Szalay et al, 1994). Confucianism understands all political relationships as falling into five categories:

between sovereign and subject, father and son, elder and younger, husband and wife, and friend and friend (Jones, 1993; Yao, 2000). Confucian ethics is believed to bring harmonious family rapport that will incontestably 'lead to a harmonious society and a peaceful state' (also see Berthrong, 1998, p. 15; Yao, 2000, p. 33). Each individual lives in the context of family, country and universe, which are all understood as being interrelated and important to the self (see Ip, 1996, p. 49). Yao (2000) emphasises that 'Confucian education is fundamentally humanistic' and the value of Confucian education is to foster 'a spirit of self-discipline, family solidarity, public morality and social responsibility' among students (p. 283). However, filial piety, as a prevailing ethic in traditional Chinese values, has been greatly criticised by those Chinese thinkers who were influenced by 'individual ideas of the Western culture' (Zhang & Bond, 1998, p. 413). Liu & Lin (1988) maintained that the achievement of filial piety prohibits individual independence, lessens creative ability and stamps out personal interest and desire.

The purpose of music education throughout Chinese history has been to promote social harmony. Emperors of Imperial China used music to promote social harmony in a hierarchical society, since harmony was thought to connote 'an orderly combination of different elements' so as to form 'a new unity' (Yao, 2000, p. 171). Music was considered in traditional Chinese society as one of the four fundamental societal functions together with morals, law and politics. Confucian ethics compared good familial relations with those between indigenous Chinese musical instruments. The Confucian social value of music stressed the bonds of kinship and social stability. Because of close associations with the conservative characteristics of Confucian society, music is thought of more in terms of ethics, rather than aesthetics (see Ho, 1996). The inclusion of moral education or character education within the music lesson raises the question of how it can be taught, and to what particular ends.

In Hong Kong, Confucian thinking is found in 'New Guidelines on Civic Education in Schools' drafted in 1996, and 'Guidelines on Civic Education for Junior Secondary', published in 1998, both of which aim to educate children to become rational, active and responsible citizens within a framework grounded in the family. Although the education of the conventional 'good citizen' is not stated in official music documents (see Curriculum Development Committee, 1983; Curriculum Development Council, 1987, 1992), this aim is considered with reference to music in the *Guidelines on Civic Education in Schools* (Curriculum Development Council, 1996), which gives examples of suitable songs such as 'Good Policemen' and 'Mr. Postman' for primary school students (p. 94). In 1999, compact discs on civic education titled 'Xianggong Shi Wo Jia' (Hong Kong is my home), sung by Hong Kong popular artists, were produced by the Government of the Hong Kong Special Administrative Region (HKSAR) and distributed to schools. This production is conducive to promoting the greater good of society, so as to encourage students to understand and practise 'responsible citizenship' and to cultivate a sense of belonging to Hong Kong. Other songs, such as those in praise of friendship and parenthood, are commonly found in both Hong Kong's primary and secondary music textbooks; for example, the Cantonese songs 'Praise My Parents', set to the slow movement theme of Haydn's Quartet, op. 76 no. 2 (Qu et al, 1995), 'Good Mother' (Yuen, 1995, p. 24), 'Good Father' (Yuen, 1996a, p. 4), 'My Parents' Love' (Wu, 1997, p. 66; Editorial Board, Hong Kong Music Publisher, 1997b, pp. 80-81), 'Home Sweet Home' (Lam & Ip, 1997, p. 46), and 'I Truly Love You (My Mother)' (Editorial Board, Hong Kong Music Publisher, 2000, p. 73).

The prescription that piety, in the form of recognising one's role in the family, taking care of one's parents, and attempting to bring honour and to avoid disgrace to the family name, should govern children's' attitudes towards their parents as well as towards their ancestors is often found in Taiwanese music textbooks. Despite the emphasis put on the family as the basis for all human relations (Ministry of Education, 1995; <http://content.edu.tw/primary/music/tn-dg/content/standard/standard. htm>), most Taiwanese music textbooks include songs that praise the mother's and parents', rather than the father's love (e.g. see various volumes of primary music textbooks published by the National Institute for Compilation and Translation; Lin et al, 1998, pp. 76-77; Shen et al, 1999, pp. 41-42; Sun et al, pp. 107-109). Other songs deliver the message of a loving family and one's longing for his/her home, such as 'My Sweet Home' (found in a music textbook for Primary 5 school students published by the National Institute for Compilation and Translation), and 'My Home is on the Hillside' (Lin et al, 1998, pp. 40-41).

In sum, the encouragement of filial piety, such as found within school music education, is one of the paramount guiding ethics regulating social behaviour in the two Chinese communities. Hong Kong and Taiwan both promulgate the idea that good relationships between family members provide the basis for social solidarity. The nuclear family remains the basis for citizenship education in Hong Kong and Taiwan music education, and the song literature still conveys to students quite traditional Chinese values, mainly concerning how children should behave in the family.

Music Education and Learning Democracy

On the one hand, 'democratic musical meaning' may refer to song lyrics with overt messages of political pluralism and/or political freedom. On the other hand, 'democratic musical meaning' may refer to a musical style that is heard to carry political meanings.

The idea of 'democracy' has widespread global support and the term 'The Third Wave' is commonly adopted to label the changes in recent decades. The prevailing notion of democracy by the beginning of the twenty-first century involves liberal participation in free elections, although these have become intimately intertwined with the infrastructure of capitalism (Torres, 1998, p. 433). Nevertheless, the definition of democratic and undemocratic countries varies between Western and Eastern politicians and scholars (see Giddens, 1993, p. 331).

The concept of democracy had never been seriously addressed by Hong Kong people before the June 4th Incident in 1989, which gave rise to the first political parties, though the direct election of the Legislation Council came later in 1992. Although democratic and political songs were popular during and after the 1989 June 4th Incident, they were not allowed in school (see Ho, 1999b). Teachers and students were illegally promoting political, popular songs and sang for the remembrance of the 1989 democratic movement. These political/democratic popular songs were a challenge to both the Chinese authorities of the PRC and the British colonial administration. In July 1990, the Hong Kong Government and the Legislative Council agreed to amend any wording concerning political activities in schools (*Fai Pao*, 21 January, 1992). The amendment of the education regulations in 1990 was innovative on the part of school management, in that it relaxed state control over political activities in schools (Morris, 1992). Moreover, wording concerning prejudicial activities was also altered in the December 1993 *Education Regulations* (No. 98). As the issue of remembering the events of 1997 came nearer, the Hong Kong Government deliberately amended the education regulations. This act was designed to liberate the overall education system, so as to reduce central control over political activities in schools.

According to Chu (1998), 'Taiwan is a society with no prior democratic experience. Its history has been one of imperial control, colonial administration, and one-party authoritarian rule' (p. 133). The decision of Chiang Ching-kuo to tolerate the launch of an opposition party in September 1986 is considered to be the beginning of the democratisation process; and the Martial Laws, under which constitutional protections of human rights and citizenship were suspended, were lifted in July 1987. Some social movements of the 1980s, such as Aborigine Rights, and the Hakka Rights Movement, were public expressions of provincial identity, and a sense of society growing autonomously with respect to the Taiwanese Government. Chen (1997) believes that the democratisation process in Taiwan has dissolved ethnic conflicts into the new nation state. In his presidential address, Chen Shibian stressed the value of democracy, freedom, and human rights that Taiwan and most developed countries enjoy, but not China.

Since 1994, the Ministry of Education has launched a series of educational reforms in support of the development of democratic citizenship education in Taiwan. These reforms include opening the textbook market to fair competition, the encouragement of autonomy for teachers, and the incorporation of democratic citizenship education in the new curriculum guidelines for the twenty-first century (Lu & Hung, 1999). Since September 1996, the music textbook market has allowed private publishing companies to produce teaching materials for both primary and secondary schools. Thus, the publication of music textbooks is no longer monopolised by the National Institute for Compilation and Translation. On 1 October 1998, the outlines of the Goals for Elementary School Curriculum were promulgated, in which the cultivation of democratic citizenship education is regarded as one of the major goals of the curriculum for grades 1-9 (i.e. students around 6-15 years old).

Comparatively speaking, Hong Kong is more cautious with its expressions of democratic ideals in official documents. Giving his comments on the ways of implementation and measures made by the Guidelines on Civic Education in Schools, Tse (1997) argues that it is ineffective to promote national and democratic education through the current social subjects. Hong Kong's music syllabuses are not politicised, do not educate for democracy, and are less concerned with peace and love than Taiwanese music syllabuses. Nonetheless, primary and secondary music education materials in Hong Kong and Taiwan do not incorporate songs dealing with topics such as justice, human rights, equality and other fundamental freedoms. In Hong Kong music education, only a few songs are in praise of world peace or the protection of the environment, and these tend to be adapted from foreign pieces such as 'It's A Small World' (Wu, 1998, pp. 36-37), 'We Shall Overcome' (Yuen, 1996b, p. 6), and 'Song of the Peace', which is adapted from Sibelius's *Finlandia Suite* (Editorial Board, Hong Kong Music Publisher, 1997a, p. 91; Lam & Ip, 1997, p. 88). According to Ho's 1999 survey of Hong Kong secondary schools (see Ho, 1999b), fewer than 40% of music teachers thought that Chinese democratic songs could be successfully introduced into the curriculum for the promotion of political freedom and democracy. Meanwhile, besides the national publications, other publishers in Taiwan also include songs emphasising loving each other, such as 'Where Is My Friend?' (Yang, 2000, p. 38), 'It's Love' (Lin et al 1998, pp. 52-53), 'The Meaning of Love' (lyrics adapted from Bible: *Corinthians 1*, chapter 13, 4-8, see Lin et al, 1998, p. 68).

The Taiwanese Government also supports the promotion of aboriginal education, and provides funds for publishing teaching materials, teacher handbooks, and audio and video cassettes. For example, the National Institute for Compilation and Translation produced two videos in 1995 on aboriginal cultures, which include songs and dances. The Taiwanese state claims that the proportional representation of indigenous local songs, including those of the aborigines, is a means towards democracy, but it could as well be understood as a move towards an insular process of nationalisation *through* localisation.

Conclusion

This chapter presents a comparative study of extra-musical learning in the music classes of the schools of Hong Kong and Taiwan, where education is geared towards democracy and citizenship at a time of unstable national identity for both communities. Taiwan has been undergoing a process of indigenisation since 1945, whilst Hong Kong's sovereignty was returned to the People's Republic of China after 1 July 1997. This chapter has argued that the transmission of extra-musical learning is essentially a response to the particular needs of these two Chinese historical-social contexts, which require their music curricula to be securely grounded in the ideology of a culturally based education for 'citizenship'. Despite different approaches to Western-based musical knowledge in schools, Hong Kong and Taiwan attempt to promote a sense of national identity and an essentially Confucian set of moral values as a central goal of school music education. The promotion of ethno-cultural nationalism in Taiwan's music education is regarded as a democratic goal for the Taiwanese state, though in practice, the educational systems of both Taiwan and Hong Kong are coloured by the global context.

Though there may be a closer correspondence between policy and practice in traditionally highly centralised systems, such as Hong Kong and Taiwan, there remains great diversity in the practices of school music teaching as to whether music teachers in these two Chinese communities conduct their non-musical teaching as prescribed by the state. At the same time, different music teachers may have quite different understandings of both democratic education and citizenship education. It remains questionable how willing or able music educators are in the two countries to put either prescribed or critical social and ethical concerns before aesthetic ones in the classroom.

References

Bantock, G.H. (1968) *Culture, Industrialisation and Education*. London: Routledge & Kegan Paul.

Bantock, G.H. (1971) Towards a Theory of Popular Education, in R. Hooper (Ed.) *The Curriculum: context, design and development*. Edinburgh: Oliver & Boyd in association with the Open University Press.

Bergen, T.J. & Mi, H.F. (1995) An Analysis and Review of Confucian Philosophy as the Basis for Chinese Education, *International Education*, 24, pp. 40-52.

Berthrong, J.H. (1998) *Transformations of the Confucian Way*. Boulder: Westview Press.

Chen, W.C. (1997) National Identity and Democratic Consolidation in Taiwan: a study of the problem of democratization in a divided country, *Issues and Studies*, 4, pp. 1-44.

Chen, W.C. (1999) Political Socialization and the Cultivation of Democratic Citizens in Taiwan: a comparative study of the political attitudes and values of junior and senior high, junior college, and college students, *Issues and Studies*, 35, pp. 36-79.

Cheng, K.M. (1997) Engineering Values: education policies and values education, in J.D. Montgomery (Ed.) *Values in Education: social capital formulation in Asia and the Pacific*, pp. 173-184. Hollis, NH: Hollis Publishing Company.

Chu, Y.H. (1998) Taiwan's Unique Challenges, in L. Diamond & M.F. Plattner (Eds) *Democracy in East Asia*, pp. 133-146. Baltimore: Johns Hopkins University Press.

Curriculum Development Committee (1983) *Music Syllabuses for Secondary Schools (Forms 1-3)*. Hong Kong: Government Printer.

Curriculum Development Council (1987) *Syllabuses for Secondary Schools, General Music (Forms 4-5)*. Hong Kong: Government Printer.

Curriculum Development Council (1992) *Syllabuses for Secondary Schools, General Music for Advanced Level*. Hong Kong: Government Printer.

Curriculum Development Council (1996) *Guidelines on Civic Education in Schools*. Hong Kong: Government Printer.

Curriculum Development Council (1998) *Syllabuses for Secondary Schools: civic education (Secondary 1-3)*. Hong Kong: Government Printer.

Curriculum Development Institute (1999a) *Ka Qiang Xue Xi : Ren Shi Zhong Guo – Fei Zheng Gui Ke Cheng* (Reinforce the learning on understanding China: informal curriculum). Hong Kong: Government Printer.

Curriculum Development Institute (1999b) *Ka Qiang Xue Xi : Ren Shi Zhong Guo – Xiao Xue Zi Yuan* (Reinforce the learning on understanding China: teaching resources). Hong Kong: Government Printer.

Editorial Board, Hong Kong Music Publisher (1997a) *Integrated Music for Secondary School*, vol. 3. Hong Kong: Hong Kong Music Publishers.

Editorial Board, Hong Kong Music Publisher (1997b) *Integrated Music for Secondary School*, vol. 2. Hong Kong: Hong Kong Music Publishers.

Editorial Board, Hong Kong Music Publisher (2000) *Integrated Music for Secondary School*, vol. 1, 6th edn. Hong Kong: Hong Kong Music Publishers.

Eliot, T.S. (1948) *Notes towards a Definition of Culture*. London, Faber.

Fai Pao (In Chinese) 21 January 1992.

Giddens, A. (1993). *Sociology*, 2nd edn. Oxford: Polity Press.

Green, L. (1988) *Music on Deaf Ears*. Manchester: Manchester University Press.

Guibernau, M. (1996) *Nationalisms: the nation-state and nationalism in the twentieth century*. Cambridge: Polity Press.

Ho, W.C. (1996) Hong Kong Secondary Music Education: a sociological enquiry, unpublished PhD thesis, London, Institute of Education, University of London.

Ho, W.C. (1999a) The Socio-political Transformations and Hong Kong Secondary Music Education: politicization, culturalization and marketization, *Bulletin of the Council for Research in Music Education*, 140, pp. 41-56.

Ho, W.C. (1999b) Hong Kong Secondary Music Education: political transition and civic education, *Music Education Research*, 1, pp. 171-189.

Ho W.C. & Fung, C.V. (1999) Music Education, Political Change and Cultural Transmission in Hong Kong and Singapore: a comparative study, paper presented at Research in Music Education, Exeter, United Kingdom, 20-24 April.

Ip, P.K. (1996) Confucian Familial Collectivism and the Underdevelopment of the Civic Person, in L.N.K. Lo & S.W. Man (Eds) *Moral and Civic Education*, pp. 39-58. Hong Kong: Institute of Educational Research, the Chinese University of Hong Kong.

Jones, D.M. (1993) The Metamorphosis of Tradition: the idea of law and virtue in East Asian political thought, *South Asian Journal of Social Science*, 21, pp. 18-35.

Kelly, A.V. (1981) Research and Primary Curriculum, *Journal of Curriculum Studies*, 13, pp. 215-225.

Kelly, A.V. (1986) *Knowledge and Curriculum Planning*. London: Harper & Row.

Kuo, C.Y. (1987) A Study on the Cultivation of Music Teachers in the Republic of China, *Bulletin of the National Institute of Educational Materials*, XII, pp. 33-88.

Lam. T.C. & Ip, S.C. (1997) *The Rhythm of Music: teacher's handbook*, 3rd edn, vol. 1. Hong Kong: Pilot Publishing Company.

Lam, T.C. & Ip, S.C. (1998) *The Rhythm of Music: teacher's handbook*, 3rd edn, vol. 2. Hong Kong: Pilot Publishing Company.

Lau, K.C. (1998) The Cultural Contents of the Secondary School Music Curricula in Hong Kong and Taiwan: a comparative study of four sets of textbooks, unpublished MEd thesis, Hong Kong: Faculty of Education, University of Hong Kong.

Lau, S.K., Lee, M.K., Wan, P.S. & Wong, S.L. (Eds) (1991) *Indicators of Social Development: Hong Kong 1988*. Hong Kong: Hong Kong Institute of Asia Pacific Studies, The Chinese University of Hong Kong.

Lawton, D. (1973) *Social Change, Educational Theory and Curriculum Planning*. London: University of London Press.

Lawton, D. (1975) *Class, Culture and the Curriculum*. London: Routledge & Kegan Paul.

Lawton, D. (1983) *Curriculum Studies and Educational Planning*. London: Edward Arnold.

Lawton, D. (1989) *Education, Culture and the National Curriculum*. London, Hodder & Stoughton.

Li, Y.T. (1998) *Taiwan Xiao Yu Yu Guo Jia Ding Wei* (Taiwan's education and its status in the country). Taipei: National Normal University Bookshop Company.

Lin, M.Z. et al (1998) *Guo Zhong Yin Yue* (National secondary music), vol. 3. Taipei: Kangkuo Chu Ban.

Liu, W.L. (1994) Inspiration of the New Curriculum in Music Education: – six aspects of music teaching and learning – listening, viewing, singing, playing, improvising, appreciating, *Journal of Taipei Municipal Teachers College*, 26, pp. 1-8.

Liu, X.M. (1999) *Ga-ji Zhong-xue: Yin-yue* (Senior secondary school: music), vol. 2. Taipei: Lung Teng Wen Fa Shi Ye Company.

Liu, Z.F. & Lin, G (1988) *Chuan Tong Yu Zhong Guo Ren* (Tradition and Chinese people). Hong Kong: Joint Publishing Company.

Lu, M.H. & Hung, J.L. (1999) Deadline Scholar Passages From 'Democratic Citizenship Education in Taiwan', *Social Studies*, 90(6), pp. 253-256; also available at:
<http://www.asiamedia.ucla.edu/Taiwan'sDemocracy/articles/Lu.htm>

Marx, K. (1976) Preface and Introduction to *A Contribution to the Critique of Political Economy*. Peking: Foreign Language Press.

Ministry of Education, Taiwan (1995) *Guomin Zhongke Kecheng Biao* (Standard Curriculum for National Secondary Schools). Taipei: Ministry of Education.

Ministry of Education, Taiwan (1997) *Education in the Republic of China*. Taipei: Ministry of Education.

Morris, P. (1992) Preparing Pupils as Citizens of the Special Administrative Region of Hong Kong: an analysis of curriculum change and control during the transition period, in G.A. Postiglione (Ed.) *Education and Society in Hong Kong: toward one country and two systems*, pp. 117-145. Hong Kong: Hong Kong University Press.

National Institute for Compilation and Translation, *Guo-min Ciao-xue Yin-yue* (Music for national primary schools), various volumes. Taipei: National Institute for Compilation and Translation.

Qu, P.X., Zheng, J.H. & Xiong, M.D. (1995) *Yinyue Tiandi* (Music world), Primary 5, vol. 2. Hong Kong: Gangxian.

Schubert, G. (1999) A New Rising Nation? The Discourse on National Identity in Contemporary China, *China Perspectives*, 23, pp. 54-64.

Shen, C.Z., Li, H.M., Lin, X.Z., Tang, B.M. & Gong, M.C. (1999) *Gao-min Ciao-xue Yin-yue* (Music for national primary schools), vol. 6. Tainan: Nan Yi Shu Ju.

Smith, A.D. (1991) *National Identity*. London: Penguin.

Storey, J. (1997) *An Introduction to Cultural Theory and Popular Culture*, 2nd edn. Hemel Hempstead: Prentice Hall/Harvester Wheatsheaf.

Sun, A.G., Wu, S.M., Lu, M.Y. & Wu, Q.Q. (1999) *Gao-ji Zhong-xue:Yin-yue* (Senior secondary school: music), vol. 1. Taipei: Sanmin Shu Ju Gu Fen Company.

Szalay, L.B., Strohl, J.B., Fu, L. & Lao, P.S. (1994) *American and Chinese Perceptions and Belief Systems*. New York: Plenum Press.

Torres, C.A. (1998) Democracy, Education, Multiculturalism: dilemmas of citizenship in a global world, *Comparative Education Review*, 42, pp. 421-447.

Tse, K.C. (1997) Social Subjects and Civic Education in Secondary Schools, *New Horizons in Education*, 38, pp. 10-14.

Tse, T.K.C. (1998) Preparing Students for Citizenship? Political Education in Hong Kong, *Education and Society*, 16(2), pp. 5-15.

Williams, R. (1983) *Keywords*. London: Fontana.

Wu, W.S. (1997) *Approach to Music*, vol. 1, 3rd edn. Hong Kong: Hong Kong Music Publisher.

Wu, W.S. (1998) *Approach to Music*, vol. 3, 3rd edn. Hong Kong: Hong Kong Music Publisher.

Yang, W.B. (2000) *Yin-yue* (Music), vol. 2. Taipei: Han Lin Publisher.

Yao, X.Z. (2000) *An Introduction to Confucianism*. Cambridge: Cambridge University Press.

Yuen, J.M. (1995) *Yin Le Chu Kai* (First step of learning music), Primary 1, 2nd vol. Hong Kong: Longman, Asia.

Yuen, J.M. (1996a) *Yin Le Chu Kai* (First step of learning music), Primary 1, 1st vol. Hong Kong, Longman, Asia.

Yuen, J.M. (1996b) *Yin Le Chu Kai* (First step of learning music), Primary 5, 1st vol. Hong Kong, Longman, Asia.

Yuen, M.M.Y. (1997) The Catholic Church in Political Transition, in J.Y.S. Cheng (Ed.) *Hong Kong Report 1997*, pp. 505-528. Hong Kong: Chinese University Press.

Zhang, J. & Bond, M.H. (1998) Personality and Filial Piety among College Students in Two Chinese Societies: the added value of indigenous constructs, *Journal of Cross-Cultural Psychology*, 29, pp. 402-417.

Other sources:

<http://content.edu.tw/primary/music/tn-dg/content/standard/standard.htm>
<http://www.cdn.tw/live/1999/09/06/text/880906e2.htm>
<http://www.taipei.com/news/20000/05/28/story/0000037814>
<http://www.mailing-list.net/cditt/chinahk/sub-hk9698.htm>

Reinventing the Past to Create the Future: the rewriting of school history textbooks in post-communist Russia

JOSEPH ZAJDA & REA ZAJDA

Social Memory and Russia's Transformation

The collapse of Communism in Russia in 1991 necessitated, among other things, the rewriting of school history textbooks, which during the communist era had been dominated by Marxist-Leninist interpretations of historical events. This article analyses the new post-communist history textbooks now used in Russian upper secondary schools, and the way the content reflects the attempts to transform the society from a communist regime to a Western-style democracy. The way the texts attempt to deal with the resulting problems of creating a new sense of national identity and citizenship during the period of transition is also discussed. The aim is to critically evaluate these new versions of Russia's history being taught in schools and their interpretation of significant events, particularly in terms of new biases or omissions. During annual research visits to Russia between 1989 and 1996, the researchers were able to observe both the use of these texts in history lessons, and the reaction of teachers and students to them.

One of the paradoxes of Russia's past 9 years of change in education from 1992 to the present could be readily observed on a micro-sociological level in the everyday life of the school and classroom. While many physical reminders of the former system's focus on Soviet-communist educational goals can still be found in the outdated texts and special purpose rooms which remain, the latest generation of schoolchildren who inhabit this environment can barely remember life under Communism.

In the last 10 years, change has been very rapid and in most schools, funding is very tight. This state of affairs is due in part to the loss of traditional sponsorship relationships between schools and the various industrial organisations, many of which have either been privatised or forced out of business by competition. The physical environment in the schools is now the last item to receive any expenditure. For this reason, relics and representations of Soviet political education in schools still dominate the decor and layout of some schools.

An example of this was observed on a 1994 visit to a country school in a town located at a distance of a 60-minute *eletrichka* ride from Moscow. We were shown a special classroom once dedicated to military training classes.[1] Giant hand-painted murals covered all four walls: their theme was the Soviet Union's military strength and pride in its achievements in military and space technology. The four-wall collage was dominated by the image of Lenin and a huge red hammer and sickle, and surrounded by heroically depicted illustrations of the various military engagements and battles fought by the USSR. The room was now relegated for use in woodwork and metalwork subjects for boys, which have now replaced the subject *Nachalnaya Voennaya Podgotovka* (Introductory Military Training) since the fall of Communism.

In the same year, we became aware that a new generation of students had very different perceptions of the recent Soviet past to those of students we recalled meeting in a Moscow history class in January 1992, immediately after the 1 January dissolution of the Soviet Union. As 17 year-olds, those anxious eleventh year, or exit class, students were still old enough for their memories of the USSR to be very fresh. They expressed concern about the nature of Russia's future relationship with the former republics of the USSR, their recent class trip to Latvia making the dissolution of the Union seem more graphic to them. They now wondered whether their new friends in Latvia would ever become their enemies. They reflected with concern that since New Year's Day, their new friends now lived in a foreign country. They all expressed uncertainty and confusion about their own country's future.

Such concerns had no resonance for a year 9 group we met 2 years later in 1994. Their subject was twentieth-century history and that is exactly what the Soviet Union had now become for them, merely part of the study of history. Their eyes seemed to 'glaze over' and none of them would attempt a response when one of us asked the group about their views of recent changes. Later, one of the teachers reminded us they were too young to remember a pre-glasnost, pre-perestroika era. They had only been 11 or 12 at the time of the dissolution of the Union and had been too young to comprehend the enormous significance of the event, which had been so disturbing to older youth and was still painful to adults. We saw that the perceptions of these Russian students of the

USSR were already being shaped through the filter of texts and documents. The USSR was knowable to them only as 'history lessons'.

Increasingly, teachers who themselves grew up under the Soviet system now face classes of youngsters whose knowledge of Soviet life is second-hand and characterised by the predominating stereotypes of stagnation, repression and secrecy, and by a new Russian 'social amnesia' which has sought to redefine the communist regime. The rapidity of the attempts to change Russia economically and politically has tended to produce in some sections of the population a 'profound change in consciousness' which in turn has been accompanied by a 'characteristic amnesia' (Anderson, 1983, p. 204).

The Search for Historical Paradigms in Post-communist Russia

Under the Soviet regime, school education, through a centralised, completely unified system of instruction, was one of the key means used to invent the Soviet state. To apply Anderson's model (Anderson, 1983, p. 205), its 'biography' or foundation narrative, beginning with its bloody revolutionary birth to its maturity in the continued project of building of the USSR, was systematically and uniformly taught in all Soviet school textbooks in history, literature and, where possible, in other subjects. Its message was also reinforced in school-based children's organisations like the Octobrists, Pioneers and the Komsomol. Political socialisation occurred in these organisations with events of history perceived as significant being reinforced by celebration and public discussion. A further chapter in the Soviet nation's biography was added to the textbooks after World War Two, with the portrayal of the Great Patriotic War as a testing by blood and sacrifice which resulted in the strengthening of the Soviet state.

Since the collapse and formal dissolution of the Soviet Union, its dominant member, the former Russian Soviet Socialist Republic, has had to invent for itself a revised nationhood based on a new, or reworked, narrative of national identity. This narrative had both to recast the role of the Soviet contribution, and to establish a new, or rediscovered, non-communist source of national authenticity and political legitimacy for the state. Along with the citizens of the Soviet successor states, and the other nations in eastern and central Europe, Russians initially saw the communist model as so discredited that there was a great pressure to distance any new national ideology from any semblance to its beliefs and practices. Russians shared with these peoples a somewhat unrealistic optimism about the power of the free market to cure all existing social and economic ills. One eastern European commentator, Zdzislaw Krasnodebski (1991), aptly diagnosed the state of public consciousness in the last days of the USSR and eastern and central Europe as one of 'waiting for the supermarkets'. Gorbachev's response to the complaints of a group of Estonian protesters in 1991 that 'you would sell your souls for a piece of sausage' accentuated the fact that a significant part of the unrest was caused by dissatisfaction with the scarcity of consumer goods. In part, this discontent helped fuel wider demands for freedom and national self-determination. Disillusionment was not long in following the collapse of communist regimes. As Alain Touraine reminded his readers in 1992, the 'all-too-easily forgotten truth is that in the West a very long period of brutal and cruel capitalism preceded the organised attempt to establish a degree of social control over the economy' (Baumann, 1994, p. 27).

Unlike the other communist states, Russia's transitional period was made even more difficult because it also lacked that unifying, if somewhat temporary, surge of social solidarity and patriotism which, in other eastern and central European countries, accompanied the sense of freedom over what was seen as an escape from the USSR's dominance. The sense of a battle for self-determination having been fought and won initially buoyed up public consciousness in difficult times. For Russia, however, the change only meant a descent into total economic chaos, growing poverty, a deeply felt loss of international status and influence, widespread accusations of blame and guilt over the repression of Communism, and a moral and political vacuum. A search for social and historical models for the nation's identity became imperative. Now, instead of interpreting history and Russia's past through the framework of Marxist-Leninist ideology, the writers of Russia's new school history textbooks had to shrink or diminish the Soviet narrative of identity and undergo a process of 'rediscovery'. The question was, what sources would be found for the nation's consciousness?

Sources of National Identity

Nation builders rarely make new myths; rather, they mine the past for suitable heroes and symbols. Lenin's Party workers resorted to borrowing religious symbols and myths of the Russian Orthodox religion and giving them a socialist interpretation, in order to attract the peasants to their ideas (Tumarkin, 1983, pp. 69-72), while Stalin, leader of a state professing atheism, reopened the churches during the darkest days of World War Two as a morale booster. Russia's immediate post-communist leaders and the intellectuals who served them also turned to religion as one of the first sources of post-communist Russian national identity and authenticity. Another early post-communist source of 'Russianness' came from the rediscovery and reworking of the history of the Romanov dynasty. On a 1992 visit, we observed that the bookshop of the Moscow Regional In-Service Teachers' Institute was already making good business selling beautifully illustrated posters of the Romanov dynasty's family tree to teachers anxious to obtain the new materials.

In their newest Grade 8 textbook, *Istoriia Otechestva* (History of the Fatherland, fifth edition), of which 2.6 million copies were circulated, Russian 14 year-olds study maps and charts to learn about the glories of Russia's *two* former imperial dynasties, the Ruriks and the Romanovs, and the contributions made by each to the growth of Russia's territory. The text also devotes considerable space to Peter the Great and his major social and economic reforms (Rybakov & Preobrazhenski, 1993, pp. 218-220). Although the students learn that under Peter the Great the Tsar's rule became absolute, he is chiefly depicted in the text as a great builder of symbolic power. His invention, the design of the Imperial Coat of Arms, the now renowned two-headed eagle symbol, was resurrected after the demise of the familiar Soviet hammer and sickle in 1991, to head official Russian documents and adorn the new parliament house. Students also learn about Peter's great administrative and modernising contribution to Russia's strength as a European naval and military power. Description of his project of building St Petersburg significantly omits any reference to his use of the forced labour of tens of thousands of serfs, although modern Russians now readily recall the massive Stalinist projects of the 1930s and their reliance on the labour of political prisoners.

Reliance on this particular historical figure in the search for national identity had further developed by 1995 when the textbook treatment of Peter the Great developed to almost cult-fostering proportions. In the 1995 prescribed history textbook for Grade 10, *Istoriia Rossii: Konets xvii-xix vek* (History of the Fatherland: the seventeenth and eighteenth centuries, Part Two), Peter the Great's reforms are portrayed as so significant that they mark a watershed in Russian cultural history, providing a natural division of the nation's history into pre-Petrian and post-Petrian periods. The text notes that according to the views of a famous nineteenth-century Russian historian, Kliuchevski, 'the whole methodology of our history was based on the evaluation of the reforms of Peter the Great' while S.M. Soloviev, another major historian, characterised Peter as the 'revolutionary on the throne' and his changes as 'revolution from above' (Buganov & Zyrianov, 1995, p. 4).

Further inspiration for national consciousness and pride is sought among past heroes of Russian history. One textbook presented to the authors by the librarian of the secondary boys' sports school was titled *The Heroes and Anti-heroes of the Nation*, edited by V. Zabrodin (1992). It contained chapters on Alexander I, Nicholas II, Trotsky, Beria, Molotov and others. Given the nature of recent changes, we were curious to see which members of this very mixed gallery qualified for either title. Trotsky's changing status from that of hero of the 1918 war in the early years of the revolution, to outcast and pariah during the late 1920s and 1930s was now apparently restored to one of genuine revolutionary and leader of people. Nicholas II, represented by the communist regime as a cruel despot and in many Western assessments as a muddled victim of history, has been elevated in this text to the role of noble martyr. The Russian media at the same time gave considerable attention to the devotion paid to his memory by followers, who regularly bring flowers and pray at the site of his murder. The linking of the last Tsar with religion in the public mind was later confirmed when he was canonised by the Russian Orthodox Church. These representations were officially encouraged by the 'reforming' government in a bid to reinforce pre-communist traditions and the Tsar's patriarchal role in history.

A post-communist revival of the notion of Eurasianism (Paramonov, 1996, pp. 27-28), which stressed Russia's distinctive identity and mission as a nation leading the Turkic (neither Slavic nor European) peoples also resurfaces in this search for the sources of national identity. An example in the prescribed Grade 10 textbook, *Istoriia Rossii* (Sakharov & Buganov, 1995, p. 8) falls within this neo-Eurasionism. It appears in the all-important method-defining introductory chapter, where the 16 year-old readers learn that 'Russia is regarded as the only Eurasian country in the world'. What is perceived as Russia's distinctive mission in interpreting and translating between the cultures of East and West is also emphasised by the authors, who note that Russia is 'a distinctive world bridge where two global civilisations meet – Europe and Asia – and their active interaction is realised'. To ensure that this point is not missed by the readers, the 12 key questions at the end of the introductory chapter include question 10, which asks, 'Russia is a Eurasian nation. Explain what this means. What effects has this Eurasian identity had on Russia's history?' (Sakharov & Buganov, 1995, p. 14).

In the ongoing search for models of national identity, attempts are made to attach these somewhat unpromising sources of twentieth-century nationhood to newer ideas of democracy, human rights and citizenship. The reforming thrust from a totalising ideology to the pluralism and individualism of late twentieth century capitalism became the central goal of the change. As reform progressed, the intellectuals charged with rewriting the Russian school history curriculum ransacked Russia's rather troubled past for more convincing sources of Russian historical authenticity. They explored such diverse themes as 'race memory' and Jungian archetypes in attempts to account for Russia's ethnic tensions. The virtues of the Cossack's historical goal in protecting the nation's borders were also rediscovered, while the perceived traditional Russian peasant sense of 'collective consciousness' was seen as a possible source of pre-communist social solidarity.

The Function and Agenda of the Rewriting Process

When we consider the rewriting or reinventing of history, both in public representation and in the school curricula, Australian historian Richard

White's comment in relation to Australian attempts in the 1980s and 1990s to redefine that nation as belonging to Asia could apply equally as well to Russia's project:

> *When we look at ideas about national identity, we need to ask,*
> *not whether they are true or false but what their function is,*
> *whose creation they are, and whose interests they serve.*
> *(White, 1981, p. viii)*

In the task of rewriting Russia's history for use in public school education, there is also an important and powerful external factor at work. In the financially struggling Institutes of the Academies, and in state tertiary institutions, the receipt of Western funding or sponsorship has become the ultimate symbol of achievement for scholars (and one of job security for the recipients and their colleagues). The funding of research and publication projects by private organisations such as the Soros Foundation, which funded the preparation of new civics courses and textbooks, carry quite legitimate, even worthy, agendas from which both the Russians and the outside sponsor can benefit. While the details of such projects may be open to discussion between the funding organisation and the Russians selected to carry it out, the ultimate goals of the projects have been conceived within the framework of value systems which are external to Russia.

To some extent, the Czech writer Milan Simecka's complaint that 'we here on the Eastern border of the West will just have to go on dutifully playing our roles as the victims and outsiders of history' (Simecka, 1989, p. 161) describes the role assigned to the people of Russia by many of these projects and the materials they are required to produce. Excluded by their nation's turbulent and autocratic past from the Western historical narrative, defined by the notion of progress – a gradual development and evolution to the Rule of Law, stable transfer of political power, human rights and parliamentary democracy – the Russians are therefore doomed to play the role of the 'deprived' and 'outsiders' in this version of the historical story. As Zygmunt Baumann commented, 'History is narrated by the strong, historiography being the narrative of their victories and the verbal display of their material power' (Baumann, 1994, p. 22). Tatiana Tolstaya summarised the Russian position thus: 'in the Russian popular imagination ... the West, where the sun goes down, is the corridor to another world, a bewitched location ... The line that divides East from West is a magic site where people are transformed' (Tolstaya, 1992, p. 25).

Such considerations understandably are not foremost in the minds of the Russian scholars who compete eagerly for the projects, partly motivated as they are by their necessitous economic circumstances. The value placed on Western funds is so high in Russia that the source of the funds is often 'the pride of the connection'. The projects are questioned critically by some Russian intellectuals but defenders of outside funding for the rewriting of Russia's history, cultural values and national identity are quick to identify and discredit these critics as extremists and ultra-nationalists. In one such project on the theme of human rights known by the acronym TACIS [2], and funded by the Soros Foundation and the Council of Europe, 70 research teams competed for a grant to produce a large number of school textbooks, workbooks and teaching guides and to jointly conduct seminars for Russian teachers and academics. The successful team, who came from the Moscow Regional Institute for In-service Teacher Training, brought funds, jobs and considerable prestige and academic authority to their institute.

Michel Foucault's concept of the *regime of truth* stresses the close link between power and truth. He reminds us that:

> *truth is not outside power ... each society has its regime of truth ... the types of discourse which it accepts and makes function as true; the mechanisms and instances which enable one to distinguish false and true statements; the means by which each is sanctioned; the techniques and procedures accorded value in the acquisition of truth; the status of those who are charged with saying what counts as true. (Foucault, 1979, p. 46)*

Examples of History Lessons

On annual research visits to the USSR and Russia between 1989 and 1996, we observed many history and social studies lessons. In a rural *shkola-litsei* near Dmitrov, a town approximately 100 km from Moscow, the history teacher had set up group work to enable a more participatory and more empowering dialogue for the final year students' task of critically evaluating the Cold War. Issues discussed included Churchill's speech on communism and the role played by Bertrand Russell in the peace protests and anti-nuclear rallies. In debating the causes of the Cold War, the teacher introduced the concept of *paradoks istorii* (the paradox of history): We did not want the war, yet we have accelerated the development of the hydrogen bomb ...

The school principal and class teacher were careful to draw our attention to the teaching method to be chosen for the lesson. In a radical departure from the lecture-type lesson style of the classes of the communist regime, the history classroom had been arranged, not with the rows of desks facing the teacher but with four tables, with six students at each. All groups were engaged in spirited debate about the Cold War and vigorous and contentious analysis of various teacher-set questions on this once politically charged theme. The encouragement of discussion and debate, in which the teacher took part as she moved around the groups, contrasted strongly with the more authoritarian lecturing style of teaching in senior classes observed in earlier years, and was clearly perceived as a fundamental change by the teacher and school principal.

In the formal oral history examination at a Moscow school, Grade 10 students were required to draw a question from a box, and, after 15 minutes' silent preparation, be prepared to answer it, and then defend their argument during questioning by a panel of teachers. This traditional examination method was considered appropriate in the new teaching climate. In this school in 1994, in a Grade 11, final year history class, the teacher covered the 1990-91 period, characterised, according to her interpretation, by 'neo-conservative politics' (*neo-conservativnaia politika*), 'return to the market economy' (*vozvrat k rynochnoi ekonomiki*) and 'decline' (*spad*) in the economy. Students were confidently using sophisticated concepts and were actively engaged in comparative and contrastive analysis of Russia and the nations in Europe.

In another history lesson observed in a Grade 9 class in a select entry Moscow sports school for boys, the topic was the serfdom system in Russia from the seventeenth century to 1861. After a 15-minute discussion, during which students were able to suggest various solutions to the problem of serfdom, especially the impact of the 1861 Manifesto of Alexander II on Russia's economy, the teacher proposed a problem to be solved: ways of achieving the emancipation of the serfs. Students were encouraged to role-play the problems facing various characters of the era.

In the same school, a Grade 11 class had earlier been given a series of questions, with each class member being required to present a brief oral report on a chosen question. The four key questions on that day were as follows.

What is meant by the Stalinist model of socialism? Use primary sources to support your evaluation.
What made the leadership of socialist countries embark on economic and political reforms?
Compare and contrast revolutions of 1989 in these countries and determine their similarities and differences.
What are the causes of industrial growth and at whose expense do they occur? Analyse the development and modernity thesis.

The text was *Noveishaia Istoriia 1939-1992* (Furaev, 1993). The book is very critical of Stalin's autocratic rule and his role during the 1941 period and World War Two. The authors note that neither the People's Congress nor the Party ratified the Secret Pact with Germany. Nevertheless, the authors pay their dues to the *narod* (the people), and their heroic role in both turning the tide of the war in 1942 with the battle of Stalingrad and in saving the world from possible Nazi domination.

At a small village school in the Voskresensk Region, near Moscow, history is also integrated into music lessons, as was observed during a Grade 7 music session. We listened to Dimitri Shostakovich's Seventhth Symphony, dedicated by the composer to the Seige of Leningrad in 1941, for Soviets, and now Russians, a heroic struggle against fascism. Students were told that in those icy days and evenings the conservatorium still continued to operate and the composer produced his *chef d'oeuvre*, while outside fellow citizens climbed onto the roof to throw off the incendiary bombs as they landed in order to prevent fires.

The questions asked by the teacher included: 'What images came to your mind when you heard the crescendo?' Is it an image of good or evil?' 'At the end you can hear noise of approaching tanks, the violins are not playing but squeaking. Explain'. What is the reason for the slow, soft beginning? Is it because the fascists are coming from a great distance? How is an image of darkness conveyed by the sound of music?' 'Part IV of the symphony communicates the triumph of good over evil', suggested the teacher. The music lesson was also a moving history lesson, depicting a heroic landmark in the history of Soviet Russia, and now still to be relived by 14 year-old students in post-communist Russia.

The Post-communist History Narrative: evaluative comments

Russia now finds it imperative both to reflect a Western orientation of culture if it is to be accepted and receive assistance, and to foster cultural elements which are distinctly 'Russian' and unique to itself. A task of working for necessary compromise or adjustment between the two is an ongoing one and is far from complete. As one history teacher remarked to us in 1992:

> *We have changed our notions of history, the old Marxist-Leninist biased textbooks have been thrown out. A difficult stage begins. What kinds of philosophy of history can one create – a Christian one or one reflecting the idealistic perspectives of Soloviev or Berdiaev, the ideas of Jacobson, or the classical French tradition or European Western philosophy? As soon as the textbooks are published, the politics may change. There will be a need for yet another authorised version of history of Russia. (Interview with Y. Yamburg, then Principal of a Secondary School in Moscow)*

What is clearly reflected here is confusion over the loss of the Soviet grand narrative, or any grand narrative at all for that matter, as well as anxiety for the speaker's own security and political future in such an unstable climate, given that he was speaking immediately after the collapse of Communism. Against this anxiety of an individual history intellectual can be contrasted the tone of recently written school textbooks which accentuate pluralism, tolerance, patience and a romantic, quasi-humanistic perception of historical events. In the foreword of one history textbook, *Istoriia Otechestva*, used in Grades 10 and 11, we read:

> *We recommend that you consider the complex and*
> *contradictory past of the nation during its earlier decades.*
> *Today the events of those years have become the subject of*
> *sharp, at times angry disputes. In our history we have both the*
> *heroism and tragedy of the Soviet people, their hopes and*
> *disappointments ... We hope that you, having learned new*
> *facts and opinions, and either agreeing or disagreeing with us,*
> *will find it necessary to work out your own viewpoints. In this*
> *task other books, periodicals and newspapers, TV and radio*
> *will help you. Remember many of those who lived during*
> *those years and who have created history are still around you.*
> Ask them. *(Ostrovski, 1992)*

In this advanced organiser, the pupils are being introduced to the complexity of historical events, the notion of plurality of perspective and approaches, and to a recognition that history does not only consist of great events, famous men and women and received versions.

In the vision of the book's authors, the young students of history will conduct a project not unlike that of E.P. Thompson's, in rediscovering the 'agency' of Soviet-Russian working people and the 'degree to which they contributed by conscious efforts, to the making of history' (Thompson, 1968, p. 13). It is an attempt to reclaim the marginalised and silent voices of those who lived Soviet history during the contested historical narrative. They are to be 'rescued' from 'the enormous condescension' (Thompson, 1968, p. 13) of the Soviet perspective, which viewed individuals in terms of their roles as members of the proletariat, peasantry, nobility, bourgeoisie and intelligentsia, and history solely through the prism of class relations. In the foreword of a Grade 10 history textbook, *Istoriia Otechestva: 1900-1940*, the authors focus on a humanistic perspective of history, as well as stressing the importance of raising questions rather than finding the right answer:

> *We attempted to reflect history as a humanist science, through*
> *a subjective perspective. There's no need to be afraid of*
> *incorrect answers. It is more important to raise new questions.*
> *(Zharova & Mishina, 1992)*

Conclusion

Post-communist history textbooks appear to have the following three ideological symbols:

the symbols dealing with Russian national and cultural identity;
the symbols of reinterpreting the past; and
the symbols of transition to pluralist democracy and capitalism.

School history textbooks are critical of Stalinism and its legacies. They present highly critical and unfavourable narrative of the Soviet regime. The students are informed of the repressive nature of Stalinism and of the equally totalitarian years of Khrushchev and Brezhnev. However, the textbooks seem to ignore the new social inequality and development after 1991. In short, the textbooks bypass the most significant area in social history – the worsening social problems, crisis in education, health, and other spheres, both private and public.

The newly rewritten history textbooks, apart from introducing the students to a variety of perspectives, also undertake a moral and didactic function in appearing to prepare the new post-communist generation for the slow, painful and frustrating process of change which they are likely to encounter during the transformation of Russia to a market economy, with its demand for privatisation, deregulation and localisation (Zajda, 1999, p. 159). In the afterword in a Grade 8 textbook we read:

> *Many trials befell the fate of the people of our land ... foreign invasions, the insult of the foreign bondage, wars, years of famine and epidemics – they had to live through it all. But their spirit of the love of freedom, patriotism and aspiration for justice was never crushed. (Rybakov & Preobrazhenski, 1993, p. 273)*

Patriotism through future ordeals and problems seems to be the message of the text, which exhorts the students to understand that 'whatever the profession you have chosen, let an active interest in the history of the fatherland be forever with you' (p. 273).

One of the problems in the rewriting of post-communist history which incorporates a new national narrative is not only the ongoing shedding of the 70-year communist heritage and encouragement of acceptance of the Western-oriented perspective on democracy, human rights and the market economy, but also in trying to respond to the forces of globalisation and modernity (Zajda, 1999, p. 160). A historical-comparative research, involving pre-1917 Soviet and post-Soviet historiography may well reveal significant departures in dominant methodologies employed.

The reinterpretation of the Russian and Soviet past has become to some extent an ideological battlefield waged between various strata of the post-communist elite. Some portray the communist legacy as a tragedy never to be repeated; others treat the recent past more in terms of nostalgia for the days of glory when a strong super-state took pride in its military and economic security and moral purity.

An unresolved tension is found in the problem of achieving both a synthesis between the Western and Russian reform in the government-dictated quest for modernity and democracy and the imperative to define elements which are uniquely Russian and contribute to a new and authentic Russian national identity. As illustrated earlier, the source of 'Russianness' is usually sought in the pre-communist past, so that Russians find themselves in the paradoxical position of trying to embrace both tradition and postmodernity.

Given that the present Russian Parliament includes the representatives of the entire political spectrum, from ultra-nationalists and Stalinists to Western liberals, prospects for the future will depend on the outcomes of the socio-economic crisis and political struggles in today's Russia. At least three scenarios are possible: (1) a 'born-again' nationalist-communist takeover, (2) a continuation of Western-style economic and social reforms, or, finally, (3) a continuation of moderate reforms by a coalition of the competing elites.

Whichever way the pendulum swings, from a more radically pro-Western, pro-capitalist, and anti-communist ideology to ultra-nationalism, Russian students are likely to be exposed to contradictory ideological influences combining pro-Western and anti-Western paradigms of individualism and nationalism, within the local hybrid of postmodernist variants of 'dead certainties', 'boundless self' and 'safe simulations'.

Note

[1] The researchers visited Russia on seven occasions between 1989 and 1996 at the invitation of what are now the Russian Academy of Sciences, Institute of Sociology and the Russian Academy of Education. They were able to visit schools, initially in 1990 and 1991 with the intervention of the Academy of Education, and later by initiating their own contacts with schools. Some schools were revisited each year and the researchers were able to observe changes in teaching methods, textbooks and school ritual over this period of rapid transformation.

[2] TACIS – refers to the Technical Assistance programme to 13 countries of Eastern Europe and Central Asia (e.g. Russia, Ukraine, Uzbekistan, etc.).

References

Anderson, Benedict (1983) *Imagined Communities: reflections on the origin and spread of nationalism*. London: Verso.

Baumann, Zygmunt (1994) After the Patronage State: a model in search of class interests, in Christopher G.A. Bryant & Edmund Mokrzycki (Eds) *The New Great Transformation? Change and Continuity in East-Central Europe*. London: Routledge.

Foucault, Michel (1979) Truth and Power, in *Michel Foucault. Power, Truth, Strategy*, ed. by Meghan Morris & Paul Patton. Sydney: Feral Publications.

Krasnodebski, Zdzislaw (1991) *Waiting for the Supermarkets, or the Crisis of Communisim* [in Polish], VII All-Polish Congress of Sociology. Warsaw: PWN.

Paramonov, Boris M. (1996) Historical Culture, in Dimitri N. Shalin (Ed.) *Russian Culture at the Crossroads: paradoxes of postcommunist consciousness*. Boulder: Westview Press.

Simecka, Milan (1989) Another Civilization? An Other Civilization, in George Schopflin & Nancy Wood (Eds) *In Search of Central Europe*. Totowa, NJ: Barnes & Noble.

Thompson, E.P. (1968) *The Making of the English Working Class*. Harmondsworth: Penguin.

Tolstaya, Tatiana (1992) Tsar of All the Answers, *Guardian*, 25 June, p. 25.

Tumarkin, Nina (1983) *Lenin Lives! The Cult of Lenin in Soviet Russia*. Cambridge, MA: Harvard University Press.

White, Richard (1981) *Inventing Australia: images and identity 1688-1890*. Sydney: Allen & Unwin.

Zajda, Joseph (1999) Adult Education and Lifelong Learning: new developments in Russia, *Comparative Education*, 35, pp. 151-161.

Russian School History Textbooks

Buganov, V. & Zyrianov, P. (1995) *Istoriia Rossii* (History of Russia, Part Two). Moscow: Prosveshchenie.

Furaev, V. (1993) *Noveishaia Istoriia 1939-1992* (Modern History). Moscow: Prosveshehenic.

Ostrovski, V., Startsev, V., Starkov, B. & Sminov, G. (1992) *Istoriia Otechestva: 1939-1991* (History of the Fatherland). Moscow: Prosveshchenie.

Rybakov, B. & Preobrazhenski, A. (1993) *Istoriia Otechestva* (History of the Fatherland), 5th revised edn. Moscow: Prosveshchenie.

Sakharov, A. & Buganov, V. (1995) *Istoriia Rossii* (History of Russia. Part One). Moscow: Prosveshchenie.

Zabrodin, V. (Ed.) (1992) *Geroi i antigeroi Otechestva* (Heroes and Villains of the Fatherland). Moscow: Informekspress.

Zharova, L. & Mishina, I. (1992) *Istoriia Otechestva* (History of the Fatherland). Grade 10. Moscow: Prosveshchenie.

Not Quite the Revolution: citizenship education in England

CLIVE HARBER

Introduction

Historically, political education for democratic citizenship has been neglected in the English curriculum. The absence of revolution, defeat in war, or colonisation and independence has meant that, unlike most other countries, England has not been forced to confront the issue of preparing its citizens for a new political system. However, the lowering of the voting age to 18 in the late 1960s and the raising of the school leaving age to 16, plus the greater availability of politics and sociology graduates in schools, helped to create a situation where there was a growth in interest and provision in this area in the 1970s and 1980s (Harber, 1987). As discussion of political education developed in the 1980s, the two main political parties became increasingly divided in their attitudes, with the opposition Labour Party supportive of political education in schools and the governing Conservative Party steadily more hostile. In 1988, the Conservative Government introduced a national curriculum which would apply to all schools and which excluded any direct form of political education for democratic citizenship.

The return of a Labour government in 1997, however, led to a major change in policy. A key aspect of Labour Party policy was the modernisation and greater democratisation of British political institutions, and education was to play a part in this. The Secretary of State for Education, David Blunkett, established an Advisory Group on Citizenship chaired by Professor Bernard Crick. This supported the introduction of what it termed 'citizenship education' as a statutory part of the curriculum. This was to be composed of three strands – social and moral responsibility, community involvement and political literacy. The Crick report stated grandly and radically that:

> *We aim at no less than a change in the political culture of this*
> *country both nationally and locally: for people to think of*
> *themselves as active citizens, willing, able and equipped to*
> *have an influence in public life and with the critical capacities*
> *to weigh evidence before speaking and acting; to build on and*
> *extend radically to young people the best in traditions of*
> *community involvement and public service and to make them*
> *individually confident in finding new forms of involvement*
> *and action among themselves. (Advisory Group on*
> *Citizenship, 1998, p. 7)*

This chapter argues that this seems rather far-fetched in the present context of education in England. The chapter attempts to set out some major problems facing citizenship education, compulsory in secondary schools from 2002, that may well blunt its impact in terms of the major contribution to the democratisation of British political culture that the Crick report aspires to.

What's in a Name?

> *It also means teaching by stealth; keeping the dreaded*
> *citizenship word, with its pious overtones, off the agenda. Part*
> *of Blunkett's vision is of a syllabus that includes voluntary*
> *work in the community, a concept that goes down like wet sick*
> *with many teenagers. (Crace, 2000)*

Why is the new subject called 'citizenship education'? In the late 1970s and during the 1980s, before the introduction of the National Curriculum, the pressure was rather for 'political education', based on a model of political literacy (knowledge, skills and values) as part of a broader study of the social sciences. 'Education for citizenship' was seen as having dated, almost imperial, connotations of passivity, loyalty, obedience and nationalism rather than the critical spirit and proclivity to political action of a political literacy approach. As the Crick report rightly states, the term came back into use in 1990 with the report of the Commission on Citizenship appointed by the Speaker of the House of Commons. This document, as Crick also notes, emphasised 'active citizenship', by which it meant 'welfare being not just provision by the state but also what people can do for each other in voluntary groups and organisations'. Furthermore, the Crick report is puzzled at the failure of the Speaker's Commission to discuss more political notions of what it means to be a citizen (Advisory Group on Citizenship, 1998, p. 10). Perhaps such coyness is understandable given Kenneth Baker's presence on the Crick Advisory Group. Kenneth Baker was the Conservative Secretary of State for Education responsible for the National Curriculum, which deliberately excluded political education (and sociology and economics) from the school curriculum and which instead relegated 'citizenship education' to a cross-curricular theme.

However, as I wrote nearer the time:

> *Just after the introduction of the national curriculum in the Education Reform Act of 1988 talk began in government circles of the need for 'active citizenship', in particular from Douglas Hurd the then Home Secretary. This was then immediately linked to education for citizenship ... In the four years since there has been much discussion of education for citizenship but little clarity as to what it is. This is because different people mean different things when they use the phrase but ... evidence suggests that the general interpretation is very mush closer to the traditional, conservative 'civics' model than to a political literacy approach. Part of the reason for this lies in the origin of the debate. It is very clear from an article written at the time by the present Secretary of State for Education, John Patten, that what the government means by 'active citizenship' is getting individual citizens increasingly to take on jobs and roles via voluntary work and charities that have previously been done by (in their terms) the 'nanny' state. It is part of the right-wing ideology of the reduction of collective social provision and the privatisation of social and economic life. Education for active citizenship in the government's terms then is about motivating young people to be active in taking on the worthy and necessary tasks left undone by the welfare state. 'Active' in this sense means supporting things as they are and does not also mean critical and informed participation in democratic political debate and action. (Harber, 1992, p. 17)*

The naming of such an initiative is important because of the signals and implicit meanings it transmits to teachers. While the Crick report places equal emphasis on three strands of citizenship education – social and moral education, community involvement and service, and political literacy – the history and existing nature of citizenship education as a cross-curricular theme and the educational context into which it is being introduced (see below) suggests that the first two strands will be much more significant than the third.

Who Will Teach It?

The interpretation of citizenship education in practice will depend on who is teaching it. Here there are big problems. If citizenship education was at least partly to employ a critical social and political perspective examining the nature of the social structures that shape our lives – the economy, 'race', gender, power structures – it would require a conceptual analysis of society based on the social sciences. This would necessitate teachers with social science degrees and social science teacher education. Yet, since 1988, only graduates with a degree in a National Curriculum subject have been allowed to enter teacher training, which effectively barred social scientists from entering the profession. Many of those teachers with social science qualifications, never a large proportion in the first place, have left school teaching. Don Rowe of the Citizenship Foundation said, 'This is a significant issue which seems to weaken the whole capacity of schools to deliver a sound social education' (Barnard, 1998). In 1999, there were only six higher education institutions offering teacher training places in social science and one in sociology (Davies et al, 1999, p. 112). Moreover, few posts in citizenship education have yet been advertised in Schools of Education in higher education, which suggests that they have not yet begun to take new initiatives in this area of initial teacher training to any significant extent. This may be because they are not convinced about the market for the subject, because the low level of funding for initial teacher education in higher education does not encourage enterprise and risk taking or because there is no guarantee that citizenship education will survive the return of another Conservative Government.

There are also problems with the processes of teacher education. If teacher education is to prepare teachers for teaching education for democratic citizenship, then it must provide student teachers with congruent experience of operating democratically, of having some say over the content and nature of their course. This is precisely what happened on one teacher education course for social science teachers in the 1980s, which began with a discussion of a number of possible ways in which the course could be run, all involving students in decision-making to some extent. However, one option which many groups chose was what was termed a 'democratic learning cooperative' where students decided completely on the curriculum of the course, when chosen topics would be covered, how and by whom (Harber & Meighan, 1986). However, the advent of much greater centralised control over teacher education through the Teacher Training Agency and the Office for Standards in Education (OFSTED: government inspectors) would make such an approach much more difficult now. Discussing the democratically organised course just described, for example, some writers have recently commented that:

> In today's climate, such radical action would be accepted only in certain modified ways. Nevertheless, some way forward must be found if we are to escape the negative mechanistic managerialism that characterises at least some of the current practice in teacher education. (Davies et al, 1999, p. 114)

In the same way that there are conflicts between the processes and practices necessary for education for democratic citizenship and the wider context of the National Curriculum in schools, so there are conflicts between the processes necessary to educate teachers of citizenship and the current centrally controlled context of teacher education.

What about existing teachers? A recent national survey of 679 teachers found that citizenship education 'barely figures as a curricular concern'. The teachers had a depoliticised or apolitical view of citizenship and overwhelmingly saw citizenship as about meeting our obligations to fellow members of a community. It was perceived as being about active concern for the welfare of others:

> *Time and time again the language of caring, unselfishness, co-operation and demonstrating respect is used to give substance to the distinguishing characteristics of a good citizen, be the context school or the wider community ... it is perhaps not surprising that the notion of participation in the community emerged as a key theme on how one discharged the responsibilities of being a good citizen. (Davies et al, 1999, pp. 50-51)*

The teachers were reluctant to get involved in teaching about controversial views and one of the most common ways that teachers thought schools could promote good citizenship was by encouraging pupils to pick up litter, though obeying school rules, coming to class on time and taking pride in your school were also seen as important. The teachers put far more emphasis on the first two legs of Crick's citizenship stool – social and moral education and community involvement – than the third leg of political literacy and were reluctant to get involved with this approach. This indicates both the likely nature of citizenship education after 2002 and the scale of professional development required if it is to be more than a rather pious and conservative exhortation to be good and help others.

Furthermore, this situation will not be helped by the Government's continuing reluctance to make sure that, despite continuing opposition from the House of Lords, Clause 28 of the 1988 Local Government Act is repealed. This legislation forbade the 'promotion' of homosexuality by local authorities. As a recent leader in the *Observer* newspaper noted:

> *It was designed solely to stigmatise one group of people on the entirely bogus basis that homosexuality can be 'promoted' in the first place. Thousands of teachers, as well as many children's charities have complained that the environment fostered by Section 28 inhibits them from challenging homophobic bullying in schools. (3 December 2000)*

Clause 28 is in complete contradiction to the stated aims of citizenship education for democracy and human rights. Moreover, given the unpredictability of open discussion, teachers will be even more reluctant to handle controversial human rights issues in the classroom until this piece of legislation is removed from the statute book.

The National Curriculum

I think in terms of experiential learning and wonder how pupils are expected to grasp the ideas of democracy and citizenship when they have been trapped in a totalitarian educational system which does not recognise their right to choose what they learn or how they learn it. Isn't the whole of their schooling a lesson in living under a dictatorship? (Clarke, 2000)

Putting citizenship education in the curriculum is aimed at educating democratic citizens. Indeed, the Qualifications and Curriculum Authority (QCA) guidelines on personal, social and health education and citizenship for Key Stages 1 and 2 note the importance of developing independence and responsibility (QCA, 2000a, p. 5). Yet, these aims are contradicted by pupils' experience of the National Curriculum as a whole where subjects, subject content and reading are centrally prescribed and routinely tested and where pupils for the majority of the time have very little opportunity to exercise independent choice or take responsibility for their own learning. Paradoxically, even compulsory citizenship education itself is the result of government fiat.

If citizenship education is about more than being preached at about democracy, then pupils must learn how to behave democratically through experience of democracy. This must involve young people having some control over their lives at school, which includes some say over what they learn, when and how. At the moment, the National Curriculum makes this very difficult by providing exactly the opposite experience, that of authoritarian imposition. A recent study of the actual operation of the National Curriculum over a 5-year period involving 7000 pupils, 250 teachers and the observation of lessons in 97 primary, secondary and tertiary educational institutions concluded that:

the National Curriculum, in operation, enforced a limited course restricted to the rote-learning of subject-specific knowledge so that pupils may perform well in written tests of memory. It is my contention that this knowledge-based, assessment driven curriculum demands didactic drill-training to ensure examination success; and that such a pedagogy suppresses the development of a critical disposition, so that the school leaver becomes a passive serf or discontented

> outlaw rather that an emancipated citizen or productive
> worker. (Griffith, 2000, p. xvii)

However, the National Curriculum is also problematic in another way. How seriously will schools take citizenship education anyway and how much priority will it be given in a context where schools are judged on exam results and their consequent places in league tables? Will the pressure on the timetable created by other national curriculum subjects, the lack of league table ranking points for citizenship plus lack of teacher expertise and enthusiasm mean that many schools will subvert citizenship education through such means as 'citizenship days' of intensive community involvement or extra history lessons?

Personal, Social and Health Education

Though the Crick report warns against simply conflating citizenship education with PSHE (personal, social and health education), it does accept that there is considerable overlap and the QCA has provided joint guidelines for Key Stages 1 and 2. In practice, given the already crowded timetable and lack of space for a new subject plus existing teacher dispositions and experience, as discussed earlier, it is likely that citizenship will often be taught through the PSHE slot. Here the problem is with the word *personal*.

In PSHE, the emphasis is on the individual and what s/he needs to survive and prosper in contemporary society and preferably not become a problem for the state. Topics dealt with, for example, might include drugs, nutrition, road safety, sex, careers, the environment, emotional literacy/feelings, personal finance and parenthood. Whilst these are important and relevant topics, there is a danger that the emphasis on the personal and the individual will mean that structural issues are played down or ignored. It is important that pupils are also encouraged to utilise a wider perspective to develop critical awareness of the social structures and forces – gender, 'race', social and economic inequality, ideology – that shape individual behaviour as well as the personal skills needed to function socially. To exemplify the difference in approach, while in PSHE health education might stress nutrition, sex education and hygiene, a social scientist would want to look at evidence on the social distribution of illness (e.g. by social class), the relationship between illness and other social structures such as housing and patterns of state and private health provision.

There is a need to combine the critical analysis of social science with the practical, individual-oriented approach of PSHE. If both approaches are not used, there is a danger that education for citizenship will be little more than a descriptive and prescriptive preparation for existing society. It is unlikely to be the exercise in democratic learning permitted by social science in the sense of an examination of a range of alternative ideas, policies and structures which helps to open pupils' minds and allows them to choose for themselves.

Democratic School Structures

Delivering a talk to 100 educationalists at the British Library, Emma, 15, and James, 16, seized control by asking the audience to stand. Distinguished delegates were then asked to sit down if their hair grew over their collar, if they wore ostentatious jewellery, or if their clothes were unacceptable in the youngsters' eyes. In the end, only a few were left standing. This emphasised, said Emma and James, how frustrating it can be when school rules are simply imposed on young people. To the amusement of the audience, one of those who reputedly fell foul of the teenagers' rules was none other than Professor Bernard Crick – former tutor of Education Secretary David Blunkett and the man who has led calls for compulsory citizenship lessons. He had to sit down because his phone was switched on. Emma and James, who both attend schools in Northumberland, were speaking on behalf of the organisation Article 12. It campaigns for recognition of Article 12 of the UN Convention on Children's Rights. This calls for authorities to take the views of children into account when taking decisions that affect them. (Mansell, 2000)

While the journalist actually got some of the details of this story wrong – Bernard Crick was asked to sit down because he didn't believe that a study of human rights was compulsory in schools – the key point remains valid. If pupils are to be educated for democratic citizenship, then they must experience it in their daily lives, not just be told about it. This means that pupils must have some role in the decision-making structures of the school. Arguably, experience in elective and decision-making procedures is the most direct and important form of education for democratic citizenship in terms of a first-hand way of learning democratic skills and values and a democratic political vocabulary. The Crick report recognised this:

There is increasing recognition that the ethos, organisation, structures and daily practices of schools, including whole school activities and assemblies, have a significant impact on the effectiveness of citizenship education.

However, although the Advisory Group considered making school councils compulsory, they rejected the idea 'for fear of overburdening schools and teachers'. Instead, they aimed to 'plant a seed that will grow' (Advisory Group on Citizenship, 1998, pp. 36, 25-26).

While there seems to be some evidence that interest in school councils is increasing and that around 50% of secondary schools and 25% of primary schools already have a council, the author of the article that provides these figures also notes that:

Somehow the idea of school councils seems oddly out of step with the flavour of education in Britain today. We're all aware of the current of authoritarianism at the heart of the government's reforms: sitting in rows and getting back to basics on the three Rs doesn't seem to fit with giving youngsters the right to speak out about things, still less to actually change them. (Moorhead, 2000)

The Government seems to be giving out mixed messages about democratic decision-making in schools. Summerhill School in Suffolk is perhaps the best known democratically run school in the United Kingdom and possibly in the world. In 1999, David Blunkett issued a notice of complaint threatening the school with closure after Summerhill had received a critical inspection report from OFSTED. The major issue was that OFSTED inspectors had used criteria they normally used when inspecting state schools and had therefore ignored the democratic philosophy and goals of the school. Although the Department for Education and Employment finally withdrew its complaints just before the case went to court, it was a salutary reminder to all other schools subject to OFSTED inspection that it is dangerous to take the practice of democratic education too seriously. Given that democratising an existing school, as opposed to setting up a new school on democratic lines, is a difficult and complex process (Trafford, 1997), the attempted persecution of Summerhill does little to encourage schools to set out on this path.

At present, as Davies demonstrates in her chapter in this book, British schools and educational authorities have got a very long way to go before they take education for democratic citizenship anything like as seriously as other European nations, such as Denmark, Germany, Holland and Sweden.

Racism

Racism is a significant and ugly aspect of Britain culture. The Macpherson report on the Stephen Lawrence Inquiry (1999) was a clear reminder that racism is currently embedded in British society and institutions and that it is the opposite of, and a threat to, democracy. Surveys regularly reveal the extent of the problem. In a survey carried out just after the Macpherson report, more than 80% thought there was 'some' or 'a lot' of racial prejudice in the United Kingdom (Johnston, 1999). In a survey carried out by the European Commission, one-third of Britons said that they were either 'very racist' or 'quite racist' while another third said they were a 'little racist' (Dutter, 1997). Racism also affects young people. Childline, a national children's support group, did a study of 1600 callers to their trauma lines and concluded that 'blatant, unrelenting racist harassment and bullying plays a large part in the daily experience of many black and ethnic children at our schools and in our streets'. A similar study 10 years before had found the same results (Trench, 1996). The European Youth Survey carried out for the satellite music channel, MTV, suggested that although racism was a problem with youth in other European countries, British youth were by far the most racist. Almost 30%, for example, disagreed that all races are equal and 26% said that they would never consider dating someone of a different colour (*Guardian Weekly*, 16 December 1997).

There is considerable evidence of racism in the education system generally (Osler, 2000a) and worrying evidence of racism amongst teachers and student teachers. In a survey of over 20,000 teachers carried out by the Commission for Racial Equality (Ranger, 1988), nearly two-thirds of white teachers and 81% of ethnic minority teachers thought there was racial discrimination in schools generally. A recent survey of 400 postgraduate students broadly representative of initial teacher education students generally suggested that up to one in 10 had racist attitudes and others complained of ideas such as anti-racism or anti-sexism being 'shoved down their throats'. Cynicism about politics was widespread. A quarter believed tension was inevitable when different races lived together. A fifth thought black people did not do enough to embrace British culture and more than a third believed positive discrimination had gone too far. The author of the report, Chris Wilkins of the University of Reading, warned that unless initial teacher education courses helped students to understand concepts like social justice, attempts to introduce citizenship education would fail to make an impact (Barnard, 1999).

Indeed, the Crick report itself has been subject to considerable criticism in regard to its failure to even mention racism and the assimilationist, patronising and somewhat colonial use of language (Osler, 2000b). However, the QCA's initial guidance for schools for citizenship at Key Stages 3 and 4 (QCA, 2000b) is an improvement on the initial Crick report, making reference, for example, to the need for schools to consider local issues 'such as particular manifestations of racism and its removal' and among key concepts to be studied, 'human rights (including anti-racism)' – though the parallel guidelines on PSHE are quiet on the need for anti-racism (QCA, 2000c).

Concern with anti-racism is a relatively new phenomenon in Britain, with many books on the subject not appearing until the mid-1980s. Moreover, this has always been a highly contested and controversial terrain. As Osler argues, while there are teachers, teacher organisations and local authorities that have promoted anti-racist education, such initiatives have been consistently attacked by the political right and its allies in the press:

> *The political right attacked anti-racism in education and presented it at one level as a distraction from what was emphasised as central, the acquisition of basic skills, and at another as a dangerous tendency which would not only undermine 'standards' but which would threaten British values and undermine British culture. (Osler, 1997, p. 22)*

Yet, if citizenship education is to be aimed at genuinely democratic citizens and society then it must explicitly confront racism in the school and the classroom. At the moment, the nature of the National Curriculum, the legacy of nearly two decades of right-wing political hegemony, the nature of initial teacher training, the shortage of teachers trained in the social sciences and teaching controversial issues, and the lack of emphasis on racism and anti-racism in QCA guidelines for the most likely curriculum slot for citizenship (PSHE) suggest that this key area will not receive the overt prominence it should have.

Assessment

Assessment is important in any curriculum area as teachers tend to start with what is going to be assessed and work backwards – teaching methods are heavily influenced by types of assessment. The QCA guidelines on citizenship at Key Stages 3 and 4 stress that 'assessment in citizenship should not imply that pupils are failing as citizens'. David Brockington, who is Chair of the citizenship education subgroup on assessment, agrees and argues that assessment in citizenship:

> *must allow individual pupils to be judged in relation to their own progress, rather than by an externally-imposed national standard. Technically, a system which is individualised rather than norm or criterion-referenced. (Brockington, 2000)*

The QCA guidelines duly state that:

> *Teachers will need to keep a record of pupils' progress and results of assessment, for example, through pupil profiles, record sheets or portfolios, to provide evidence of progress towards the attainment target. Pupils should be encouraged to review and record their own progress, and develop other skills in managing their learning through use of the national record of achievement and progress file. (QCA, 2000b, p. 25)*

While this is something to be supported in principle, the problem is that it is hard to reconcile it with the type of assessment required for the rest of the National Curriculum and it would not be surprising if students and teachers attached little importance to citizenship-style assessment unless major reform of National Curriculum assessment is forthcoming:

> *Even though its advocates swear blind that citizenship is*
> *about the practicalities of life, the only practicalities that*
> *many schools are interested in are GCSE results. And although*
> *Blunkett has said that citizenship teaching will be assessed –*
> *though there are no details at present – unless a last-minute*
> *rabbit is to be produced out of the hat, there are going to be no*
> *league table ranking points at stake. (Crace, 2000)*

The Crick report and the QCA guidelines put considerable emphasis on participation in voluntary groups in the community as a key aspect of citizenship education, and Brockington (2000) stresses the importance of assessing the process of community activity in citizenship education. However, in practice, in British society, with its attendant popular press and its market-driven school league tables, this could involve schools in some difficult choices. If community participation is important and the right to choose is a significant aspect of democracy, what happens when a pupil or pupils choose to volunteer to work for a local gay rights organisation? Or a 'legalise cannabis' organisation? Or an anti-immigration group? All perfectly legal organisations but likely to bring bad publicity for a school with potentially negative effects on pupil recruitment. Perhaps pupils interested in community involvement will fast learn the limits of freedom in a democracy.

What Happens if the Conservatives are Returned to Power?

A major problem with education for democratic citizenship in Britain is that, as argued in the introduction, it is the subject of serious party political division. The present initiative is occurring very much because there is a Labour Government in power. The Conservative Party Government of 1979-97 was consistently hostile to the social sciences and political education in schools. From the mid-1980s, publications emanating from right-wing groups close to the Conservatives sought to minimise informed discussion of politics by young people by repeatedly attacking the whole idea of schools being involved in political education (Scruton et al, 1985; O'Keeffe, 1986). One right-wing group, for example, the Campaign for Real Education, opposed the teaching of sociology, politics, peace studies, world studies and political education, was critical of anti-racism and anti-sexism and claims to have been influential in the framing of the National Curriculum (Hempel, 1988). While this may well have some truth in it, the Secretary of State for Education who introduced the National Curriculum, Kenneth Baker, claims that a key influence was Mrs Thatcher's hairdresser:

*On the curriculum she did have views, which as far as I could
see came from her hairdresser or it may have been her cleaner
who lived in [the left-wing run London borough of] Lambeth,
who was worried that her children were going to be educated
by a lot of Trots ... She believed basically that all one needed
in the national curriculum were English, mathematics and
science. (Sunday Tribune, Durban, 2 June 1996)*

The Conservative Party has always been unenthusiastic about a
genuinely open and realistic political education that uses evidence and
encourages young people to make up their own minds for the simple
reason that this has been perceived as a potential threat to their 'natural'
(and historically empirical) hegemony in the political system. If schools
do not openly and democratically tackle social and political ideas, then
they serve to reproduce the existing dominant values of the surrounding
society and political culture, which the Conservative Party has seen as
primarily favouring itself. It is not, therefore, surprising that the National
Curriculum introduced in 1988 deliberately excluded social and political
education. Schools and teacher education institutions will rightly now
be cautious about wholeheartedly investing time, money and personnel
in citizenship education as set out in the Crick report if there is even a
possibility that the Conservative Party will be returned to office. Michael
Portillo's (until 2001 shadow Chancellor of the Exchequer) statement in
January 1997 (supported by the Prime Minister, John Major) calling for
cadet corps to operate in all schools because military discipline and good
citizenship go hand in hand (Nahra, 1997) is a salutary reminder of times
not so past.

Conclusion

At the moment, citizenship education looks like the seed that did not fall
on fertile ground. The main problem is that it is being introduced into an
education system that is currently undemocratic and does not have
anything like the congruent structures, procedures, values, assessment
and staffing required to make it a significant contribution to changing
British political culture. If it is to survive and succeed, it will need long-
term political commitment and resourcing, which is by no means certain
or secure. It is just possible that the contradictions it might help to reveal
will eventually contribute towards the demise of present, wider,
regressive educational policies. But I won't hold my breath while I wait
to see.

References

Advisory Group on Citizenship (1998) *Education for Citizenship and the Teaching of Democracy in Schools* (The Crick Report). London: Qualifications and Curriculum Authority.

Barnard, N. (1998) Missing Sociologists Threaten Reform, *Times Educational Supplement*, 20 February, p. 14.

Barnard, N. (1999) One in Ten Trainees Has Racist Attitude, *Times Educational Supplement*, 16 April, p. 24.

Brockington, D. (2000) Citizens Are Hard to Judge, *Times Educational Supplement*, 28 April, p. 22.

Clarke, F. (2000) Democracy Has to Be Lived to Be Learned, *Times Educational Supplement*, 20 October, p. 15.

Crace, J. (2000) The New Citizens, *Guardian*, 15 February, p. 2.

Davies, I., Gregory, I. & Riley, S. (1999) *Good Citizenship and Educational Provision*. London: Falmer Press.

Dutter, B. (1997) One Third of Britons Admit to Racism and Xenophobia, *Weekly Telegraph*, 24-30 December, p. 19.

Griffith, R. (2000) *National Curriculum: national disaster*. London: Routledge Falmer.

Harber, C. (Ed.) (1987) *Political Education in Britain*. London: Falmer Press.

Harber, C. (1992) *Democratic Learning and Learning Democracy*. Ticknall: Education Now.

Harber, C. & Meighan, R. (1986) Democratic Methods in Teacher Training for Political Education, *Teaching Politics*, 15, pp. 179-187.

Hempel, S. (1988) The Real Consumer Backlash, *Times Educational Supplement*, 29 July.

Johnston, P. (1999) Eight in Ten Say UK Has Racism Problem, *Weekly Telegraph*, 10-16 March, p. 15.

Macpherson, W. (1999) *The Stephen Lawrence Inquiry*. London: Stationery Office.

Mansell, W. (2000) Pupils Discipline Professor, *Times Educational Supplement*, 28 April, p. 20.

Moorhead, J. (2000) Kids Rule, *Times Educational Supplement*, 24 October, p. 7.

Nahra, C. (1997) Citizenship is Not Just Cricket, Teachers Warn, *Times Higher Education Supplement*, 31 January, p. 12.

O'Keeffe, D. (Ed.) (1986) *The Wayward Curriculum*. London: Social Affairs Unit.

Osler, A. (1997) *The Education and Careers of Black Teachers*. Buckingham: Open University Press.

Osler, A. (2000a) Citizenship, Human Rights and Cultural Diversity, in A. Osler (Ed.) *Citizenship and Democracy in Schools*. Stoke-on-Trent: Trentham Books.

Osler, A. (2000b) The Crick Report: difference, equality and racial justice, *The Curriculum Journal*, 11, pp. 25-37.

Qualifications and Curriculum Authority (QCA) (2000a) *Personal, Social and Health Education and Citizenship at Key Stages 1 and 2: initial guidance for schools.* London: QCA.

Qualifications and Curriculum Authority (QCA) (2000b) *Citizenship at Key Stages 3 and 4: initial guidance for schools.* London: QCA.

Qualifications and Curriculum Authority (QCA) (2000c) *Personal, Social and Health Education at Key Stages 3 and 4: initial guidance for schools.* London: QCA.

Ranger, C. (1988) *Ethnic Minority School Teachers: a survey of eight local education authorities.* London: Commission for Racial Equality.

Scruton, R., Ellis-Jones, A. & O'Keeffe, D. (1985) *Education and Indoctrination.* Harrow: Education Research Centre.

Trafford, B. (1997) *Participation, Power-Sharing and School Improvement.* Nottingham: Educational Heretics Press.

Trench, A. (1998) Britain's Dirty Little Secret, *Sunday Times*, 29 March, p. 18.

Values and Citizenship: cross-cultural challenges for school and society in the Asian Pacific Rim

ELWYN THOMAS

Introduction

In company with many countries around the world, nations of the Asia-Pacific region have seen quite a remarkable revival in citizenship education, often referred to as Civic Education (Advisory Group on Citizenship [AGC], 1998; Torney-Purta et al, 1999; Print, 2000). The main thrust in this part of the world is one of getting students involved and informed about civic education as a means of engendering democratic citizenship and the awareness of a civil and humanitarian society, which is rapidly becoming part of a global culture. The search for a set of so-called civic values has been at the cutting edge of much of the work carried out by several countries in the region, with the purpose of eventually enriching the school and college curriculum. There has been a growing consensus since the late 1980s, especially amongst the Asian members of the Pacific Rim, such as Singapore, Japan, Malaysia and Indonesia, to re-examine the whole field of values education, as part of curriculum development (Thomas, 1996, 1997). This consensus was strengthened further in the 1990s, in response to the need to institutionalise some form of citizenship education which reflects democratic principles and civic values, and which could be an essential part of schooling (Huntington, 1997; Montgomery, 1997; Cogan & Derricott, 1998).

This chapter will be limited to examining the place of cultural values in citizenship education, and it will be argued that a meaningful and worthwhile strategy for citizenship education would be enhanced by a cross-cultural analysis of the values that may be included in programmes that aim to promote citizenship in schools and the wider community. The chapter will fall into three parts. The first part will examine the nature of cultural values within the context of citizenship, from a comparative perspective; the second part will analyse some key cross-cultural dimensions with reference to the inclusion of values as part of citizenship education; and the third part will provide a background to the intercultural role of educators, in the light of the cross-cultural analysis presented in the earlier parts of the chapter. In the analysis which follows, I will draw on my experience of researching values education in several countries of the Asian Pacific Rim as a teacher educator. The terms citizenship education and civics education are used interchangeably.

Cultural Values and Citizenship
Education in Comparative Perspective

Values are not only the basis of everyday existence, giving guidance and direction to our lives, but they are one of the key elements in the process of education and schooling. The place of values and values education is central to the development of democratic societies, and education has a key role to play in this development. Putnam (1995) and Montgomery (1998) have argued that values play a particularly crucial role in the development of 'social capital', which provides the potential and possibly the driving force behind the notion of a democratic society.

Values are perceived by social psychologists as a central core construct, which relates to moral concepts, and to specific attitudes, as peripheral elements. Cummings (1997) sees values as being general, enduring, abstract and procedural, the latter including such notions as the common good, power, affection and rectitude. The work of Schwartz (1994), who carried out cross-cultural research on values, emphasised the guiding nature of values. I have also examined the potential of researching values cross-culturally (Thomas, 2000a).

Education plays a key role in the transmission of values (Cheng, 1997; Thomas, 1997) and so it would follow that citizenship education, which would include political, cultural and moral values within its brief, could play a significant part in the acquisition and underpinning of a sense of civic values and democratic principles, so essential in the future development of a nation's citizenry. Therefore, educators have a responsibility to lay the foundations of democratic citizenship during the years of schooling, which can act as a catalyst for its further development, so that when students enter adulthood and the world of work, they will be able to build a society from a basis of shared values. There have been several attempts at analysing values related to citizenship education. The work of Allport et al, (1960) developed a values categorisation which delineated economic, aesthetic, social, political and religious forms. Marshall (1973) distinguished between civil, political and social components to citizenship. There have been at least two key international studies related to the place of values in civics and citizenship education, namely the Citizenship Education Policy Study of Cogan & Derricott (1998), and the work of Torney-Purta et al (1999), who conducted the International Association for the Evaluation of Educational Achievement (IEA) study on civic education across 24 countries.

A study reported by Print (2000) identified and compared civic-related policies, and the civic value statements within the policies, as expressed by a number of governments in the Asia-Pacific Region. The study was conducted in Australia, the USA, Thailand, Taiwan, Japan and Hong Kong, and addressed particularly how values were translated at the classroom level through civics education. It was found that Asian members appear to emphasise the need for developing the 'good person' linked to the 'good of the state'. In contrast, non-Asian countries emphasised human rights, democratic values and the historical background to their constitutional development. These different approaches in the way values are linked to citizenship will be examined cross-culturally below.

Cross-cultural Dimensions to Citizenship Education

Two key cross-cultural dimensions pervade both the theory and practice of cross-cultural psychological research, and have an important bearing on a cultural values component of citizenship education. The two dimensions include *individualism-collectivism* (I-C), and *universalism-relativism* (U-R). Before we examine each dimension, it would be useful to clarify briefly the polar nature of cross-cultural dimensions. The I-C and U-R dimensions are polarities that reflect substantive cross-cultural behavioural research that has been conducted in many parts of the world over the past few decades. The view of the author is that polarities provide useful benchmarks in analysing cross-cultural behaviour. However, one should always be mindful that context plays a key role in the way cross-cultural behavioural specificities or commonalities are manifested, and what value, if any, they may have for an effective cross-cultural analysis. For instance, in strong collectivist cultures such as Malaysia and Thailand, when it comes to pupil performance in examinations, strong individualistic patterns of behaviour come to the surface as part of individual achievement reflecting contextual fluidity. Let us now turn to both cross-cultural dimensions.

The Pervasive Nature of Individualism-Collectivism: a dilemma for citizenship education

To understand culture and cultural differences, writers such as Bhawuk & Brislin (1992), Hofstede (1980) and Hui (1990) have cited the distinction between individualism and collectivism as being amongst the most important concepts in interpreting interactions during intercultural encounters. The distinction between the two concepts is based upon the different goal priorities which a person wishes to pursue. As far as individualistic societies are concerned, e.g. the USA, Canada, the United Kingdom, most persons have been brought up to put themselves and their ambition before anything else. Generally, group goals are of a lower order of priority than those of the individual. In collective societies, e.g. Malaysia, Zimbabwe, individual goals are less important than that of the group, and great value is put on conforming and honouring group norms, before self-interest. The seminal work of Hofstede (1980) provided a view of culture which consisted of five categories, of which individualism-collectivism was a key category. The other categories included power-distance, uncertainty-avoidance, masculinity-femininity and Confucian dynamics.

Trompenaars (1993) also included within his seven categories of culture individualism-collectivism. More recently, Kagitcibasi (1997) has pointed out that the most important distinction between individualism and collectivism is the emphasis which is placed on the feeling and opinions of group members, and the 'psychological closeness' between a person and others. In collectivist societies generally, there is more concern about how decisions made by one member of a group will affect others. On the other hand, decision taking for individualists is much more of a personal affair and, apart from immediate family and close friends (in some circumstances), they are not worried about if and how decisions will affect others.

A key factor in trying to understand the nature of citizenship in a collective society is that persons will tend to treat the society as a collective, in the same way as the nature of the home is regarded as a collective culture. This is the accepted collectivist notion of society in countries like China and Japan, and is in stark contrast to the individualist's position, who pursues his or her own goals, and makes decisions as far as *possible*, independent of a group, institution and the wider society.

Sharing of knowledge, skills and materials, and a strong measure of conformity are typical collectivist characteristics. However, a sharing of rewards on an equity basis (i.e. rewards distributed on the basis of a person's contribution) is more favoured by individualists. On the other hand, equality of rewards (i.e. all persons receive the same) is more common amongst collectivist cultures. Meeting the goals of a programme of citizenship education that ranks society and the good of the nation as a high priority is much more likely to concur with a collectivist culture.

In institutions like the school, office or factory, the collective will tends to come before the wishes of the individual. A collectivist culture will also possess a 'psychological closeness' which plays a key role in family and in work. In collectivist societies, institutional or organisational culture is often a natural extension of the home collectivist culture. The strong familial ties of persons from collectivist societies, labelled *familism,* transfer naturally across into the group, as shown by research carried out in India by Sinha (1994) and in Uruguay by Negandhi (1984). However, group affiliations tend to be strongly based on obligation between group members and a dominance of group decision-making, leaving little opportunity for any form of individualism. Therefore, these features play a significant role when it comes to examining citizenship education in societies that are more collectivist. For instance, notions like national identity, social cohesion and societal cooperation are amongst the most common subjects of civics programmes in countries like Taiwan and Singapore.

In a close examination of the Singapore Civics and Moral Education programme (CME), there is a preponderance of modules which emphasise the importance of collectivism. Modules such as Belonging Together, Loving my Family, Building Bonds and to some extent Unity in Diversity reflect the collectivist emphasis of Singapore's civics education. The remaining two modules on The Growing Me and Becoming a Better Citizen give opportunities for secondary school students to express a certain degree of individualism, although it seems that individualism is mostly relegated to citizenship training in the latter module. The whole CME programme is an eclectic mix of moral values and citizenship training, and the more recent National Education (NE) launched in 1997 by the Prime Minister, Goh Chok Tong, puts an even greater emphasis on nationhood rather than individualistic features such as democratic freedom and rights of the individual.

Chew (1998) discusses the impact of the CME on schools, and it seems that while individualism is played down in most of the modules, the key collectivist message of national belonging is not getting through either, as a survey of school students and teachers revealed. It was found that CME ranked below academic and assessment goals in schooling. This indicates that with all the emphasis on a CME programme, with its strong collectivist orientation, individualism and self-improvement, manifested through the very competitive examination system, is clearly a formidable factor to be reckoned with. It is clear that there is an imbalance between collectivist and individualistic goals, which, according to Chew, 'poses a most severe challenge for any values programme in Singapore'. It seems that collectivism is actually getting in the way, as there are too many stakeholders and participants who influence classroom decision-making. There is an insufficient emphasis on how students and teachers as individuals can interpret for themselves the cultural values which are part of the civics programme.

More recently, the notion of 'active citizenship' is currently being debated in Singapore as part of the the Singapore 21 report. This is a vision of the Republic in the twenty-first century. This report, with its five key ideas (*Every Singaporean matters, Strong families, Opportunities for all, The Singapore heartbeat, and Active citizens*), is seen to act as a compass for the new millennium. If these ideas were to be implemented as part of a future civics programme, it would show that a collectivist stance would be maintained by the Singapore Government, in spite of what surveys of secondary school students reveal.

Han (2000), in her discussion of the 21 Report, raises the issue of *voluntarism* in the context of political participation as part of citizenship education, and compares it to the notion of 'active citizenship' in Britain. In the British context, students are encouraged to have a more individualist approach to active citizenship, challenging the status quo through weighing up evidence before speaking and acting. Han suggests that this type of voluntarism would be unacceptable in Singapore, as it would not fit in with the local context. In other words, it would be too individualistic, diluting the strong collectivist notion of an active citizenship. Clearly, there are very different conceptions of what an active and participatory citizenship means in a society like Singapore, which reflects both a Confucian Heritage Culture (CHC) coupled with a policy of linking civics with national identity; this coupling has the implication of using citizenship education as a vehicle for promoting the nation as a collective par excellence!

In Taiwan, which is perceived as a monocultural society, social diversity is not an issue, but collectivism is nevertheless an important part of the civics education curriculum, which is extended to cover national identity, much as in Singapore. The new civics education in Taiwan also attempts to attain a balance and consensus between issues such as individualism versus society, freedom versus order, diversity versus uniformity, and identification versus criticism (Liu, 2000). However, social cohesion, a key ingredient of a collectivist culture, is the most emphasised values component of the civic curriculum, with democratic values coming second. The structure of the new civics programme must also be seen in the context of the changing relationship with the People's Republic of China (PRC), which is changing its democratic stance vis à vis the existing communist ideology. But Taiwan is at pains to point out that its powerful neighbour is much less democratic than currently is the case for Taiwanese society.

From an analysis by Morris & Morris (2000) of Hong Kong's Guidelines for Civic Education (produced in 1985 and 1996), it is clear that even with the changes anticipated before the handover in 1997, as well as those that have taken place since, a strong collectivist theme runs through the civics curriculum. Care for parents, sense of duty to family, moral responsibilities for the neighbourhood and support for the common good form a strong basis for educating the young people of Hong Kong as we enter the new millennium. In other words, in spite of a marked political change in the former British Colony's status, traditional collectivist values continue to endure as in previous decades. This collectivist emphasis is reflected in the school civics programme in phrases like 'contributing citizens' and 'to participate actively in civic affairs'. The change in Hong Kong's status from colony to being part of China has meant that the change has permeated key aspects of civics education for schools along rather subtle lines. For instance, much of the new approach to civic education is not seen as being *overtly* nationalistic in the direction of PRC, but in the way culture has been used as a gloss, emphasising traditional Chinese family values, and the importance of understanding the special features of Chinese culture. However, reading between the lines of the 1998 syllabus, one is left with little doubt that Chinese national identity, which is a strong cultural notion, is the ultimate goal for the future of Hong Kong's young citizens.

As far as individualism is concerned, the section of the civics programme that deals with *self-cultivation* shows how the emphasis from the 1985 version has changed from treating the individual in terms of character formation, and the importance of individual responsibilities to the community, to subsuming the individual as part of the social order through self-discipline, rather than a more active and participatory approach to citizenship, in which free thought would be a salient feature.

An analysis of civics education using the I-C dimension provides an interesting perspective on the way young people are prepared for citizenship in Hong Kong, Taiwan and Singapore. The I-C polarity is evident in the approaches to citizenship in all three countries. The fact that the three countries are firmly CHCs underlines the long held view that individualism is subordinated to the collective will, even with the growing influence of global culture, and the opportunities this holds for the individual who comes into contact with the wider world through the mass media and especially the Internet. Achieving goals of collegiality, staff cooperation and sharing of ideas and practices amongst staff reflects strong collectivist attributes and fits well with a collectivist version and approach to civics education. For highly individualistic cultures, characteristics of individualism such as self-reliance, autonomy, independence and self-confidence relate well with citizenship programmes that emphasise human rights and responsibilities, freedom of the individual and the right to question government actions and policies.

However, where citizenship education may need to embrace more collectivist notions, in societies that have a strong culture of democratic individualism, policy-makers and educators will need to work out a balance between the need for individualism and collectivism, so that a culture-specific and global mix would be the desired outcome.

Let us now examine the second of our cross-cultural dimensions, namely universalism-relativism (U-R).

Universalism-Relativism: a challenge for citizenship education

The notions of universalism and relativism have a key place in cross-cultural psychology, cultural psychology and social anthropology. In cross-cultural psychology, writers like Triandis (1978, 1979) and Lonner (1980) refer to universals as psychological rather than cultural, as they confine their scope to human activity, rather than to the products of that activity. Both Lonner and Triandis have argued that the search for psychological universals is perhaps one of the highest priorities for cross-cultural psychologists to tackle, hopefully leading to better global understanding of human behaviour. For an eminent cross-cultural psychologist such as Jahoda (1980), the value of universals lies mainly in their potential for cross-cultural comparisons.

The argument goes that the proven existence of universals would help to test the generality of psychological theories and principles, giving a greater predictive capacity for explanations of human behaviour (Jahoda, 1980). Amplifying Jahoda's views further, this predictive capacity may ultimately inform what constitutes a 'global culture', and, germane to our present concerns, the possible impact on citizenship education in schools. However, research about the universality of human behaviour is in its early stages, with the added complication that there is no consensus amongst workers in this field about what value research into universals will bring. For example, workers such as Scribner & Cole (1973), Davidson (1994) and Schweder (1990) have stressed the importance of intra-cultural and indigenous approaches to behaviour in different cultural contexts as being more useful. For these researchers, the search for universals provides little about cultural interaction, which is one of the key goals of studying the influence of culture on our daily lives.

While the link between cultural universals and a values component of citizenship education is a close one, it appears that the term 'universal', when used by educators, often refers to values that have a universal appeal, rather than being a constant feature of a person's behaviour. This is in contrast to the notion and approaches used by many cross-cultural psychologists. The notion of universality when applied to cultural values is a notion that has socially desired outcomes which are part of global culture. For instance, values such as a love of freedom, working for world peace and promoting democratic ideals amongst schoolchildren are some of the values that would constitute the so called universal cultural values, and are often described as 'core values' by educators. Values such as honesty, tolerance and cooperation would also be included as core values in many countries, especially those in South-east and East Asia, where such values are intimately bound up with the collectivist cultural mosaic. However, values such filial piety, well-being, righteousness and respect for age would be considered as being more culture-specific, and are generally not thought to have such an universal expression. In this sense, these values would also constitute a 'core' but within a narrower cultural context – in other words, they would be relativistic values.

Recent developments in the Asian region show that in countries like Malaysia (Mukerjee, 1988), Singapore (Gopinathan, 1988; Thomas, 1990, 2000b), Myanmar and Vietnam (Thomas, 1996) and Thailand (Thomas, 1996; Pitiyanuwat & Sujiva, 2000) there have been conscious efforts to arrive at varying degrees of consensus when it comes to drawing up a values education curriculum, which reflects the need to include both universal as well more culture-specific values. However, which values (be they universal or culture-specific) should be considered relevant for their inclusion in a values education programme remains a key problem for these and other countries in the region. The problem becomes even more acute where the selection and subsequent inclusion of values is integral to citizenship or civics education.

Let us analyse recent attempts to develop a balance between universal (or core) cultural values and the relativistic (more culture-specific) values in citizenship education which can be developed to meet the political, economic and sociocultural changes facing some of the south and north-east nations making up the Asia-Pacific Rim.

In Thailand, civics and values education is identical with citizenship education, and, as well as emphasising nationhood and reflecting the strong Buddhist religion of the country, the programme also encourages students to look outside the borders of Thailand to her regional neighbours and the world beyond. Universal values which relate to the good world citizen have been superimposed on the local needs for the development of 'good' Thai citizens as well. It was found by Buranasiri (1989) that students agreed strongly with including aspects of world citizenship such as respect for one's rights and freedoms, acceptance of different cultures, developing a model of the good world citizen and the promotion of world peace as part of citizenship education.

In Taiwan also, the emphasis on more global concerns reflecting universal values such as a belief in co-existence between different cultural groups, toleration and respect for cultural diversity and the pursuance of democratic ideals are elements that are included in the 1994 civics education programme. As in the case of Thailand, students are being encouraged to look beyond the boundaries of their country, and become acquainted with more global and universalistic values, in order that they will be become not only 'good' Taiwanese citizens, but regional and 'world' citizens as well. Universal values are also being promoted within Hong Kong with the inclusion of mutuality, which emphasises values such as betterment of humankind, and the understanding of human rights and responsibilities.

In Singapore, there is little explicit reference to universal values being part of civics education. It appears that developing a national identity is still a priority, before reaching out to more global and international concerns. In an analysis by Otsu (2000) of the Japanese civics curriculum, the notion of universal cultural values is subsumed under core values, but even so, there is little or no extension of these core values into the wider global arena, and student exposure to them appears to be minimal. This is perhaps strange, since Japan has made laudable efforts to make its values education programmes have a universal appeal (Thomas, 1990, 1997). However, it could be that Japanese educators are being encouraged to look nearer home in reassessing their national identity, with the impact of globalisation and with recent socio-political indicators which have questioned the policies after World War Two, to reform Japan's previous civic education and the strongly pervasive nationalistic values which typified it.

While educators and researchers into cross-cultural behaviour have differing agendas to the meaning of universalism and relativism, much of the research and writing on the subject from both cultural and cross-cultural viewpoints provides educators with a valuable perspective on the study of values education in the context of citizenship. The use of the U-R polarity, and the way different cultural contexts can throw light on the changing nature of universals, provides useful guidelines for educators to draw up values programmes for all societies and especially those that are multicultural.

Developing Intercultural Educators as an Essential Part of Citizenship Education for the Future

Justifying the inclusion of new and more diverse cultural values, alongside well-established values as part of citizenship education in many Asian Pacific Rim countries, is posing as many challenges for educators from this region as it is in Western countries (Thomas, 1996). However, the nature of the challenges is different because the starting points from which collectivism and individualism are experienced in Western and non-Western societies are so wide apart. In most Western countries, upholding so-called institutions such as the family, respect for democratic institutions such as freely elected parliaments, and active participation in local democracy have become seriously eroded. While the rights of the individual and freedom of expression have become ever more demanded by Western youth, the responsibilities that go hand in hand with these rights are not always accepted by them. In fact, the challenge for Western educators is to persuade young people that rights linked to responsibilities is the only feasible choice, if we are to have a society which works by mutual consent. A key challenge for the Western educator, as far as citizenship education is concerned, is to engender a greater sense of societal collectivism and a toning down of the excesses of individualism.

For educators in the Asian Pacific Rim, having to engender the collective will, and maintain respect for institutions like the family, the school, community and the state, are values that are already well-established features of civic and family life. However, the key challenge for the Asian educator is to deliver a form of civics education which gives opportunities for learners and teachers to discuss the role of participation in decision-making affecting environmental, social and societal issues. Opportunities also need to be given for young people to question and reassess the role of authority, and create new ways of participating constructively in local as well as national issues. In other words, the processes of correction and compensation are now tilted towards a more individualistic stance, so that active democratic citizenship may become a reality.

Turning to the issue of universal versus relativistic values, it is clearly important for educators, wherever they teach, to realise that in an increasingly global world, there is a need to recognise the growing universal appeal of certain values. For instance, values linked to a code of conduct affecting child pornography and female circumcision, codes of practice relating to fair trade through the Internet, appropriate values linked to the rights of minorities, freedom of speech, sexual orientation and gender are clearly becoming universal concerns which sooner or later will be classified as universal values. These newer values, alongside existing universal cultural values, will hopefully be included as part of citizenship education programmes throughout the world, which would certainly make the task of educators more challenging, but also a task that appears to be essential.

While the search for universal values will clearly become more intensive as globalisation gains pace, one must not forget that citizenship is also about local values. Balancing both sets of values will be a major challenge for the success of most citizenship education programmes. However, the success of a balanced citizenship education, as far as its values content is concerned, should not only be seen in terms of what happens in school, but how it makes sense when students leave school for the wider world. Amongst the main causes for past failures of such programmes has been a patent absence of school-community links. As ever, the role of teachers will be crucial in getting the balance right and even more important, seeing that citizenship education for young people is relevant and worthwhile for future life in the community. Clearly, the preparation of effective and dedicated educators who will be tuned in to the intercultural dynamics of a multicultural society will be pivotal in the success of any programme that is aimed at the education of the future citizen. Meeting the cross-cultural challenges discussed in this chapter will no doubt form an essential part of the preparation of teachers, whose role it will be to make citizenship education meaningful as well as culturally relevant.

References

Advisory Group on Citizenship (1998) *Education for Citizenship and the Teaching of Democracy in Schools*. London: Qualifications and Curriculum Authority.

Allport, G., Vernon, P. & Lindzey, G. (1960) *Study of Values*, 3rd edn. Boston: Houghton Mifflin.

Bhawuk, D. & Brislin, R. (1992) The Measurement of Intercultural Sensitivity Using the Individualism and Collectivism Concepts, *International Journal of Intercultural Relations*, 16, pp. 413-436.

Buransiri, S. (1989) Opinions Concerning Characteristics of World Citizenship of Secondary School Students in Bangkok Metropolis, unpublished master's thesis, Graduate School, Chulalongkorn University.

Cheng, K.M. (1997) Engineering Values: education policies and values transmission, in J. Montgomery (Ed.) *Values in Education: social capital formation in Asia and the Pacific*. Hollis, NH: Hollis Publishing.

Chew Oon Ai, J. (1998) Civics and Moral Education in Singapore: lessons for citizenship education? *Journal of Moral Education*, 27, pp. 505-524.

Cogan, J. & Derricott, R. (Eds) (1998) *Citizenship for the 21st Century: an international perspective on education*. London: Kogan Page.

Cummings, W. (1997) Promoting Human Rights in East Asian Values, in J. Montgomery (Ed.) *Values in Education: social capital formation in Asia and the Pacific*. Hollis, NH: Hollis Publishing.

Davidson, G. (1994) Cultural, Cross Cultural or Intercultural? Comment on Lonner, Dasen & Segall, *Cross Cultural Psychology Bulletin*, 28, pp. 1-4.

Gopinathan, S. (1988) Being and Becoming: education for values education in Singapore, in W.K. Cummings, S. Gopinthan & Y. Tomoda (Eds) *The Revival of Values in Education in Asia and the West*, pp. 131-145. Oxford: Pergamon.

Han, C. (2000) National Education and 'Active Citizenship': the implications for citizenship and citizenship education in Singapore, *Asia Pacific Journal of Education*, 20, pp. 63-72.

Hofstede, G. (1980) *Culture's Consequences: international differences in work related values*. Beverly Hills: Sage.

Hui, C.H. (1990) Work Attitudes, Leadership Styles, and Managerial Behaviours in Different Cultures, in R.W. Brislin (Ed.) *Applied Cross Cultural Psychology*, pp. 186-208. Newbury Park: Sage.

Huntington, S. (1997) After Twenty Years: the failure of the third wave, *Journal of Democracy*, 8, pp. 1-12.

Jahoda, G. (1980) Theoretical and Systematic Approaches in Cross Cultural Psychology, in H.C. Triandis & W. Lonner (Eds) *Handbook of Cross Cultural Psychology*, vol. 3. New Jersey: Allyn & Bacon.

Kagitcibasi, C. (1997) Individualism and Collectivism, in J.W. Berry, M.S. Segall & C. Kagitcibasi (Eds) *Handbook of Cross Cultural Psychology, Vol. 3, Social Behaviour and Applications*, pp. 1-49. Boston: Allyn& Bacon.

Liu, M. (2000) Civic Education in Taiwan, *Asia Pacific Journal of Education*, 20, pp. 73-81.

Lonner, W. (1980) The search for psychological universals, in H.C. Triandis & W. Lonner (Eds) *Handbook of Cross Cultural Psychology*, vol. 3. New Jersey: Allyn & Bacon.

Marshall, T. (1973) Citizenship and Social Class, in T. Marshall (Ed.) *Class, Citizenship and Social Development*. Chicago: University of Chicago Press.

Montgomery, J. (Ed.) (1997) *Values in Education: social capital formation in Asia and the Pacific*. Hollis, NH: Hollis Publishing.

Montgomery, J. (Ed.) (1998) *Human Rights: positive policies in Asia and the Pacific Rim*. Hollis, NH: Hollis Publishing.

Morris, P. & Morris, E. (2000) Constructing the Good Citizen in Hong Kong: values promoted in the school curriculum, *Asia Pacific Journal of Education*, 20, pp. 36-52.

Mukerjee, H. (1988) Moral Education in a Developing society: the Malaysian case, in W.K. Cummings, S. Gopinthan & Y. Tomoda (Eds) *The Revival of Values in Education in Asia and the West*, pp. 147-162. Oxford: Pergamon.

Negandhi, A.R. (1984) Management in the Third World, *Advances in International Comparative Management*, 1, pp. 123-154.

Otsu, K. (2000) Civics Education in Japan: values promoted in the school curriculum, *Asia Pacific Journal of Education*, 20, pp. 36-52.

Pitiyanuwat, S. & Sujiva, S. (2000) Civics and Values Education in Thailand: documentary analysis, *Asia Pacific Journal of Education*, 20, pp. 82-92.

Print, M. (2000) Civics and Values in the Asia-Pacific Region, *Asia Pacific Journal of Education*, 20, pp. 7-20.

Putnam, R. (1995) Bowling Alone: America's declining social capital, *Journal of Democracy*, 6, pp. 65-78.

Schwartz, S.H. (1994) Beyond Individualism/Collectivism: new cultural dimensions of values, in U. Kim, H.C. Triandis, C. Kagitcibasi, S-C Choi & G. Hoon (Eds) *Individualism and Collectivism: theory, method and applications*, pp. 85-119. Thousand Oaks, CA: Sage.

Schweder, R.A. (1990) Cultural Psychology: what is it? in J.W. Stigler, R.A. Schweder & G. Herdt (Eds) *Cultural Psychology: essays on comparative human development*. Cambridge: Cambridge University Press.

Scribner, S. & Cole, M. (1973) Cognitive Consequences of Formal and Informal Schooling, *Science*, 182, pp. 552-559.

Sinha, J.B.P. (1994) Cultural Embeddedness and the Developmental Role of Industrial Organisations in India, in H.C. Traindis, M.D. Dunette & L.M. Hough (Eds) *Handbook of Industrial and Organisational Psychology*, 2nd edn, vol. 4, pp. 727-764. Palo Alto: Consulting Psychologists Press.

Thomas, E. (1990) Filial Piety, Social Change and Singapore Youth, *Journal of Moral Education*, 19, pp. 192-205.

Thomas, E. (1996) Teacher Education in South East Asia: prospects for a North-South dialogue with a difference, in C. Brock (Ed.) *Global Perspectives on Teacher Education*, pp. 123-151. Wallingford: Triangle Books.

Thomas, E. (1997) Teacher Education and Values Transmission: cultural dilemmas with difficult choices, in K. Watson, C. Modgil, S. Modgil (Eds) *Educational Dilemmas: debate and diversity*, pp. 246-259. London: Cassell.

Thomas, E. (2000a) Researching Values in Cross Cultural Contexts, in R. Gardner, J. Cairns & D. Lawton (Eds) *Education for Values: morals, ethics and citizenship in contemporary teaching*. London: Kogan Page.

Thomas, E. (2000b) *Schooling and Culture: building bridges between research, praxis and professionalism*. Chichester: John Wiley.

Torney-Purta, J., Schwille, J. & Amadeo, J. (1999) *Civic Education across Countries: twenty four national case studies from the IEA Civic Education Project*. Amsterdam: International Association for the Evaluation of Educational Achievement.

Triandis, H.C. (1978) Some Universals of Social Behaviour, *Personality and Social Psychology Bulletin*, 4, pp. 1-16.

Triandis, H.C. (1979) The Future of Cross Cultural Psychology, in A.J. Marsella, R.G. Tharp & T.J. Ciribowski (Eds) *Perspectives on Cross Cultural Psychology*. New Jersey: Academic Press.

Trompenaars, F. (1993) *Riding the Waves of Culture*. London: Brealey.

PART FIVE

Adult Learning

While the book started with the voice of children and college students, it completes the circle by focusing on the learning of democracy and citizenship by adults. As Maria Fischer & Janet Hannah point out in their opening chapter, in adult education, the promotion of democratic participation and active citizenship has been a pervasive theme in both the liberal and radical traditions. However, the chapter contrasts the economics-driven 'lifelong learning' with the enlightenment or critical practice tradition. It uses the case of the innovative training programme of the Brazilian metalworkers' union to illustrate that vocational training programmes in capitalist societies need not be slavishly driven by supply-side considerations, nor antithetical to the 'adult education of engagement' in which learners are viewed as agents of social and political change.

John Holford & Palitha Edirisingha's chapter also looks at a diversity of possibilities in adult learning: it describes the beginning of a research project in six European countries to examine what 'active citizenship' and governance mean, and how learning to be an active citizen can occur in a number of different contexts within a country. Some initial observations include a general concern at a rising 'democratic deficit', that is, that mechanisms of democratic government no longer work effectively partly because people no longer trust them. The need to 'remoralise' citizens clearly resonates with accounts in other parts of this book on the promotion of civic values.

The book ends with a chapter by Peter Jarvis, the President of BAICE for 2000-01, who provides a broad review of globalisation, citizenship and the education of adults. This too looks at the intersection between the changing nature of citizenship and the changing nature of learning. The Brazilian study which opened this section would support Jarvis's optimism about the possibilities for learning active citizenship through education. This will not be sudden, but the 'learning society' is recognised as crucial in combating social exclusion as well as the more negative and anti-democratic forces of globalisation.

(Re)constructing Citizenship: the Programa Integrar of the Brazilian Metalworkers' Union

MARIA CLARA BUENO FISCHER & JANET HANNAH

Introduction

Internationally, the concept of 'citizenship' is highly topical, forming the backdrop to debates about how to stimulate political activity and civic participation within recently democratised political systems and democracies concerned about growing levels of political apathy and social exclusion. Although there is no single accepted definition of citizenship, Benn & Fieldhouse (1998) suggest that 'a reasonably representative definition of citizenship can be taken as how an individual activates him or herself to be able to consciously influence their own situation and the situation of others in a democratic society' (1998, p. 44). Martin (2000) reminds us that there are two major traditions of citizenship in Western thought, and that a healthy democracy requires the exercise of both traditions. The liberal tradition enshrines the notion of the individual participating in the politics of the state by exercising the right to vote, whilst the civic republican tradition is collectively based, a social practice carried out within social movements and communities. Martin contends that 'the debate about citizenship is a debate about democracy, i.e. the kind of society we live in and the kind of society we want to live in' (2000, p. 12).

Schools are recognised as important sites for instilling in our children the attitudes and values conducive to active citizenship, and 'citizenship education' is now a feature of the British National Curriculum. In adult education, the promotion of active citizenship has been a pervasive theme in both the liberal and radical traditions, and as Benn & Fieldhouse (1998) state, 'the promotion of democratic participation and active citizenship is a frequent preoccupation of adult educators' (p. 41). It is therefore hardly surprising that the renewed political interest in citizenship has been accompanied by growing debates amongst adult educators about its relationship with adult education theory and practice (Bron et al, 1998; Johnston, 1999; Martin, 2000).

In recent years, however, the dominant discourse and policy framework within which adult education is located has become that of 'lifelong learning' in which education and training to meet the requirements of the economy is a central driving force. The concept of 'lifelong learning' has proved remarkably geographically and politically mobile, being adopted by governments all over the world. Whilst there may be specific nuances in interpretation and application of the concept, the economic imperative is always central.

Referring to Britain, but undoubtedly applicable elsewhere, Hyland argues that:

> *there is a world of difference between education and training provision driven by economic objectives and the sort of learning proposed by the adult education tradition – concerned with 'enlightenment' (Simon, 1990) and the fostering of 'critical practice ... and direct engagement in definable concrete projects for social change' (Collins 1991, p. 119). (1994, p. 138)*

The contention that lifelong education as a concept is fundamentally constructed to serve economic ends is echoed in Martin's identification of the two dominant discourses of citizenship in contemporary adult education policy and practice. He argues that:

> *both are fundamentally economistic in the sense that they posit at the centre of our conception of lifelong learning the idea that human beings are essentially economic animals – creatures of the cash nexus. The first discourse constructs the adult learner as worker or producer ... The second discourse of citizenship constructs the adult learner as consumer or customer. (2000, p. 12)*

Inherent in the first discourse is the belief that education and training is the key to competitiveness in increasingly competitive global markets. The emphasis is on training for work, irrespective of whether jobs actually exist, 'the point being that where there is no work, the discipline of the work ethic must nevertheless be maintained' (Martin, 2000, p. 12). Whilst the first discourse of citizenship is based on a supply-side approach to lifelong learning, the second discourse focuses upon the demand side. In this approach, adult education is a commodity to be bought and sold in the market according to individual tastes and lifestyle preferences. Whilst these two discourses dominate current policy and practice in the United Kingdom and beyond, it must be borne in mind that the liberal and radical traditions have historically been significant, and continue to find spaces today. From a radical perspective, Keith Jackson (1995) adopts a position similar to that of Collins, quoted earlier, when he refers to the 'adult education of engagement' (quoted in Martin, 2000) in which the adult learner is positioned, not as a producer or consumer, but as a political agent and social actor.

There would appear to be an implicit assumption amongst proponents of the 'adult education of engagement' that this is a practice associated with social movements and community education. With its specific focus on the learner as worker or producer, vocational training may not be considered fertile ground for the practice of 'the adult education of engagement'. However, Hyland (1994) and Butler (2000) remind us that there is no intrinsic reason why vocational education should be restricted to the narrow, instrumental approach with which it is generally associated today. Adopting Peters's (1978) justification of education 'as involvement in worthwhile activities', Hyland points out that, in principle, this is capable of applying equally to so-called vocational as well as academic activities, and quotes Dearden, who states that:

A process of training could be liberally conceived in such a way as to explore relevant aspects of understanding, and in a way which satisfies the internal standards of truth and adequacy. (1990, p. 93, quoted in Hyland, 1994, p. 117)

The case of the Programa Integrar of the Brazilian metalworkers' union illustrates that vocational training programmes in capitalist societies need not be slavishly driven by supply-side considerations, nor antithetical to 'the adult education of engagement' in which learners are viewed as agents of social and political change. However, it is perhaps significant that the example of the Programa Integrar has emerged in Brazil, where the radical approach remains strong in contemporary social and popular movements, as Kane notes in relation to his study of the Brazilian Landless People's Movement, the MST:

The MST's educational work shows strong continuity with the recent, radical past in Latin American popular education. All education is considered political and whether it happens to be in campaigning, organizing co-operatives, tackling illiteracy or running specialist courses, every aspect of MST practice is underpinned by the desire to politicize, raise critical awareness and encourage the emergence of 'subjects' of change. (2000, p. 45)

Like the MST's educational programme, the Programa Integrar of the metalworkers' union is also firmly rooted in the desire to politicize, raise critical awareness and encourage the emergence of 'subjects of change'. Of particular interest here is its overt commitment to the active promotion of the exercise of citizenship (cidadania) in the Brazilian economy and society. Before going on to present and discuss the Programa Integrar, a brief overview of the economic and political context in which it operates is presented.

The Economic and Political Context

Brazil is the world's eighth largest economy, with an estimated population of 170 million. Vast and diverse, it is commonly divided into five geographic regions, which vary from the heavily industrialised south and south-east regions to the huge, but sparsely populated, northern region, which contains the tropical rainforest. Between them, the south and south-east produce more than 75% of the nation's gross domestic product. Brazil is infamous for its unequal wealth distribution: the poorest 20% of the population share 2.6% of national income, whilst the richest 10% have 48.7% (Inter-union Department of Statistics and Socio-economic Studies [DIEESE], 2000). Agricultural employment continues to decline rapidly – in the last 30 years approximately 30 million people have migrated from the country to urban areas seeking employment (Central Unica dos Trabalhadores [CUT – Brazil's largest trade union centre], 2000). Manufacturing industry is in crisis, with workers experiencing large-scale redundancies and employment insecurity arising from intensifying competition and the spread of subcontracting. The informal economy is growing at an alarming rate, and it is now estimated that 50% of all jobs are found in the informal sector (DIEESE, 2000). Access to education is also highly uneven, corresponding to the 'local systems for the poor and global systems for the rich' identified by Ilon (1994, p. 102), in which the majority of the population receives an inadequately resourced state education that makes them 'marginally competitive for low-skilled jobs', whilst a small elite benefits from a private education that makes them globally competitive. As discussed below, Brazil's metalworkers have experienced an average of only 3 years of school education.

Also of importance to understanding the context and significance of the Programa Integrar is the fact that Brazil is still in the process of democratising itself. Military rule ended in the mid-1980s and a new constitution was agreed in 1988, but old attitudes and practices from the fascist era still linger in the labour market and employment relations. However, the current Brazilian Government recognises the need to rebuild 'civil society' and promote the 'citizenship dimension' and is creating spaces and opportunities within society to actively participate in this process. Sectors of the Brazilian trade union movement are snatching these spaces and constantly arguing for more to become available. The Programa Integrar, to which we now turn, indicates how potentially powerful such opportunities can be.

The Programa Integrar – origins and rationale

The Programa Integrar is operated by the metalworkers' union – the Centro Nacional de Metalurgicos (CNM) which is affiliated to Brazil's largest trade union centre, the Central Unica dos Trabalhadores (CUT). CUT is committed to the radical transformation of power in Brazilian society, and actively challenges public policies within and outside the factory, seeking the generation of alternative forms of work and employment that aim to redefine control of the productive process. These wider transformational aims are important to understanding the policies and practices adopted by CNM/CUT in relation to vocational training, debates about which are located within wider discussions about the economic, political and social development of Brazil.

Levels of unemployment and the growth of casual and informal work are viewed as equally serious questions by trade unions and other social organisations. This is stimulating discussion not only about education, but also about potential alternatives for the Brazilian economy, including the creation of alternatives to salaried employment, which is in crisis. Thus, re-emerging in Brazil and in other Latin American countries is the discussion about, and establishment of, cooperatives. These include job creation worker cooperatives and, in many cases, the search for products to serve human society. Universities, social movements, unions and even the Government have entered into this debate. Diverse practices and interpretations are currently leading to debates about the limits, possibilities and contradictions of such experiences within the context of the restructuring of production and the intensification of competition within the capitalist economy. As discussed below, identifying opportunities to strengthen and expand this sector is an important aspect of the Programa Integrar.

Informing these attempts to influence the economic, political and social development of the country is a commitment to the creation of conditions for, and exercise of, *cidadania*, or citizenship. This is a term commonly used by the social and popular movements in Brazil, and can be understood as:

> *Deriving from, and therefore intrinsically connected to, the concrete experience of social movements. In the organization of these social movements, the struggle for rights – such as the right to equality through the right to be different – constitute the fundamental base for the emergence of a new notion of citizenship. This concrete experience then accumulates into a wider emphasis in the construction of democracy, but more than this, in its extension and strengthening ... As a*

*consequence of these two dimensions, a third arises: the fact
that she (the citizen) organizes a strategy for democratic
construction, of social transformation, creating a nexus
between the dimensions of culture and politics. (Dagnino,
1994, p. 104)*

The quotation highlights the significance of citizenship for the social and popular movements, and the wider political horizon in which the struggle for rights such as democracy in the relations of work and control over public resources is situated. In this context, the nature of relations between the state and civil society has had considerable weight in the discourse and social practice of many organisations. There is a culture being constructed in Brazilian society in respect of the rights of men and women to benefit from and to create rights, as well as the necessity of understanding the meaning and the differences between 'state' and 'public'. Therefore, the making of public policy and the allocation of state resources are becoming increasingly understood as the responsibility of society, and not only the organs of the administration of the state apparatus. Thus, different collective bodies are pursuing and discussing forms of popular participation that complement, but also question, the traditional forms of representative participation.

Until very recently, vocational training was viewed by employers and the state as the private concern of capital (Arroyo, 1996, p. 1), and trade unions had no official role. Nevertheless, there are a number of historical examples of trade unions becoming involved in vocational education and training (Manfredi, 1997). In recent years, new negotiating spaces have begun to open up with the Government and with the employers. These are, however, only occasional and the workers are struggling to extend them:

*The negotiating challenge lies in the capacity of the trade
unions to present proposals for vocational training in the face
of the new forms of the production and organisation of goods
and services. These need to be considered together with
questions that go beyond simple preparation for work.
(DIEESE, 1998, p. 9)*

A unique opportunity for the trade union movement to accept this challenge and present a proposal for a radical experiment in vocational training arose when, in the mid-1990s, the Government invited interested parties to bid for public money to fund vocational training. The metalworkers' union quickly saw the possibilities that this offered, and submitted a successful bid to establish a vocational training programme – the Programa Integrar – that represented a radical departure from the norm. In relation to metalworkers, that 'norm' was very limited access to opportunities to undertake skills or personal development of any kind, with the exception of training in the operation of new production technologies on the shop floor when it was considered necessary by management. Operating in the manufacturing sector of the economy, which has suffered a series of recurrent crises and mass redundancies, huge numbers of metalworkers have lost their jobs in recent years and the threat of unemployment is ever-present for those who remain in work. High levels of job insecurity, allied with low levels of basic education, conspire to produce poor prospects for employed and unemployed metalworkers alike. Faced with this harsh economic reality, the union seized the opportunity to access state funding to launch a radical programme that combines education and training with social action.

The Principles and Objectives of the Programa Integrar

Thus, the Programa Integrar was born with the policy decision of the Third National Congress of Metalworkers in 1995, 'with the aim of developing and planning vocational training and reinforcing the relations between unions and unemployed workers' (CNM/CUT, 1998a, p. 12). There was an understanding amongst the metalworkers' leadership that:

A vocational training project – whether for the unemployed or employed worker – ought to seek integration with a new reality of production. In contrast to the models of training as instruction, the project would have to train the worker within a wider concept of citizenship. (CNM/CUT, 1998a, p. 12)

Since its inception, therefore, the programme has incorporated a strategic vision of the construction of the citizenship of the workers through intervention in the development of public policy, principally in relation to policies concerning the creation of work, wealth and education and in the unions' role in their negotiation. The conception of vocational training on which the programme is founded is expressed in the following quotations.

Vocational training must be placed under the responsibility of the workers and be integrated into the regular system of teaching in the more general struggle for a public education that is free, secular and unitary. Public and free with the state assuming its responsibilities, but with the effective participation of society in issues concerning pedagogical and administrative development. (CNM/CUTRS, 1998, p. 52)

In contrast to the restricted view of training as a response to considerations of profit, vocational training should be of interest to the worker, and satisfy the many needs of the human being.

> *We believe that the critical, educated and contemporaneous worker, from the point of view of the innovations which humanity has developed, is not a consequence of the process of production, but a consequence of citizenship. Therefore, we are training the whole worker. Not because it is required by production, but because we view (him [the worker]) as a critical being, with understanding of the world, with an informed vision. This is fundamental for a free (man), for the whole (man). On this basis, we also work in the cultural dimension, of understanding, of absorbing the knowledge which humanity has produced, as fundamental to a just society. The Programa Integrar is part of this conception: that the human being should be free, be able to actively participate and to control these dimensions which, historically, were always only possibilities for the dominant classes. To understand culture, to know poetry, to understand the classics, to understand the advances of technology – not only for profit, but as complete and whole human beings – is fundamental, and this concept is the foundation stone of the Programa Integrar as a whole. (CNM/CUT, 1998a, p. 43)*

Embedded in the quotations is a holistic and rounded view of education, strongly influenced by the work of Paulo Freire, that overcomes the apparent opposition between vocational training and general education. Although the work of Dewey has not been an overt influence in the development of CUT's pedagogy, it is interesting to note that the emphasis on the exercise of citizenship echoes Dewey's early twentieth-century vision. Writing in 1916, he expressed a holistic approach to education and training that encompassed:

> *The development of artistic capacity of any kind, of specific scientific ability, of effective citizenship, as well as professional and business occupations, to say nothing of mechanical labour or engagement in gainful pursuits. (1996, p. 307)*

Echoes of this vision can be discerned in the guiding principles of the programme, which are as follows.

> *1. It is the responsibility of the state to guarantee public, quality education.*

> *2. Public resources, applied honestly, must be directed towards meeting the interests of the workers.*

3. Unemployment is a political-economic question, arising from the model of development pursued, and not a personal problem or due to a lack of training.

4. Connections must be made between training/action/the construction of citizenship and the strengthening of the trade union movement.

5. Connections must be made between vocational training and technological qualifications of the first and second levels.

6. The knowledge of the worker must be recognized and valued.

7. Vocational training is not restricted to the factory.

8. Training is interdisciplinary.

9. The worker is viewed as a complete, integral human being.

10. A project based on these principles must be recognized as still in the process of construction, and therefore likely to suffer limitations arising from traditional methods of training,
(CNM/CUT, 1998b, pp. 14-15)

Connected with the strategy and its underlying principles, the objectives of the programme are as follows:

1. to develop amongst the unemployed the consciousness that they can and must struggle for their reinsertion into the world of work, discovering new alternatives;

2. to offer learning opportunities which help to develop understanding of:
– the world economic crisis
– the rise of neo-liberal politics in the government of nations
– the significance and effects of economic dependency
– the role of new technologies in the production process
– the implementation of the restructuring of production within companies
– the new dimensions of trade unionism;

3. to promote study and group relations as a means of respecting the person, facilitating the development of knowledge and widening social relations;

4. to combine the certification of the first grade scholar with the commitment of study and group and community participation;

5. to make clear the new aspect of trade unionism, committed now to the formulation of policies for vocational training combined with citizenship (cidadania);

6. to develop knowledge on the basis of a social pedagogy, adopting a methodology which will facilitate the development of mature, critical consciousness;

7. to position, through group action and participation in civil society, the search for alternative work and the struggle to overcome social injustice;

8. to increase understanding that unemployment will be confronted more effectively with greater knowledge and a collective force committed to initiatives for the generation of employment and wealth. (CNM/CUT, 1998b, p. 16)

Underpinning the above objectives is the view of the worker/learner as a whole person: a political agent and social actor as well as a producer. It combines the practical need to enhance workers' job security and employment prospects with the development of active citizenship – the effort to create a more just society, and the search for alternative forms of work and employment. Producer, consumer and financial cooperatives (credit unions) are trying to break free of the chains of the market, attempting to organise themselves into economic organisations 'whose labour processes can represent the seeds of a new culture of work that could be conceived as a mode of production, distribution and consumption of goods and resources which would provide an alternative to capital' (Tiriba, 1998, pp. 198-199). These organisations have been labelled 'Organizacoes Economicas Populares' – OEPs. According to Singer (1998), 'workplaces which have as their principal objective the guarantee of work for all members, and not for profit, already employ 10,000 workers in the country [Brazil]' (*Zero Hora*, 21 November 1998). The OEPs, in association with CNM/CUT and other supportive trade unions and social movements, are trying to identify an appropriate education and training strategy to meet their objectives. Once again, this endeavour would find support in the writings of Dewey, who believed that:

any scheme for vocational education which takes its point of departure from the industrial regime that now exists, is likely to assume and to perpetuate its divisions and weaknesses, and

thus become an instrument in accomplishing the feudal
dogma of social predestination. (1996, p. 318)

CNM/CUT is therefore working in partnership with other progressive bodies, and a number of organisations contribute in different ways to the implementation of the Programa Integrar. These include the Inter-university Foundation for the Study and Research of Work (UNITRABALHO); the Inter-union Department of Statistics and Socio-economic Studies (DIEESE) and the Federal University of Rio de Janeiro (UFRJ) Postgraduate Programme in Engineering – COPPE. Through the pedagogical approach described in more detail below, groups of workers/learners/citizens explore alternative possibilities for the development of work and employment opportunities. Strategies to pursue these alternatives through campaigns and action are also devised in the workshops, activating a dynamic relationship between education, training and action for social change.

The Implementation of the Programa Integrar

The Programa Integrar consists of three central strands – the first is directed towards the training of the unemployed, the second for those in employment and the third for trade union leaders. The programme for the unemployed has as its focus strategies for the creation of work and wealth (CNM/CUT, 1998b, p. 44) For those in employment, the focus is on the workplace, based on negotiating and agreeing qualifications as an item on the union agenda. 'Learning laboratories' and 'joint workshops', described below, bring both employed and unemployed workers together. Both, of course, also deliver training in skills relevant to metalworkers, and this provision is identified through 'participatory research for negotiating vocational training', undertaken in partnership with employers to identify the requirements for vocational upgrading of the workers to meet the needs of productive restructuring. The researchers include the trade unionists in these companies with the technical support of the university, and the results form the basis of bipartite negotiations about the appropriate training courses for the workers. According to the Secretary for Training of CNM/CUT:

We really want to discuss everything with the employers: the
curriculum, the methodology, the timetable, the financing.
Everything arising from the research done on the factory floor,
the real necessities of the workers. (CNM/CUT, 1998b, p. 40)

The third element – the programme for trade union leaders – encompasses the elements present in the other two, but is deeper and wider in scope.

The pedagogical assumptions on which the programme is based are also relevant to understanding its significance in promoting citizenship and the emergence of 'subjects of change', and are synthesised in the sixth principle described earlier. To recap, this principle is 'to develop knowledge on the basis of a social pedagogy, adopting a methodology which will facilitate the development of mature, critical consciousness' (CNM/CUT, 1998b, p. 14).

The recognition of the workers' knowledge has a fundamental place in the programme, directly influencing the approach of the educators in the classroom and, consequently, the curriculum. There is one instructor, an ex-metalworker, who, together with a male and female tutor, administers the classes as well as all of the content to be developed through dialogue with the knowledge of each participant (CNM/CUT, 1998b).

The curriculum integrates the experience of the worker in the construction of knowledge and formally recognises (through the award of a certificate) what has been acquired by the worker in the course of his (and less commonly, her) life. The programme seeks to redeem 'the original notion of the curriculum which signified a passage, incorporating the experience of life of the worker and of struggles in the content and process of interdisciplinary teaching and learning' (CNM/CUT, 1998b). The curriculum seeks to integrate general learning with the development of technical competence. This integration has the objective of breaking with the established practice in the Brazilian education system where the children of rich parents receive a general education, whilst those of the working class can afford to access only vocationally oriented education. As mentioned earlier in relation to the rationale for launching the Programa Integrar, it should be borne in mind that the average number of years spent in school education by a metalworker in Brazil is only 3 years. Therefore, the formal content of the CNM/CUT courses:

> *Emerge from a process of deep reflection that combines the*
> *concepts and content of the courses with the lived experiences*
> *of the worker in the process of production. (CNM/CUTRS,*
> *Programa Integrar RS, 1998, p. 4)*

The curriculum of the programme is not only part of this integrated approach to human development, but is also providing its participants with basic education and basic vocational training.

In the course materials, the curriculum is represented by a diagram in the form of a circle, showing the approach to the curriculum adopted by the programme. At the centre is the theme of the restructuring of production. This is surrounded by five subthemes – mathematics (180 hours), management and planning (120 hours), reading and interpreting designs (120 hours), information technology (160 hours), and work and technology (120 hours). In approaching each of these topics, tutors and participants articulate, in the same process, concepts, participants' knowledge and collective action. Permeating all is general knowledge. Basic common questions link each of the five topics and the central theme. For example, in work and technology, the question addressed is the nature of relations in the world of work.

Another feature of the regular courses is their flexible, modular structure, which respects time and rhythm in the lives of the unemployed. Complementing the courses are the so-called 'learning laboratories' and workshops. Learning laboratories are sociocultural events of many types that allow the participants to develop their knowledge of society: the functioning of industry, public organisations, alternative forms of employment and wealth, and participation in cultural events. The sustainable development workshops, meanwhile, serve to widen awareness and plan action in relation to alternatives for sustainable local and regional development. The target participants of the workshops are employed and unemployed workers irrespective of industry or level of education, and popular organisations that already exist, or are in the process of being formed:

> *In sum, members of diverse associations for which the agenda of local development could, even indirectly, be adopted by an increasing number of citizens of every city. (CNM/CUTRS, 1998, pp. 18-19)*

Already, the sustainable development workshops are yielding positive outcomes: local projects have been developed to construct alternative forms of regional and local sustainable development that incorporate vocational training as an element.

In relation to the structure of the management and delivery of the programme, there are variations in how it is operated in the states. The state of Rio Grande do Sul can be taken as an example. Here, there is a management group, a Consultative Committee, a technical coordinator responsible for 'establishing the classrooms, developing partnerships, planning, coordinating and taking part in the discussions about the restructuring of production, its historical context and alternatives in the labour market' (CNM/CUT, 1998b, p. 28). There is also a pedagogical assistant and an executive assistant, an administrative sector, a research and dissemination sector, a pedagogical coordinator within every local centre and, in the classroom, a tutor (from the network) and an instructor (an unemployed metalworker).

A broad, and necessarily limited, picture of the Programa Integrar is presented above. Some aspects of the evaluation of the programme will now be described, based on documentary and interview evidence collected at both national level and in one of the participating states, Rio Grande do Sul. There is still a limited amount of information available, but it is nevertheless possible to draw some conclusions about the impact and significance of the Programa Integrar to date.

The Significance of the Programa Integrar

CNM/CUT evaluates the programme in different ways: the learning outcomes identified by the worker and the actions stimulated by the programme (institutional impact), the creation of bonds of solidarity amongst the unemployed, the establishment of effective relations between workers' groups and centres of study and research, and the organisation of actions and events in which the dynamics of the restructuring of production are discussed (CNM/CUT, 1998b, p. 16). According to Fernando Lopes, the Education Secretary of CNM/CUT, the programme has fulfilled initial expectations in valuing and accrediting workers' experience, and the objective of making the unemployed worker 'included' rather than 'excluded' through collective action has also been realised. Another positive aspect of the programme has been that the achievements of the unemployed are occurring through union action. Fernando Lopes also identified as positive the experience that the workers are having in administering public resources. However, it was acknowledged that one of the 'rather complicated' aspects was the generation of work and wealth (CNM/CUT, 1998b, p. 45).

In the state of Rio Grande do Sul, those responsible for the programme identified a number of positive outcomes during interviews. These ranged from the award of certificates to the regaining of self-esteem and the creation of a collective identity amongst the unemployed. It was also believed that participants had developed a greater understanding of public policies in relation to vocational training and the generation of employment and wealth. In some cases, this had resulted in practical action leading to the identification of market and job creation opportunities.

It was also suggested that the programme presented a number of innovatory aspects. These included the efforts to integrate technological knowledge with the demands of the worker and the collective search for alternatives to unemployment, and the contribution to the development of citizenship (cidadania) in the workers already excluded or in the process of being excluded from the labour market (CNM/CUTRS, 1998, pp. 8-9).

Conclusion

In conclusion, it is argued here that the Programa Integrar is an innovative and highly significant attempt to reintegrate elements that have historically been segregated in capitalist societies. These are: preparation for work and a general education, the adult learner as producer or the adult learner as political agent and social actor, employed workers and unemployed workers. Central to the entire programme is the concept of 'citizenship' that goes beyond the narrow, economistic discourses inherent in 'lifelong learning', challenging them on their most solid territory of vocational training. Thus, the Programa Integrar reconciles the positioning of the adult learner as a worker or producer with the positioning of the learner as a political and social actor – it proves that they need not be mutually exclusive. This simultaneous positioning of the learner as producer, political agent and social actor overcomes the essentialism associated with 'the adult education of engagement' based on positioning the learner as an agent of political and social action on the one hand, and vocational training's 'economistic discourse'of the learner as producer on the other.

It is also innovatory in its attempts to identify and create concrete economic alternatives based on solidarity, representing a living example of how appropriately designed vocational education and training has the potential to question and shape visions of work for the future. In combining these various elements in a programme that actively seeks to influence public policy and instigate economic and social change, it is not merely a training ground, but a theatre in which active citizenship is being exercised.

References

Arroyo, M. (1996) Educação básica, profissional e sindical – um direito do trabalhador, um desafio para os sindicatos. Belo Horizonte: Escola Sindical 7 de Outubro, Seminar paper presented at Escola Sindical, 4 June.

Benn, R. & Fieldhouse, R. (1998) The Role of Adult Learning in Promoting Active Citizenship in Britain in the Twentieth Century, in A. Bron, J. Field & E. Kurantowicz (Eds) *Adult Education and Democratic Citizenship*. II Krakov: Impuls Publisher.

Bron, A., Field, J. & Kurantowicz, E. (Eds) (1998) *Adult Education and Democratic Citizenship*. II Krakov: Impuls Publisher.

Butler, E. (2000) Knowing 'Now', Learning Futures: the politics and knowledge practices of vocational education and training, *International Journal of Lifelong Education*, 19, pp. 322-341.

Collins, M. (1991) *Adult Education as Vocation*. London: Routledge.

Centro Nacional de Metalurgicos (CNM)/Central Unica dos Trabalhadores (CUT) (1998a) *Resoluções do 4ºCongresso dos Metalúrgicos da CUT*. São Paulo: CNM/CUT.

Centro Nacional de Metalurgicos (CNM)/Central Unica dos Trabalhadores (CUT) (1998b) *Programa Integrar: formação e qualificação para o trabalho*. São Paulo: CUT.

Centro Nacional de Metalurgicos (CNM)/CUTRS (1998) *Considerações sobre o Programa Integrar*. Porto Alegre: Mimeo.

Central Unica dos Trabalhadores (CUT) (2000)

Dewey, J. (1996) *Democracy and Education*. New York: Free Press.

Dagnino, E. (1994) Os movimentos sociais e a emergência de uma nova noção de cidadania, *Anos 90:pol'tica e sociedade no Brasil*, pp. 103-115. São Paulo: Brasiliense.

DIEESE (Inter-union Department of Statistics and Socio-economic Studies) (1998) Pesquisa DIEESE no. 14: *Formação Profissional: um novo espaço de negociação*. São Paulo: DIEESE.

DIEESE (Inter-union Department of Statistics and Socio-economic Studies) (2000) <http://www.dieese.org.br> (accessed 2 March 2001).

Hyland, T. (1994) *Competence, Education and NVQs: dissenting perspectives*. London: Cassell.

Ilon, L. (1994) Structural Adjustment and Education: adapting to a growing global market, *International Journal of Educational Development*, 14, pp. 95-108.

Jackson, K. (1995) Popular Education and the State: a new look at the community debate, in M. Mayo & J. Thompson (Eds) *Adult Learning, Critical Intelligence and Social Change*, pp. 182-203. Leicester: National Institute of Adult Continuing Education.

Johnston, R. (1999) Adult Learning for Citizenship, *International Journal of Lifelong Education*, 18, pp. 176-190.

Kane, L. (2000) Popular Education and the Landless People's Movement in Brazil (MST), *Studies in the Education of Adults*, 32, pp. 36-51.

Martin, I. (2000) Contesting Citizenship, in J. Thompson, M. Shaw, & L. Bane (Eds) *Reclaiming Common Purpose*, pp. 12-13. Leicester: National Institute of Adult Continuing Education.

Manfredi, S. (1997) Experiências e projetos de formação profissional entre trabalhadores brasileiros, *Educação e Sociedado*, XVIII(60), pp. 117-143.

Movimento Sem Terra (MST) (2001) http://www.sanet.com.br/~semterra/mstl.htm (accessed 8 March 2001)

Tiriba, L.V. (1998) Economia popular e produção de uma nova cultura de trabalho: contradições e desafios frente à crise do trabalho assalariado, Frigotto (Ed.) *Educação e crise do trabalho: perspectivas de Final do século*, pp. 189-216. Petropolis: RJVOZES.

Adult Learning, Active Citizenship and Governance in Europe: theoretical, methodological and policy perspectives

JOHN HOLFORD & PALITHA EDIRISINGHA

Introduction

This chapter discusses some key theoretical and methodological issues arising in the investigation of how adults learn 'active citizenship' and 'governance' in Europe.[1] Its purpose is modest: to outline the project's theoretical perspectives and preliminary investigations.

The premise of the project is that the attitudes, skills and behavioural patterns which equip adults to participate actively as citizens, and to conduct tasks of governance and social and economic regulation, are not learned simply – nor even primarily – through formal or targeted educational provision. They are constructed – learned incidentally – in socio-institutional and cultural processes. The project therefore has four key elements.

It reviews and analyses the meaning of 'active citizenship' and 'governance', and the nature of related learning policies, at the European level and in a cross-section of six European countries.
It examines how learning to be an 'active citizen' occurs in a series of contexts. These will be located within each of four primary 'domains' of social life (work, the state, civil society, and the private domain), in each of the six countries. Learning of citizenship and governance will be analysed in terms of three key dimensions (effectivity, responsibility, and identity).
It will develop a framework which will (a) enable professionals to identify and design effective formal, non-formal and informal citizenship and governance educational intervention strategies, and

(b) permit effective evaluation of interventions, in each case having regard to both aims and context.

It will disseminate the findings through manuals, print-based and online materials, and training events, through establishing partnerships and other forms of collaboration which support professional networks of 'citizenship educators'.

Rationale

The European Union (EU) has set itself two key policy aims: closer integration on a basis of participative citizenship, and competitiveness in the global economy. Education and training have been given key roles in each of these. Achieving a simultaneously democratic, tolerant and inclusive – yet globally competitive – Europe is a challenging aim. Yet, the design of educational interventions and policies has been constrained in a number of ways.

First, educational intervention strategies have focused too strongly on formal structures (i.e. chiefly primary and secondary schooling). The increasing emphasis in European and national policies on 'lifelong learning' in the 'learning society' raises the question of how strategies for informal and non-formal political education can be elaborated.

Second, educational curricula and policies have concentrated on narrow definitions of politics (especially as state related). Recently, social scientists (for example, Giddens, 1991 and Beck, 1997) have stressed work and civil society as domains of life experience, and explored links between traditional forms of political participation and the personal, private domain. Learning theorists also have emphasised 'situational' or 'contextual' influences on learning (cf. Jarvis, 1987; Lave & Wenger, 1991; Biggs & Moore, 1993; Wenger, 1998). However, the implications of such perspectives for learning citizenship and governance have been little explored.

Third, educational strategies have in the past seen agency in citizenship and governance as derived chiefly from primary ideological affiliations (socialism, Christianity, etc.) Recent scholarship has, however, emphasised more subjective or pragmatic affiliations (gender, ethnicity, migration, pollution, etc.) in contemporary Europe (Lyotard, 1984; Benhabib, 1992; Bauman, 1993). Diversity in identities is therefore increasingly important in analysing agency.

Fourth, European policy envisages not only political and social aims – integration on the basis of social inclusion – but also economic competitiveness. Many authors (e.g. Beck, 1992; Beck et al, 1994) stress the risky character of contemporary social transformations. They argue for identifying new balances between economic aims and social priorities such as active citizenship. As Sennett (1998) has argued, the nature of work organisation in contemporary capitalist economies may itself lead to declining levels of social participation and active citizenship.

Fifth, in order to be able to understand exclusion as well as stimulate active citizenship, knowledge of specific and local contexts is needed. While Europe's economic, political and social objectives are relatively well established, little is known of how educational intervention for adults currently occurs, or should take place, in the diverse contexts in which these objectives must be achieved.

Sixth, the principle of subsidiarity applies strongly to education, which is governed by the national (and/or subnational) legislation of EU member states. Yet, Europe faces simultaneous pressures toward both integration and relative uniformity (globalisation, political integration, monetary union, etc.), and fragmentation and diversity (regional, local, cultural, ethnic and linguistic identities, subsidiarity, etc.)

The research examines how notions of citizenship and governance are learned by adults in a series of contexts. These are distinct in terms of national and regional location, and social, economic and political domain.

Formal education for citizenship (i.e. in schools) has itself faced uncertainties as 'modern' conceptions of citizenship have been displaced or eroded by social change. Citizenship education can no longer be simply integration into a community of enlightened citizens with shared values – if only because sheer diversity seems to render the aim unachievable. From a postmodern perspective, moreover, classic 'modern' statements about the nature of citizenship (e.g. Marshall, 1950) appear as 'metanarratives' (Tsang, 1996). The mainstream response – a 'competence' approach, centring on decision-making ability (Crick & Porter, 1978; Porter, 1981, 1996) – has been criticised for its inability to develop critical awareness of prevailing socio-institutional and historical conditions. Drawing on the work of Habermas (1987, 1991) and Freire (1970, 1996) among others, Giroux and McLaren have argued that 'border pedagogies' provide a more acceptable base for citizenship education today (Giroux, 1983, 1987, 1992; Giroux & McLaren, 1986, 1994).[2]

Research Questions and Methods

The project seeks to provide answers to a number of research questions.

How are practices and concepts of 'active citizenship' and 'governance' being reshaped under current conditions of social transformation, such as 'Europeanisation' and globalisation?
How are the notions of 'active citizenship' and 'governance' articulated in policy within the countries studied, within the EU, and within relevant other international organisations (e.g. Council of Europe), and how have the notions evolved historically into their present forms?

What connections have been drawn, within these policies, between 'active citizenship' and dysfunctional citizenship in the political (state) domain, and related notions of active and non-participation in regulation in other (work, civil, and private) domains?

What is the mutual articulation of 'effectivity', 'responsibility' and 'identity' in the formation of citizens with a real capacity as agents of change?

How do processes of learning for citizenship and governance vary between men and women, and between selected age-cohorts?

To what extent does adult learning in formal, non-formal and informal education contribute to the development of new balances between economic development and civic involvement?

What approaches to education for active citizenship and governance have predominated, or been advocated, in policy at the various levels of governance? What have been the prime modes of intervention (formal, non-formal, and informal), and what has been their effect on different individuals and sectors in society? How far have these addressed citizenship and governance as gendered notions?

What new approaches to educational intervention for active citizenship and governance are currently being developed given current changes in societal contexts? Which approaches should be fostered in view of the challenges with which Europe is confronted?

What modes of educational intervention have proved most effective for learning citizenship and governance? What modes are likely to prove most effective in the future?

The research project employs participative methods. Educators, policy-makers, designers of learning materials, agents of change, and other end-users play a key role throughout the project through a series of advisory panels. A life history method is used to explore how adults learn about citizenship and governance, and focus groups are used to identify intervention strategies. The manuals, materials, training events and other elements of the dissemination strategy will be developed in association with the advisory panels and focus groups. Feedback and dialogue mechanisms will ensure end-user input in research perspectives, in the design and orientation of outputs, and in the overall strategy for embedding project findings in 'citizenship educator communities'.

Theoretical Framework

Learning about citizenship and governance can, of course, occur in a very large number of contexts. The importance of social context for adult learning is a widely accepted view in the literature. In addition, the importance of particular contexts, such as the workplace (Marsick, 1987; Marsick & Watkins, 1990) or social movements (Finger, 1989; Holford, 1995), have also been shown. While broad definitions of learning context can be presented quite simply, their boundaries, however, are frequently ill defined.

Contexts of Learning

The research is based on a typology which permits detailed comparative analysis of specific social contexts in which learning occurs. This sees learning as occurring within four primary contexts (or 'domains') – *work, the state, civil society* and *the private domain* – derived from major traditions in social theory (cf. *Sociaal en Cultureel Rapport*, 1996, p. 538). Each domain can itself be broken down in a number of ways. (For instance, the domain 'work' comprises the entire spectrum of work experiences: clearly, the learning contexts of senior managers of transnational corporations, 'knowledge workers' in SMEs [Small and Medium Enterprises], hospital maintenance staff, and so forth, will vary.)

Within each, a learning context will be identified which is strongly influenced by current forces of rapid social change. Each context permits the investigation of the gender dimension in learning, and the analysis of power relationships in the analysis of learning. For pragmatic reasons, the research focuses on the dimensions of work, the state, and civil society; the private domain is explored only incidentally.

Dimensions of Learning

Within each of the learning contexts selected, the research investigates three key dimensions of learning: *effectivity, responsibility* and *identity*. These are related to constructs of governance and citizenship, and derived from principal themes in learning theory and social theory (cf. Bloom, 1956; Crittenden, 1978; Giddens, 1984). In addressing empirically the dimensions of identity and responsibility, they also relate to theorisations of gendered differences in learning approaches and contexts of knowledge (Belenky et al, 1986; Code 1991, 1995).

The dimension of *responsibility* has been central in traditional political learning (and education). The nature of responsibility is shaped by recent and current social transformations. Authoritarian, and even welfare, states assume responsibility for their citizens in problematic ways, organising moral obligations in ways for which they are often ill equipped. Wolfe (1989), for example, argues that new welfare states' intervention in civil society makes the organisation of obligations to distant strangers more difficult. Related arguments can be found in the work of Levinas (1991), Taylor (1991) and Melucci (1996). Learning responsibility is a vital and problematic aspect of learning citizenship.

Typically, learning citizenship and governance in our late modern society can be seen as comprising two shifts. On the one hand, there is a de-ideologisation of politics and a more pragmatic concentration on concrete social issues. This shift is sometimes discussed as the instrumentalisation of political learning. So, in late modern political learning, the dimension of *effectivity* comes more to the foreground. On the other hand, the diminishing role of politics also leads in citizens to a more personal commitment with particular issues and particular forms of participation. These more personalised forms of politics can be found, in particular, in the new forms of learning citizenship and governance outside the domain of the state.

Within such forms of political, economic, or civic participation, the element of *identity* building and self-realisation becomes stronger. In late modern social philosophy, in contrast to instrumentalisation, this shift is sometimes referred to as the aestheticisation of politics. The nature of identity learning arises especially in relation to changes in the nature of identity – local, regional, ethnic, transnational, and so forth – in the European context. However, the analysis and understanding of identity has substantial roots in social theory (Goffman, 1959; Habermas, 1989; Giddens, 1991; Lash & Friedman, 1992; Potter, 1996). Melucci (1996) argues that there is a sense of something lacking in persons which leads them to question who they are. In terms of education for governance and citizenship, important elements in identity learning are the development of social skills and feelings of social commitment and the development of an open attitude.

Modes of Learning

In relation to each of these learning contexts and dimensions of learning, the project investigates the effectiveness of actual and potential interventions in terms of three principal modes: *formal, non-formal* and *informal* (Coombs & Ahmed, 1974). This categorisation permits the application of mainstream educational theory to such concepts as the *learning society* and *lifelong learning*, providing an established and more precise categorisation, which is less liable to conceptual slippage than 'lifelong learning' and similar terms.

The Analytical Matrix

Combining the three main elements enables an analytical matrix to be derived for the research. This matrix, resembling a three-dimensional cube, allows the research team to analyse specific combinations of *domain of learning, dimension of learning agency* and *mode of intervention*. A total of 36 combinations (4 x 3 x 3) is theoretically feasible, each providing a logically distinct point for comparative analysis. (As explained earlier, the research focuses for pragmatic reasons on three dimensions – work, the state, and the civil society.) The combinations enable the team to explore strengths and limitations in educational approach, and to evaluate policies and intervention strategies. The matrix will be refined and simplified during the research process, so that a version of it can be applied readily in educational practice, planning and policy decisions.

In order to understand exclusion as well as to stimulate active citizenship, knowledge of particular and local contexts is needed. While Europe's economic, political and social objectives are now relatively well established, little is known of how educational intervention for adults currently occurs, or should take place, in the diverse contexts (national, domains) in which these objectives must be achieved. The matrix should provide a basis for a structured and internationally comparable body of knowledge about educational strategies across these domains and national contexts.

Research Methodology

Research Locations

The research is being conducted in six European countries (five EU member states – Belgium [B], Spain [E], the Netherlands [NL], Finland [FIN], and the United Kingdom [UK], plus the Republic of Slovenia [SI]). The countries have been selected to provide an illuminating cross-section of European states in terms of geographical and demographic size, economic and industrial structure, political and cultural institutions and history, and period of membership of the European Union and Communities. This permits a cross-cultural analysis of citizenship and governance education in terms of political, economic and social power.

A number of (chiefly quantitative) social and political indicators have been used to ensure that the selected countries provide an appropriate range of contrast, both historical and contemporary. The indicators include features such as date of accession to the EU, length of continuous democratic government, population, population density, gross domestic product per capita, industry as percentage of total employment, main religious affiliations, divorce rate, births outside marriage, suicide rate (men), unemployment, students at third level per 100,000 population and television receivers per 1000 population.

Main Phases of the Research

Exploration and planning. The research programme comprises five phases: exploration and planning, biographical methods, focus groups, scientific interpretation, and dissemination of findings. During the first phase, each partner engaged in a preliminary audit of existing networks relating to citizenship and governance education. This provided information for the identification of learners and educators for later phases. Advisory panels of about 10 members were established. Members are drawn from such areas as national and local government policy-making, adult and school education, industrial and commercial training, media and new learning professions, not-for-profit and religious organisations, and employers and trade unions.

Life history and biographical methods. Life history and biographical methods (a major theme in recent empirical methods on adult learning; see e.g. Alheit, 1996; Antikainen et al, 1996; Dausien, 1996; West, 1996; Eriksson-Stjernberg, 1998) are designed to provide a fuller understanding of the nature of the mutual articulation of 'effectivity', 'responsibility', and 'identity' in the learning of active citizenship and governance within the three domains (work, state, civil society). The research project will reconstruct the life histories of a sample of learners, and will analyse these in terms of the nature, context and periodisation of their learning of citizenship and governance. A total of 96 learners have been selected, 16 in each country. These learners are drawn from the three selected learning contexts.

The prime criterion for selection of these learners has been that they, in their own social environment, can be considered active as citizens in one of the three domains. Examples of these might be trade union representatives or team leaders (work domain), environmental activists, lay members of religious organisations, or club secretaries (civil society), and social workers, welfare rights officers and local political party activists (state). However, in each learning context in each country, one or two adults have been selected on the basis that they do *not* appear to be 'active citizens' (according to traditional or dominant definitions). This is designed primarily to provide a point of comparison or contrast, but also to serve as a basis for exploration of other, perhaps unrecognised, ways in which men and women are, and learn to become, agents of change.

The learners were selected on a theoretical sampling basis, with a balance of two age cohorts: those aged 25-40 and 55-70. These age cohorts permit exploration of the hypothesis that patterns of civic commitment and learning of citizenship have changed significantly over the last 2-3 decades. The hypothesis stems from a theoretical underpinning of the project: the significance of the late twentieth-century transformation from 'classic modern' to 'late modern' or 'postmodern' social conditions. The 55-70 age-cohort underwent its primary and secondary socialisation before 1965, while the 25-40 age-cohort would have been born between 1960 and 1975, and become adults in years from the late 1970s to the early 1990s. The latter may be seen as a 'postmodern' or 'late modern' generation, and the research will permit exploration of the implications of this transition for the learning of governance and citizenship.

There is an equal representation of female and male learners in each country (though for arithmetical reasons, the balance cannot be precisely achieved within each specific learning context). This permits investigation of the hypothesis that notions of active citizenship are gendered, and that female modes of activity and collaboration are excluded from definitions of legitimate 'activity'.

The interviews address issues of how and why attitudes to citizenship are learned, and in what contexts. They also explore issues of periodisation in learning. Interviews also address why adults do not learn to be 'active', why some learn to be active in 'illegitimate' or 'dysfunctional' ways, and what learning processes lead people to cease to be active. The influence of formal, informal and non-formal education is considered.

Focus groups. Focus groups are to be used to transform the results of the biographical and documentary stages of the research into effective intervention strategies. Over recent years, focus group research has become established as an effective method in empirical social inquiry (Morgan & Spanish, 1984; Krueger, 1994; Morgan, 1997; Morgan & Krueger, 1997; Barbour & Kitzinger, 1998). Specifically, however, focus groups have been established as a reliable, valid and cost-effective method for the formulation of effective intervention strategies in various aspects of the education and training of adults (van der Veen & van Netten, 1997).

In each region, three focus groups will be formed, one within each of the selected three domains (work, state and civil). Each of these groups will consist of 8-10 experts drawn from different aspects of education and learning, which relate to the selected learning context. The definition of 'education and learning' used for this purpose will be a broad one, and will include not only teachers and other adult educators, but also community development workers, management consultants, 'change agents', as well as professionals in the media, developers of learning packages, etc.

Within each focus group, there will be an equal representation of men and women. However, in order to explore the possibility that the effectiveness of intervention strategies may vary by gender, further focus groups will be formed, one consisting entirely of men, the other entirely of women.

Scientific interpretation, dialogue and dissemination. The fourth phase of the project will interpret the empirical data, providing links between the data collected in the two empirical phases (biographical; focus groups), and develop analyses which combine these data in new perspectives and insights for both national and international purposes.

The final phase addresses the need to build on the participation of citizenship and governance educators and policy-makers within the project, and to draw them further into the analysis and shaping of outputs. This is designed to disseminate the perspectives, data and materials developed during the project, to enable the project outputs to play a role in strengthening professional communities of 'active citizenship educators', but also to strengthen further professionals' and end-users' role in making the project outputs appropriate and user-friendly.

Emerging Issues

Grappling with Definitional Complexities

This chapter has presented some key theoretical and methodological issues underpinning the project, which investigates how adults learn 'active citizenship' and 'governance' in Europe. During the first 6 months of the research, several issues emerged, mainly related to key concepts and methodology.

As a collaborative exercise, it was important to establish a consensus on operational definitions of key concepts such as 'citizenship', 'active citizenship', and 'governance'. This kind of consensus is needed so that the team has a shared understanding of the research, and to underpin the selection of 'active citizens' for the life history interviews.

A potential divergence in understanding of the concepts stems, *inter alia*, from varying national understandings, and from how the concepts translate from English. For example, the Finnish translation for the name of the project (Kansalasiseksi Kasvaminen Euroopassa) would translate back to English as 'to develop as a citizen in Europe'. The Finnish partners advise that there is 'no sensible Finnish expression' for 'governance' in this context.

One further example deserves mention. In English, it is possible to distinguish between the meanings of the words 'governance' and 'government'. Although the distinction is in many respects one of nuance, and dictionary definitions overlap in substantial ways, *governance* can be used in relation to issues to which *government* does not typically refer. Table I sets out a number of dictionary definitions.

Although at first sight these appear very similar, closer inspection reveals that although the meanings overlap to a very large degree, there are some interesting areas of contrast. In particular, *government* tends to be used to refer to institutions ('the government has stated its view on such-and-such'), while *governance* is more commonly associated with processes of governing. Not being closely associated with specific institutions, and as a word which has rather fallen from use until the last few years, *governance* is also a rather plastic term, quite readily moulded to the ends desired by its users.

'Government' (From Webster)	'Governance' (From various dictionaries)
The person or persons authorised to administer the laws; the ruling power; the administration.	Exercise of authority; control; government; arrangement.
The body politic governed by one authority; a state; as, the governments of Europe.	The state of being governed.
The right or power of governing; authority.	
The act of governing; exercise of authority; administration of laws; control; direction; regulation; as, civil, church, or family government.	The act, process, or power of governing; government: 'Regaining a sense of the state is thus an absolute priority, not only for an effective policy against ... terrorism, but also for governance itself'.
The mode of governing; system of polity in a state; established form of law.	

Table I. Dictionary definitions of government and governance.

In this light, the fact that *governance* has been adopted by those advocating certain broad political agendas is hardly surprising – but does make the quest for an unambiguous 'scientific definition' still more complex. This is particularly true in the European context, where governance has been adopted – for example – as part of an agenda to recast the role of the European Commission. Thus, we find a recent European Commission paper asserting that:

> *the situation at national state level in terms of democratic representation and of effectiveness is [not] as healthy as is often contended in terms of the model of parliamentary democracy. To the contrary, there is a growing awareness that the ever wider control and monitoring functions claimed by centralised national governments are at odds with their actual abilities and that these functions are being diffused among an ever more complex array of actors who defy description in terms of this traditional model. But while these new modes of governance lack accountability in these terms, their development is often testament to their technical effectiveness and efficiency as well as their flexibility in comparison with the traditional forms of government. (Lebessis & Paterson, 1997, p. 9)*

They are also seen as having 'potential' for providing alternative forms of 'accountability' and 'representation'. This line of thinking has been taken up by Romano Prodi, President of the European Commission, in attempting to revitalise the relationship between 'Europe' and its people.

> *I believe Europe needs a new division of labour – a new, more democratic form of partnership – between civil society and the other actors involved in governance. I call this new partnership 'Network Europe'. It means EU institutions, national governments, regional and local authorities and civil society interacting in new ways: consulting one another on a whole range of issues; shaping, implementing and monitoring policy together. It means citizens having a greater say at all levels.*
>
> *But if civil society is to play an effective part in European governance, we have to ensure that European policy initiatives are debated in Europe-wide fora. The media must be involved, obviously, but also trade unions, business associations, churches and all the various non-governmental groupings which make up civil society. (Prodi, 2000)*

In effect, therefore, various key terms used in the research must serve both a conceptual or analytical role within the research project, while they have simultaneously been adopted by political actors and now form part of the 'programmatic baggage' of contemporary politics. The example of governance has been given here; much the same might be said of 'active citizenship'.

Of course, several key terms have also been the subject of philosophical debate and political contest over centuries, even millennia: the notion of *citizenship* is a clear example. Many recent discussions commence with the work of T.H. Marshall, who saw citizenship as consisting of 'three parts, or elements' that were 'dictated by history even more clearly than by logic': civil, political and social. More recently, the Council of Europe has identified legal, political and psychological dimensions of citizenship. But European debates about citizenship date back at least to ancient Greece, and these debates demonstrate – if nothing else – that citizenship can be understood from various political and ideological standpoints.

Key contributions to debates about citizenship come in recent years from feminist approaches. According to Preece (2000), the generic features of a gender perspective on citizenship include consideration of power relations, manifested through the use of language, behaviour and internalised meanings; the experience of being a woman, as described by women (drawing out issues of identity and subjectivity); how people create a sense of agency from their interpretations of conflicting discourses; representations of women, men, gender and racial difference, and other forms of inequality through text and media; the need to look beyond the 'normal'; and frameworks which emphasise experience as interpreted in context.

Some Initial Observations

At this stage of the research, it is possible to give only a few examples of some of the themes which appear to be emerging. Among these are the following.

In all countries studied, the welfare state is a key problem issue, intimately connected both with governance and with the nature of citizenship. The nature of the problems emerging is by no means surprising. The escalating cost of public services and the growing problems and complexity of managing the public sector are commonplaces of socio-political debate over the past quarter century. But linked to this is the nature of citizenship in the welfare state, where citizens are also consumers and customers.

There is a general concern at a rising 'democratic deficit': the sense that established mechanisms of democratic government no longer work effectively, and that in part they fail to work because the people no longer trust them. There are, of course, many aspects to this, and the democratic deficit is articulated in rather different ways in the different countries. Nevertheless, the concern is general. And stemming from it, we find quite a widespread concern to 'remoralise' citizens: the feeling (at least on the part of those who govern) that if citizens have lost confidence in government, ways must be found of regenerating their sense of community spirit and collective responsibility.

There is a widespread interest in mechanisms which will decentralise the processes and institutions of government. This is clearly linked to the concern to 'remoralise' the citizenry. It emerges in different forms in various countries, but across the countries we study, there have been experiments with 'direct' democracy, such as citizens' forums, and growing attempts to encourage the voluntary sector and non-governmental organisations to play an active part in social processes such as welfare provision.

Finally, all countries showed – though in nationally specific ways – growing concern with the politics of migration, ethnicity and identity.

At the same time, some very distinct features emerge, which confirm how significant national cultural contexts are in the study of citizenship and governance. We will remark on only three.

In countries – in our sample, Spain and Slovenia – where democracy has been quite recently established, the experience of the transition to democracy is marked, and plays a powerful part in popular conceptions of citizenship and governance.

In Belgium and the Netherlands, the notion of citizenship as having been constructed within a 'pillarised' society is very important, and by the same token, the erosion of pillarised structures and identities – 'depillarisation' – is seen as a critical contemporary trend, with profound implications for the understanding of citizenship.

In the Netherlands, the importance of the *poldermodel* – a form of governance, involving the pursuit of compromise, consensus and harmony at every level – is marked. But it is seen as variously positive and negative: 'the treacle state' is both supportive and constraining.

Early indications support the need for research on citizenship education and the learning of citizenship among adults. Although studies of formal civic education are becoming much more common, and there are in some countries well-established traditions of study of non-formal – community – adult education, *learning* citizenship and governance remains very seldom studied. And this is particularly true of learning of citizenship by adults.[3]

Notes

[1] The chapter stems from the project, 'Education and Training for Governance and Active Citizenship in Europe: analysis of adult learning and design of formal, non-formal and informal educational intervention strategies', funded under the European Union's Fifth Framework programme. This chapter draws on the project proposal, which was drafted by J. Holford and R. van der Veen, with support and advice from other members of the project team, in particular, P. Jarvis, M. Laitinen, V. Mohorcic Špolar, J. Preece and D. Wildemeersch.

[2] This project does not involve empirical research within the school context. However, the ways in which learning in formal education (i.e. chiefly as children or young adults in school) has a continuing impact on adults' constructs of active citizenship and governance, and on how they conduct their roles as citizens, are addressed.

[3] The project website (http://www.surrey.ac.uk/Education/ETGACE/index.htm) includes information about progress and papers emerging from the research.

References

Alheit, P. (1996) Changing Basic Rules of Biographical Construction: modern biographies at the end of the twentieth century, in A. Weymann & W. Heinz (Eds) *Society and Biography: interrelationships between social structure, institutions and life course*, pp. 111-128. Weinheim: Juventa.

Antikainen, A., Houtsonen, J., Kauppila, J. & Huotelin, H. (1996) *Living in a Learning Society: life histories, identities and education*. London: Falmer Press.

Barbour, R. & Kitzinger, J. (Eds) (1998) *Developing Focus Group Research: politics, theory and practice*. London: Sage.

Bauman, Z. (1993) *Postmodern Ethics*. Oxford: Blackwell.

Beck, U. (1992) *Risk Society: towards a new modernity*. London: Sage.

Beck, U. (1997) *The Reinvention of Politics: rethinking modernity in the global social order*. Cambridge: Polity Press.

Beck, U., Giddens, A. & Lash, S. (1994) *Reflexive Modernization: politics, tradition and aesthetics in the modern social order*. Cambridge: Polity Press.

Belenky, M.F., Clinchy, B.U., Goldberger, N.R. & Tarule, J.M. (1986) *Women's Ways of Knowing: the development of self, voice and mind*. New York: Basic Books.

Benhabib, S. (1992) *Situating the Self: gender, community and postmodernism in contemporary ethics*. Oxford: Polity Press.

Biggs, J. & Moore, P. (1993) *The Process of Learning*. Sydney: Prentice-Hall Australia.

Bloom, B.S. (1956) *Taxonomy of Educational Objectives: the classification of educational goals*. New York: David McKay.

Code, L. (1991) *What Can She Know? Feminist Theory and Construction of Knowledge*. London: Cornell University Press.

Code, L. (1995) *Rhetorical Spaces: essays in gendered locations*. London: Routledge.

Coombs, P. & Ahmed, M. (1974) *Attacking Rural Poverty: how nonformal education can help*. Baltimore: Johns Hopkins University Press.

Crick, B. & Porter, A. (Eds) (1978) *Political Education and Political Literacy*. London: Longman.

Crittenden, B. (1978) Autonomy as an Aim of Education, in K.O. Strike & K. Egan (Eds) *Ethics and Educational Policy*, pp. 107-108. London: Routledge & Kegan Paul.

Dausien, B. (1996) *Biographie und Geschlecht. Zur biographischen Konstruktion sozialer Wirklichkeit in Frauenlebensgeschichten* (Biography and gender. on biographical construction of social reality in female life histories). Bremen: IBL Forschung 1.

Eriksson-Stjernberg, I. (1998) Emotions in Life-long Learning, *Nordisk Pedagogik*, 18(2), pp. 65-76.

Finger, M. (1989) New Social Movements and their Implications for Adult education, *Adult Education Quarterly*, 40, pp. 15-22.

Freire, P. (1970) *Pedagogy of the Oppressed*. Harmondsworth: Penguin.

Freire, P. (1996) *Pedagogia da Autonomia. Saberes necessários à práctica educativa*. São Paulo: Paz e Terra.

Giddens, A. (1984) *The Constitution of Society: introduction of the theory of structuration*. Berkeley: University of California Press.

Giddens, A. (1991) *Modernity and Self-identity: self and society in the late modern age*. Cambridge: Polity Press.

Giroux, H.A. (1983) Critical Theory and Rationality in Citizenship Education, in H. Giroux & D. Purpel (Eds) *The Hidden Curriculum and Moral Education: deception or discovery?* pp. 321-360. Berkeley: McCutchan.

Giroux, H. (1987) Citizenship, Public Philosophy, and the Struggle for Democracy, *Educational Theory*, 37(2), pp. 103-120.

Giroux, H. (1992) *Border Crossings: cultural workers and the politics of education*. New York: Routledge.

Giroux, H. & McLaren, P. (1986) Teacher Education and the Politics of Engagement: the case for democratic schooling, *Harvard Educational Review*, 56, pp. 213-238.

Giroux, H. & McLaren, P. (Eds) (1994) *Between Borders: pedagogy and the political of cultural studies*. New York: Routledge.

Goffman, E. (1959) *The Presentation of Self in Everyday Life*. Harmondsworth: Penguin.

Habermas, J. (1987) *The Theory of Communicative Action*. Vol. 2. *Lifeworld and System*. Cambridge: Polity Press.

Habermas, J. (1989) *The New Conservatism*. Cambridge: Polity Press.

Habermas, J. (1991) *The Theory of Communicative Action*. Vol. 1. *Reason and the Rationalization of Society*. Oxford: Polity Press.

Holford, J. (1995) Why Social Movements Matter: adult education theory, cognitive praxis, and the creation of knowledge, *Adult Education Quarterly*, 45(2), pp. 95-111.

Jarvis, P. (1987) *Adult Learning in the Social Context*. London: Croom Helm.

Krueger, R.A. (1994) *Focus Groups: a practical guide for applied research*, 2nd edn. Thousand Oaks: Sage.

Lash, S. & Friedman, J. (Eds) (1992) *Modernity and Identity*. Cambridge: Polity Press.

Lave, J. & Wenger, E. (1991) *Situated Learning: legitimate peripheral participation*. Cambridge: Cambridge University Press.

Lebessis, N. & Paterson, J. (1997) *Evolutions in Governance: what lessons for the Commission? A First Assessment*. European Commission, Forward Studies Unit Working Paper. Available from:
http://europa.eu.int/comm/cdp/working-paper/evolution_in_governance.pdf

Levinas, E. (1991) *Totality and Infinity*. Dordrecht: Kluwer.

Lyotard, J-F. (1984) *The Postmodern Condition: a report on knowledge*. Manchester: Manchester University Press.

Marshall, T.H. (1950) *Citizenship and Social Class, and Other Essays*. Cambridge: Cambridge University Press.

Marsick, V.J. (1987) *Learning in the Workplace*. London: Croom Helm.

Marsick, V.J. & Watkins, K.E. (1990) *Informal and Incidental Learning in the Workplace*. London: Routledge.

Melucci, A. (1996) *The Playing Self*. Cambridge: Cambridge University Press.

Morgan, D.L. (1997) *Focus Groups as Qualitative Research*, 2nd edn. Thousand Oaks: Sage.

Morgan, D.L. & Krueger, D.L. (1997) *The Focus Group Kit*. Vols 1-6. Thousand Oaks: Sage.

Morgan, D.L. & Spanish, M.T. (1984) Focus Groups: a new tool for qualitative research. *Qualitative Sociology*, 7, pp. 253-270.

Porter, A. (1981) Political Literacy, in D. Heater & J. Gillespie (Eds) *Political Education in Flux*. Beverley Hills: Sage.

Porter, A. (1996) The Aims of Education for Citizenship, in L.N.K. Lo & S.W. Man (Eds) *Research and Endeavours in Moral and Civic* Education, pp. 1-10. Hong Kong: Hong Kong Institute of Educational Research, Chinese University of Hong Kong.

Potter, J. (1996). *Representing Reality*. London: Sage.

Preece, J. (2000) The Learning of Citizenship and Governance: a gender perspective, in J. Holford & P. Edirisingha (Eds) *Citizenship and Governance Education in Europe: a critical review of the literature. Report to the European Commission*, pp. 21-31. Guildford: School of Educational Studies, University of Surrey.

Prodi, R. (2000) Towards a European Civil Society. Second European Social Week, Bad Honnef, 6 April. Speech/00/124: http://www.europa.eu.int/rapid/start/cgi/guesten.ksh?p_action.gettxt=gt&doc=SPEECH/00/124|0|RAPID&lg=EN

Sennett, R. (1998) *The Corrosion of Character: the personal consequences of work in the new capitalism*. New York: Norton.

Sociaal en Cultureel Rapport 1996 (1996) Rijswijk: Sociaal en Cultureel Planbureau.

Taylor, C. (1991) *The Ethics of Authenticity*. Cambridge, MA: Harvard University Press.

Tsang, W.K. (1996) Citizenship Education, Modernity and Postmodernity: a sociological analysis, in L.N.K. Lo & S.W. Man (Eds) *Research and Endeavours in Moral and Civic Education*, pp. 11-38. Hong Kong: Hong Kong Institute of Educational Research, Chinese University of Hong Kong.

van der Veen, R.G.W & van Netten, H. (1997) *Informeel leren in sociaal-cultureel werk*. Utrecht: NIZW.

Wenger, E. (1998) *Communities of Practice: learning, meaning and identity*. Cambridge: Cambridge University Press.

West, L. (1996) *Beyond Fragments: adults, motivation, and higher education: a biographical analysis*. Washington, DC: Taylor & Francis.

Wolfe, A. (1989) *Whose Keeper? Social Science and Moral Obligation*. Berkeley: University of California Press.

Globalisation, Citizenship and the Education of Adults in Contemporary Society

PETER JARVIS

Traditionally, society has been regarded as having two distinct spheres – the state and civil society – the former being public and the latter the private – by which we mean that it lay beyond the sphere of the state, such as the ownership of private property, non-governmental organisations, and so on. Traditionally, the state has been the mechanism through which a people in a specified territory has been governed, and in democratic societies citizens have been free to enter and play a role within the public sphere and they also have had some rights in determining who will rule them. As Habermas (1989, p. 85) points out, the:

> *public sphere of society stood or fell with the principle of universal access. A public sphere from which specific groups would be* eo ipso *excluded was less than merely incomplete; it was not a public sphere at all. (Emphasis in original)*

Three criteria were essential for citizens to enter the public sphere: being male, having a good education and property ownership. Over the years, as societies have become more democratic, these restrictions on entry have declined but not disappeared. Until recently, power has resided in the public sphere. However, through the process of globalisation, the structures of society are undergoing profound changes, which in their turn are affecting the power relations. This chapter seeks to examine the relationship between citizenship and the education of adults as a result of these changes. It has three parts: globalisation, the changing nature of citizenship and the education of adults. The chapter argues that formal education will continue to reproduce the social structures but that there is a major place for learning, especially that which has occurred in radical adult education organisations.

Peter Jarvis

Globalisation

The process of globalisation, as we know it today, began in the West (USA followed by western Europe) in the early 1970s. There were a number of contributory factors, such as the development of sophisticated information technology through the Star Wars programme, competition from Japan, the General Agreement on Tariffs and Trade (GATT) and the breakdown of the Bretton Woods agreement, the oil crisi, which dented the confidence of the West, and so on. Corporations began to transfer capital and relocate manufacturing around the world, seeking the cheapest places and the most efficient means to manufacture, and the best markets in which to sell their products. Those who control capital (not own it) constitute the major powers in the global market, which has expanded rapidly because of the advances in information technology. The information technology revolution took off, with one development leading to another, as Castells (1996, p. 51f.) demonstrates. He makes the point that 'to some extent, the availability of new technologies constituted as a system in the 1970s was a fundamental basis for the process of socio-economic restructuring in the 1980s' (p. 52).

The driving force of social change is information technology driven by those who control capital – both financial and intellectual. More significantly, however, the corporations have been able to create an international division of labour and to generate a competitive international market. Suddenly the state, the public sphere, has been undermined and one element from the private sphere has assumed more power than the state. Indeed, the structures of the world have changed, made possible by the formation of joint stock companies in the first instance. Now these have changed and the most successful ones control capital, both financial and intellectual, and consequently information technology; transnational corporations have transformed capitalism. Controlling capital and information technology is the mechanism of corporate dominance worldwide. What has not become globalised is the apparatus of the state, so that governments are now almost incapable of regulating the global market or its substructure. Beck (2000, p. 11) actually suggests that globalisation is 'the *processes* through which sovereign national states are criss-crossed and undermined by transnational actors with varying prospects of power, orientations, identities and networks' (italics in original). That they do so with little intervention being possible by any state is most significant for our understanding of the public sphere. Castells (1996), however, has argued that the state still has a place to play in a not-completely free but extremely competitive global market. Now global society has three spheres: the global market, the state systems and the private sphere.

Consequently, there is a need to create a world society – a transnational civil society – as opposed to the global market. Such a society would ultimately need a world system of governance, which will

292

be hard to achieve. Citizenship would have to be transnational, but at present, there are few opportunities to be a world citizen, although there is an increasing number of social movements that are assuming a global role, such as the feminist, ecological and environmental movements. But these are early days for global citizenship since most states still seek to protect their own territorial integrity and politicians their own power base. It is, however, an increasingly significant debate of which educators should be aware and in which they should play their part.

At present, the transnational corporations alone function as if the world is already united. The law of the transnational is the law of the global market, whereas the laws of the states are still apparently controlled by the democratic (or not so democratic) governments. But the global market has simply bypassed the laws of the states, and as Bauman (1999, p. 156) argued, this has resulted in less active citizenship:

> *Once the state recognizes the priority and superiority of the laws of the market over the laws of the* polis, *the citizen is transmuted into the consumer, and a 'consumer demands more and more protection while accepting less and less the need to participate' in the running of the state. (Emphasis in original)*

There is a danger in this that Habermas (1954, p. 359) warns about: 'the public sphere is a warning system with sensors that, though unspecialized, are sensitive throughout society'. When the sensors are not operating, then the public sphere seems irrelevant to the private and people no longer seek to participate in it. The laws of the global market undermine all forms of democratic activity.

Marshall (1950), who thought that capitalism and citizenship were incompatible, was still optimistic enough to think that the profits of capitalism could fund citizens' welfare, which he regarded as one of the rights of citizens which enabled them to live the life of a civilised being according to the standard prevailing in society. But in the global society, there is no way of enforcing these rights – if they exist – and so there is no welfare and even free education is being undermined. Even in countries where there has been welfare, it is now being reduced, and so the socially excluded get poorer.

The Changing Nature of Citizenship

Marshall (1950) regarded citizenship as functioning within three spheres: the private, the public and the social. Turner (1990) also started from the distinction between private and public, but recognised that there is also an active-passive dimension. Consequently, he suggested that a conservative view of citizenship is that it is passive and private whereas a more radical form is active and public. His four forms of citizenship are:

passive democratic – acts in the public space and allowed from above;

revolutionary – acts in the public space and comes from the people;

plebiscitary authoriarian – acts in the private space and is allowed from above;

liberal pluralism – acts in the private space and comes from the people. (1990, p. 200)

The passive (conservative) form of citizenship has been encouraged by right-wing governments (by whatever name they go) and is being practised by many people living in such societies. This has, paradoxically, actually allowed the state itself to be rolled back and rendered even more ineffective in the face of globalisation. As the global market gains even more power, so the state continues to abdicate its welfare responsibility.

The capitalist discourse is prevalent; even people are human capital. Human beings are useful if they are employable, but there are problems if they become redundant and there is no welfare. Indeed, it is almost as if employability is itself a symbol of citizenship, and being employed is a means of entry into a new dimension of citizenship – citizenship of the corporation. Meister (1998, pp. 95-98) actually describes how the companies not only utilise the language of, but train new employees in, corporate, citizenship with its hidden curriculum of global capitalist culture.

She quotes the director of the University of Chicago Hospital (UCH):

Our vision in creating the orientation program for UCH was to develop a program where our employees could learn to be good citizens. To us, a good citizen moves beyond performing just the job tasks. Rather a good citizen acts like he/she is the owner of the business, desires to satisfy customers, understands that customer satisfaction comes from how the job is done, and takes responsibility for continually striving to do a better job. (1998, p. 95)

Employed individuals become corporate citizens and even though they do not own the business, they act as if they do. They are educated to be active and further the corporate mission, while they may well remain passive and private citizens of the state itself. Indeed, Bauman (1999, p. 169) suggests that the power of the state has diminished to such an extent that it is toothless to protect its citizens in the face of global economic demands, and so, what of citizenship within local civil society?

Herein lies the nub of the contemporary problem of citizenship – traditionally, the active citizen has worked for the good society and the common good, whereas the corporate citizen now works for the corporate good and individual gain.

Indeed, Riley (1992, p. 209) perhaps summarises this discussion about welfare of the socially excluded quite succinctly:

> *Citizenship, especially when invoked in the same breath as the welfare state, embodies a purposeful dream that has never been fully realized. The question is how far this egalitarian drive within citizenship remains convincing as an aspiration, given the proliferation of claims for the recognition of difference. Yet this strong ideal within citizenship is unlikely to fall into neglect because it insists on some standard of rights which inhere in each person, simply by virtue of that person's being in society.*

For the most part, therefore, we can see that citizenship is a problematic concept in a rapidly globalising world and the concern for this world and its peoples has been overtaken by the concern for the corporation and individual gain in a great deal of political rhetoric and corporate discourse. In this situation, the democratic processes are being overturned and there is an increasing need to rediscover active citizenship in which men and women can work together for the common good, especially for those who are excluded as a result of the mechanisms of the global market.

The Place of Education and Learning in Global Society

Education is increasingly being seen as a way through which people can learn to become active citizens. Some educators often refer to education as if it is a single, homogeneous entity, However, a number of years ago, I drew a distinction in curricular models: education from above and the education of equals (Jarvis, 1985, pp. 48-50), although my analysis is only one amongst a number that have started from similar perspectives (see, for instance, Freire, 1972; Griffin, 1978).

Currently, however, there is a blurring of the differences between education and learning. Within the rhetoric of the learning society, the term 'learning' appears to be being used in an institutionalised form, as if it were education. Learning, however, is individual whereas education is social: the blurring of the terms places more emphasis on individual and less on social responsibility for education. For the remainder of this chapter, education refers to all institutionalised forms of learning and learning to the human processes whereby individuals acquire knowledge, etc. and develop their own human being as a result. I now want to discuss these two forms of learning separately.

Education (Institutionalised Learning)

Institutionalised education may be classified as 'education from above' – it is a system of initiating individuals meeting the system needs. Its content is selected from the system's culture by those given the power and authority so to do, its methods are usually didactic (whether it be face-to-face or through distance modes), the learning is examined and a certificate of achievement (sometimes but wrongly related to ability) awarded. This is a public recognition of achievement, the right to perform a job, to be a member of an association or organisation, and so forth. There is a sense in which this form of education is, *ipso facto*, reproductive. Indeed, we have to consider the economic rationale of those (corporations or states) who invest in education, if their overall aim is not in some way to be reproductive in social and cultural terms.

Educational systems are institutionalised and controlled systems of learning. Bourdieu (1973, p. 84) wrote:

> *By making social hierarchies and the reproduction of these hierarchies appear to be based upon the hierarchy of 'gifts', merits, or skills established and ratified by its sanctions, or, in a word, by converting social hierarchies into academic hierarchies, the education system fulfils the function of legitimation which is more and more necessary to the perpetuation of the 'social order' as the evolution of the power relationship between classes tends more completely to exclude the imposition of a hierarchy based upon a crude affirmation of the power relationship.*

Bourdieu's thesis of social and cultural reproduction was echoed by Althusser's (1972), amongst others. It is, perhaps, significant that more recently, Giddens (1998, pp. 109-110) made the point that education is not able to reduce the inequalities in society. If the system (corporate, state or other) wants passive, or conformist, citizens, then it will reproduce the status quo.

Nevertheless, idealists have placed great hopes in education being a means by which active citizens can create a more democratic and equal society. Beveridge (1944, p. 256), for instance, echoing the famous 1919 Report, wrote:

> *Learning should not end with school. Learning and life must be kept together throughout life; democracies will not be well governed till that is done. Later study should be open to all, and money, teaching and opportunities must be found for that*

as well. In the development of education this is the most
important, if not the most urgent, of all tasks of reconstruction.
The needs of civilised men are illimitable, because they
include the wise, happy enjoyment of leisure.

A very similar position is held by Ranson (1994), who sees the learning society as one in which all people can be active citizens and play a democratic role. But, for many, the learning society is an educative one. There is certainly a major place in society for a wide provision of education which might help socially excluded women and men find a place in contemporary society; it might also help make others aware of the importance of active citizenship and being involved in community development issues.

Learning

Learning is uncontrollable inasmuch as it occurs within people, even when they learn in a controlled educational setting. Dovey (Dovey & Onyx, 2001) demonstrated how workers in South Africa were able to use the education and training that they were receiving in the workplace to play a role in civil society.

Teaching and learning among equals, where there is no control of the outcomes, is the form that traditional adult education has frequently assumed. Many adult education institutions have been closely related to social movements. For instance, Highlander (Adams, 1975; Horton & Freire, 1990) played a major role in the American civil rights movement, and the Canadian Association of Adult Education (Selman, 1991) endeavoured to create a more democratic Canada after World War II. In addition, the feminist movement, which is also about the education of equals approach, has played a major role in helping women to become more active citizens. All of these movements have had a vision of a better society.

Conclusions

I am not so naive as to think that the vision of a better society and a good life for all will be more attractive to many people in the face of corporate and individual gain, or that active involvement is more enjoyable than passive citizenship. I am not as optimistic as many that education will suddenly produce active citizens, or cease to play its traditional reproductive role. However, I am optimistic that people will continue to learn about ways in which they can be citizens through the educational system, and that non-governmental organisations and other movements will continue to offer an education of equals that enables some members of society to play active citizenship roles (whether they are at local, state or international level) in this global society.

In addition, the democratic processes that still exist, but are being eroded by globalisation, might eventually force the state, even a superstate, to play a more independent role and seek to regulate the transnational corporations. Then it might genuinely develop that form of education that education theorists have written about for many generations:

> The peculiarity of truly human life is that man [sic] has to create himself by his own voluntary efforts; he has to make himself a truly moral, rational, and free being. This creative effort is carried on by the educational activities of slow generations. Its acceleration depends upon men consciously striving to educate their successors not for the existing state of affairs but so as to make possible a better future for humanity. (Dewey, 1916, p. 95)

References

Adams, F. (with Myles Horton) (1975) *Unearthing Seeds of Fire*. Winston-Salem: Blair.

Althusser, L. (1973) Ideology and Ideological State Apparatus, in B.R. Cosin (Ed.) *Education, Structure and Society*. Harmondsworth: Penguin.

Bauman, Z. (1999) *In Search of Politics*. Cambridge: Polity Press.

Beck, U. (2000) *What is Globalization?* trans. P. Camiller. Cambridge: Polity Press.

Beveridge, W. (1944) *Full Employment in a Free Society*. London: George Allen & Unwin.

Bourdieu, P. (1973) Cultural Reproduction and Social Reproduction, in R. Brown (Ed.) *Knowledge, Education and Social Change*. London: Tavistock.

Castells, M. (1996) *The Rise of the Network Society* (vol. 1 of *The Information Age: economy, society and culture*). Oxford: Blackwell.

Dewey, J. (1916) *Democracy and Education*. New York: Free Press.

Dovey, K. & Onyx, J. (2001) Generating Social Capital at the Workplace, *International Journal of Lifelong Education*, 20.

Freire, P. (1972) *Pedagogy of the Oppressed*, trans. Myra Bergman Ramos. Harmondsworth: Penguin.

Giddens, A. (1998) *The Third Way*. Cambridge: Polity Press.

Griffin, C. (1978) *Recurrent and Continuing Education – a curriculum model approach*. Nottingham: University of Nottingham Department of Adult Education.

Habermas, J. (1954) *Between Facts and Norms*, trans. W. Rehg. Cambridge: Polity Press.

Habermas, J. (1989) *The Structural Transformation of the Public Sphere*, trans. T. Burger assisted by F. Lawrence. Cambridge: Polity Press.

Horton, M. & Freire, P. (1990) *We Make the Road by Walking*. Philadelphia: Temple.

Jarvis, P. (1985) *The Sociology of Adult and Continuing Education*. London: Croom Helm.

Marshall, T.H. (1950) *Citizenship and Social Class and Other Essays*. Cambridge: Cambridge University Press.

Meister, J. (1998) *Corporate Universities* (revised and updated). New York: McGraw-Hill.

Ranson, S. (1994) *Towards the Learning Society*. London: Cassell.

Riley, D. (1992) Citizenship and the Welfare State, in J. Allen & P. Lewis (Eds) *Political and Economic Forms of Modernity*, pp. 179-227. Cambridge: Polity Press.

Selman, G. (1990) *Citizenship and the Adult Education Movement in* Canada. Vancouver: Centre for Continuing Education, University of British Columbia.

Turner, B.S. (1990) Outline of a Theory of Citizenship, *Sociology*, 24, pp. 189-218.

Notes on Contributors

Dr Lore Arthur is a lecturer in the Centre for Educational Policy and Management at the Open University with responsibilities for postgraduate teaching and research in lifelong learning. She is the coordinator for lifelong learning within the Doctorate in Education programme. Her research and publications cover lifelong learning, comparative education and intercultural communication with, in the main, reference to Germany and Britain.

Archana Choksi was the project manager for the DIET project and now works as an education consultant. She and Caroline Dyer have worked as a collaborative North-South team for nearly 10 years and have published extensively together. Renu Moyade and Neetu Purohit were members of the research project team, working with DIET staff and teachers in Madhya Pradesh and Rajasthan, respectively.

Lynn Davies is Professor of International Education and Director of the Centre for International Education and Research in the School of Education, University of Birmingham. Her current research interests are in democratisation of education and in education and conflict, and she is involved in projects in the Gambia, Malawi, Kosovo and Bosnia as well as continuing work on school councils and pupil democracy in the United Kingdom. She is currently Chair of BAICE.

Dr Caroline Dyer is Senior Research Fellow in International Education at the University of Manchester, United Kingdom and co-editor of the journal *Compare*. She has been researching aspects of Basic Education in India for the last 10 years, and has particular interests in the implementation of policy, education for nomadic and migrant groups, and the professional development of primary teachers and teacher educators.

Palitha Edirisingha is a research fellow at the School of Educational Studies, University of Surrey. Currently he is engaged in an EU-funded research project on Active Citizenship and Governance in the European context. His previous research includes open and distance education with particular emphasis on developing countries, and the use of interactive media for learning.

Dr Clara Fischer has many years' experience of working in popular movements and trade union education in Brazil. After completing a PhD on Brazilian trade union education at the University of Nottingham in 1997, she became a lecturer in the Centre for Human Sciences at UNISINOS, a University in the State of Rio Grande do Sul, Brazil.

Michael Fielding is Reader in Education at the University of Sussex, United Kingdom, where he is currently setting up a Centre for Educational Innovation. His two main research interests are the development of the 'person-centred school' and the radical potential of student voice in educational transformation. His recent book, *Taking Education Really Seriously: four years' hard labour* (Routledge Falmer, 2001), provides a searching, appreciative critique of the educational record of the United Kingdom's New Labour Government.

Dr Janet Hannah is a senior lecturer in comparative education and deputy director of the Centre for Comparative Education Research in the School of Continuing Education at the University of Nottingham. Her teaching and research interests are in the field of comparative education, and in recent years, she has engaged in research and published on workers' education and higher education in Britain and Brazil, and refugee education in the United Kingdom and Australia.

Clive Harber is Professor of International Education in the Centre for International Education and Research, School of Education, University of Birmingham. From 1995 to 1999, he was Professor of Education and Head of the School of Education, University of Natal, Durban, South Africa. His research and publication interests are education and political development in Africa and education for democracy internationally. His most recent book is *State of Transition: post-apartheid educational reform in South Africa* (Symposium, 2001).

Wai Chung Ho did her MA in music education, followed by a D.Phil in music education, at the Institute of Education, University of London. She is currently Assistant Professor in the Department of Music and Fine Arts, Hong Kong Baptist University. She lectures on curriculum issues, principles and applications of music education, and applications in creative music communication. Her current research is on comparative education, gender research in music education and music teaching and learning.

John Holford is Professor of Adult Education, Director of Research and Head of Lifelong Learning in the School of Educational Studies at the University of Surrey. His career has been in adult education, including periods with the University of Hong Kong and the Workers' Educational Association. He has written on trade union education, learning theory, lifelong learning, community education, and adult education in South-east Asia. His current research interests include adult learning for active citizenship.

Keith Holmes is the membership secretary of BAICE. He is completing a PhD at the University of Bristol Graduate School of Education, sponsored by the Economic and Social Research Council. Formerly a volunteer teacher in Jamaica and South Africa, he has recently co-authored, with Dr Michael Crossley, *Educational Development in the Small States of the Commonwealth* (Commonwealth Secretariat). His doctoral dissertation is on research capacity in small states, with special reference to Saint Lucia in the Eastern Caribbean. Interests include education policy in the Caribbean and the implications of post-colonial theory for social and educational research.

George Hudson has taught in secondary schools and also had a career as an educational researcher at the National Foundation for Educational Research and Sheffield City Polytechnic. Since 1978, he has been a senior lecturer in educational studies at University College Worcester. His main field of interest is the relationship between schooling systems and society.

Peter Jarvis is Professor of Continuing Education at the University of Surrey, and Adjunct Professor of Adult Education at the University of Georgia, USA. He was President of BAICE in 1999-2000. His main areas of interest are learning theory, lifelong education and lifelong learning, and social-philosophical perspectives on all aspects of the education of adults. One of his books, *Adult Learning in the Social Context*, gained an international award for Adult Education Literature. His most recent books are *Learning in Later Life* and *Universities and Corporate Universities: the higher learning industry in global society* (both Kogan Page, 2001). He is also the founding editor of the *International Journal of Lifelong Education*.

Professor Kenneth King is Director of the Centre of African Studies and Professor of International and Comparative Education, University of Edinburgh. He has published extensively on education, training, the informal sector and aid.

Gerison Lansdown is a children's rights consultant. She was the founder director, in 1992, of the Children's Rights Development Unit, now the Children's Rights Alliance for England, established to promote implementation of the UN Convention on the Rights of the Child. She has published and lectured widely on the subject of children's rights, both nationally and internationally. She is on the executive boards of the Children's Discovery Centre in east London and UNICEF-UK. She is a consultant for the UNICEF Innocenti Research Centre in Florence and for Rights for Disabled Children, an international working group established with the support of the Committee on the Rights of the Child.

Wang Meifang is an associate professor in the Institute of Educational Science at Shandong Teachers' University, China. Her research interests are in the field of social and cognitive psychology and she has acted as an adviser to schools on moral education. She is current studying for a PhD at Beijing Normal University on children's understanding.

Dr Rob McBride is now in the School of Development Studies (including the Overseas Development Group) in the University of East Anglia. Much of his earlier activity was in the field of teacher education, in which he has published widely. In the new school, he has been able to develop his interests in applied cross-cultural research, the education of the marginalised, and educational improvement in low income countries. He has just completed the first stage of research into the educational needs of orphans in Malawi and has new projects researching the development of university teaching in Bangladesh and the education of street children in more than one country.

Dr Simon McGrath is a research fellow at the Centre of African Studies, University of Edinburgh. His teaching, research and consultancy interests are in education and skills development policy; the informal sector; and knowledge, aid and development.

Svend Poulsen-Hansen has been Deputy Secretary-General of the Danish National Commission for UNESCO since 1994. He is Secretary of subcommittees for Culture and for Education. He has worked as an Assistant Professor at Copenhagen University and Copenhagen Business School, and done a number of consultancies in eastern and central Europe as well as in Denmark.

Julia Preece is a senior lecturer at the University of Botswana where she is conducting a study on HIV/AIDS and gender issues in the workplace. She is also responsible for coordination of gender issues in a pan-European research project into the Education and Training of Governance and Citizenship in Europe, which is being managed from the University of Surrey, her previous place of employment. She has published extensively on issues of social exclusion. Her latest publication, co-authored with Ann-Marie Houghton, is *Nurturing Social Capital amongst Excluded Communities: a kind of higher education* (2000)

Marcia Prieto is Professor of Social Foundations of Education and Qualitative Research Methods at the Institute of Education of the Universidad Catolica de Valparaiso, Chile. Her research interests are related to education for democracy and citizenship and teacher education.

Dr Michele Schweisfurth is a lecturer in international education at the School of Education, University of Birmingham. Her research and teaching interests lie in teachers' responses to educational reform, particularly in developing countries undergoing political democratisation. Her forthcoming book, *Teachers' Experiences of Democracy: policy and practice in South Africa and Russia* (Symposium, 2001), deals with these themes.

Ikuko Suzuki is currently a D.Phil student at the University of Sussex Institute of Education, working on a thesis about the participation of parents in education in primary schools in Uganda. She has taught at secondary schools in Japan and Kenya and has working experience in East African countries.

Dr Elwyn Thomas is an international education consultant, specialising in teacher education, curriculum development and staff training in higher education He also carries out research into cultural aspects of educational development. He is at present working on research and development projects in north and South-east Asia. He was former chair of the Department of International and Comparative Education, Institute of Education, University of London and recently held Senior Fellow and Visiting Professor status at the Singapore Nanyang Technological University.

Joseph Zajda is Director of the Institute for International and Comparative Education, the School of Education, the Australian Catholic University (Melbourne), where he also teaches courses in the sociology of education, global studies in education and educational research methods. He edits *Curriculum and Teaching, Education and Society*, and *World Studies in Education* for James Nicholas Publishers. His recent books include *Education and Culture* (co-edited with M. Secombe), *Learning and Teaching, Curriculum, Culture and Teaching*, and *Education and Society*, 3rd edn (2001).

Rea Zajda majored in politics, anthropology, and sociology, and she won the Frieda Cohen prize for the best dissertation at the University of Melbourne. She is the Publisher and Managing Director of James Nicholas Publishers, where she also edits *Educational Practice and Theory*, and *Information, Theory and Society*, and serves as Managing Editor of the *Journal of Postcolonial Education, Information Technology, Education and Society*, and *Information, Theory and Society*.